# Pawlet
### VERMONT
# for One Hundred Years

*Hiel Hollister*

HERITAGE BOOKS
2012

# HERITAGE BOOKS
*AN IMPRINT OF HERITAGE BOOKS, INC.*

**Books, CDs, and more—Worldwide**

For our listing of thousands of titles see our website
at
www.HeritageBooks.com

A Facsimile Reprint
Published 2012 by
HERITAGE BOOKS, INC.
Publishing Division
100 Railroad Ave. #104
Westminster, Maryland 21157

Copyright © 1999 Heritage Books, Inc.

Entered according to Act of Congress, in the year 1867,
by Hiel Hollister,
In the Clerk's office of the District Court of the United States,
for the District of Vermont.

— Publisher's Notice —
In reprints such as this, it is often not possible to remove blemishes from the original. We feel the contents of this book warrant its reissue despite these blemishes and hope you will agree and read it with pleasure.

International Standard Book Numbers
Paperbound: 978-0-7884-1243-1
Clothbound: 978-0-7884-6953-4

# INTRODUCTION.

In the intervals of severe and exacting manual labor, we have gathered the materials of this work, and collated and grouped them together in their present form. Were we to make pretensions to scholarship, the character of this work would not invite its exercise.

Our aim has been to rescue from the fast thickening mists of forgetfulness, and to release from the domain of tradition such fragments of our early history as are not already shrouded by the dark clouds of oblivion. And judging that any history of the town would be incomplete that did not come down to the present time, while we have reached back to the earliest dawn of our existence, we have followed the line of history to its latest period. Our materials would have justified a more extended work, particularly in the department of Family Sketches, but we judged, whether rightly or not, that sins of *omission* were more pardonable than sins of *commission*. In our limited acquaintance with local histories prepared by others, it has not been our fortune to meet with one that commended itself to our judgment as a model worthy of imitation. Hence we were compelled to construct a plan of our own which has at least the merit of novelty.

Instead of continuous narrative and detail of facts we have served it up in instalments, grouping together in distinct chapters the facts and statistics pertaining to each subject embraced in the province of history. We are ourselves better pleased with the *plan* than with its *execution*.

While the elderly lady or gentleman will turn over the pages of this book to find some fact, or incident, or name only, perhaps of some associate, friend, or loved one, who has "gone before," we look to the children of the present day, and to their successors, whom the tide of time in coming years, shall bring to the surface, to play their allotted parts on the stage of life and retire behind the scenes, for a proper appreciation of our labors.

The sentiment that inspired the poet who wrote *This is my own my native land*, lies deep in every human breast, and he is an exception, wherever his lot may be cast, whose inmost soul does not thrill at the thoughts of home.

In the department of Family History we have taken a wide range, and have brought under fire and levelled our guns at six generations of our citizens with an occasional shot over the border.

Some critics may think we are too minute in these sketches, and others will wonder that so many facts of equal interest are omitted. To Capt. Noah Gifford we acknowledge our indebtedness for his efficiency in gathering materials for this department.

We have "swung round the circle," and exhausted our invention in the introduction and discussion of subjects relevant to our purpose. But we forbear. Who ever reads a preface?

# Pawlet for One Hundred Years.

## TOPOGRAPHY.

This town is situated in the southwestern corner of Rutland county, and has Wells on the north, Danby on the east, Rupert on the south, and Hebron and Granville, N. Y., on the west. It is six miles square and contains 23,040 acres. It lies in north latitude 43° and 23'. It took its name, we may presume, from its principal river, which was spelled by early writers Paulette and Paulet. It is divided from north to south, nearly through its centre, by a high range of mountains, which is flanked on the west by an auxiliary range of less height, while on the southeast it touches on Danby and Dorset mountains. The mountains in the principal range are known as South mountain, which extends into Rupert, North mountain, extending into Wells, Middle mountain, between that and Haystack, and its most prominent mountain, Haystack.

This mountain rises abruptly towards the north part of the town and nearly in its centre east and west. It is accessible in carriages, within one hundred rods of its summit, and has become a favorite place of resort. From its rock-crowned summit, in a clear day, a prospect of surpassing loveliness is presented. On the east are the Green mountains, seen at intervals over an intermediate range, the glory of the state, clothed in perennial verdure whose frowning ramparts no enemy ever scaled and whose rugged slopes the foot of slavery never trod.

On the north, nearly at its foot, is Lake St. Austin, on whose placid surface is photographed every leaf, tree and feature of the overhanging cliffs, with an accuracy no artist need hope to rival. Farther north lies Lake Bombazine, fronting the battle ground of Hubbardton, the severest action ever fought in the state.

Northwest, in the blue of the far distance, rise the snow-clad points of the Adirondac, at whose base repose the ashes of John Brown, whose self-sacrificing devotion to his view of right and justice was the initial step towards melting every fetter on this continent, and whose spirit "marching on" appears destined to remove tyranny and oppression from the universe.

On the west are the mountains that encircle Lake George and fringe the Sacandaga and the upper Hudson.

Southwest are the mountains that skirt the valley and plain of Saratoga, from whose bosom gush its health-giving waters. On the south are the green hills that environ the bloody field of Bennington, through whose gateway many of our citizen soldiers passed to their everlasting rest.

The limits here outlined embrace eminently classic and historic ground. Here, more than a century ago, the question of supremacy on this continent between France and England, and of the ascendancy of the Protestant over the Romanist was decided at the point of the bayonet. Here in 1777, at Saratoga, was fought the battle that virtually decided the revolutionary question, as it opened the way for the recognition of our independence by France and secured its assistance in our struggle.

Here in 1814, on the waters of the Saranac and the bosom of Champlain, the army of the enemy was sent reeling back to Canada while its navy was snugly moored in Whitehall harbor. Who of our older citizens failed to visit that fleet the following winter?

Lakes and rivers, mountains and valleys, field and forest lie intermingled in this grand panorama, while dotted all over this broad landscape are thousands of peaceful and luxurious homes.

The principal river is the Pawlet or Mettowee, which rising in Dorset and crossing the corner of Rupert winds its devious course diagonally through this town,—like a silver thread wrought in emerald,—to its ocean home.

Its principal tributaries are Flower brook, which rising in Danby flows into it near the village, and Indian river, which rising in Rupert bathes the southern border of the town and joins it in Granville. Besides, it receives the waters of Lake St. Austin and Wells brook, which enter it near the northwest corner of the town. Water-power available for mills abound on all these streams. Springs of the purest water are every where met with, and brooks and rivulets water every ravine and valley.

The surface of the town in its virgin state was clothed with a luxuriant growth of forest trees. On the alluvials grew the sycamore and the elm; in the swamps and marshes the hemlock, tamarac and black ash, while on its hill sides and mountain slopes flourished the pine, sugar maple, beech, birch, several species of oak, etc. Its mountain heights were crowned with spruce and cedar. The early settlers, thoughtless of the needs of this generation, consigned to the log-heap many a towering pine and stately oak whose value if left to the present time could scarcely be estimated. The soil of the town partakes of all the different elements known to geological science. While gravelly loam preponderates, limestone, clay, slate and silex in all their combinations every where abound. Hence it is adapted to all the various fruits, grains, roots and grasses of this latitude.

The leading interest in the first fifty years was the raising of grain and cattle for market. In process of time grazing came more in vogue as less exhaustive of the soil, and the dairy and sheep-fold supplanted the grain-field. At present the tide sets strongly in favor of the dairy and other branches of husbandry are made subservient to it.

## FIRST SETTLEMENT.

The town was granted to Jonathan Willard and sixty-seven others by Governor Benning Wentworth of New Hampshire, in a charter bearing date August 26, 1761. It was substantially a free gift, being coupled only with the following easy conditions, to wit: "That each proprietor should plant and cultivate five acres for each fifty acres he may hold within five years from the date of the charter on penalty of forfeiture of his right. That before any division of land was made among the grantees a tract of sixty-eight acres for town lots, as near the centre of the town as possible, should be reserved, and one acre should be allotted to each grantee;

## First Settlement.

the rent of which should be one ear of Indian corn annually at Christmas. After the expiration of ten years each proprietor was to pay the Crown one shilling, proclamation money, annually, for each hundred acres he might hold, or in that proportion, forever."

The following reservations were also made: "To his Excellency Benning Wentworth a tract of land containing five hundred acres, marked B. W. in the plan; one share for the incorporated Society for the Propagation of the Gospel in Foreign Parts; one share for a Glebe for the Church of England; one share for the first settled Minister of the Gospel, and one share for the benefit of schools in said town."

Also there was a provision that all white and other pine trees suitable for "masting the Royal Navy" should be reserved for that use.

The revolution which took place soon after the settlement of the town nullified all these provisions of the charter, but did not have the effect to deprive the grantees of their rights.

But few of the grantees ever settled in town or even visited it. Jonathan Willard came here in 1761 or 1762 and made some clearings. [For a detailed account see "Jonathan Willard."] The proprietors in 1768 donated fifty acres to Simon Burton as first settler, and thirty acres to William Fairfield second settler, and twenty acres to ——— as third settler. The earliest records now known bear date July 29, 1768, but they refer to prior records. At that meeting Reuben Harmon was moderator and Simon Burton, clerk. The first allotment of land was fifty acres to each proprietor. This was followed in a few years by another and still another allotment until all desirable land was appropriated. There seems to have been no regular system of surveys, hence a great many gores and parcels were left out to be afterwards appropriated by him who should first locate them. We find no record of the location of the sixty-eight town lots.

The peculiar circumstances attending the settlement and proprietorship of the town gave rise to a class of speculators or land-jobbers, who buying of the original grantees, many times for a nominal sum, sold out to actual settlers at a heavy advance. In fact the wild lands in this town cost the settler an immoderate price, which being bought mostly on time weighed heavily against the prosperity of the town for many years. The average price was about ten dollars per acre, but in some instances thirty dollars were paid. We must bear in mind that money was not then plentiful and was worth three times as much as at the present time. A large share of the town was settled in forty acre lots.

The troubles in New York which will be referred to hereafter, was another hindrance to the settlement of the town. As there were double claimants to the title to the soil timid buyers hesitated to invest. In 1770 there were but nine families in town and the progress of settlement was slow until after Burgoyne was defeated at Saratoga, and what was left of the British forces were driven south of the Hudson. This together with the resolute stand taken by Ethan Allen in withstanding the claims of New York encouraged settlement and the town rapidly filled up. Many soldiers of the revolution who in the course of their service had visited the town, were so pleased with it, that on their release from the army they came directly here.

## WAR.

### Section 1—*French and Indian.*

The war between England and France which was waged in this vicinity was closed before the location of the town, and tradition persistently fixes on Indian hill in the west part of the town as the theatre of bloody conflicts during that war or immediately preceding it. The most commonly accepted version of the tradition is that Gen. Putnam, while at Fort Edward, was ordered to proceed to the east and dislodge a force of French and Indians who were lurking in the vicinity of Lake St. Austin, which was a favorite fishing ground of the Indians. This party encamped on Indian hill and fortified a natural breastwork of rock and awaited the approach of the enemy whose camp fires were seen at a distance. The enemy commenced the assault the next day and a fierce battle ensued in which the enemy at first had the advantage. Many were killed, some on our side taken prisoners, but afterwards retaken. The rock which constituted their breastwork is still shown and it is said several persons were buried near it.

Several of our first settlers were in the French and Indian war, among whom were Daniel Branch, David Willey and James Uran.

### Section 2—*Revolutionary.*

Our citizens sympathized with the other towns on the Grants in the controversy with New York; but we have no distinct account of any organization of a military force until 1777, when a military station was in existence which was for a time a frontier post. When Burgoyne came up from Canada sweeping all before him, most of the settlers north of us fled to the south and some of our citizens joined in the stampede. Most of them, however, soon returned and the presence of such gallant officers as Col. Warner and Col. Herrick soon reassured them.

During this year (1777) Col. Herrick's famous regiment of Rangers, the prototype of the whole family of Rangers which have figured so largely in our national history, were organized here. They were the terror of all the country round. They "hung like a gathering cloud on his flank," as Burgoyne said in one of his despatches. They obstructed his advance by felling trees in Wood creek, and rolling large stones in his path so that he was compelled to cross Fort Ann mountain with his heavy train of artillery on a road then and now almost impassable. They harrassed his rear, and though, of course, unable to cope with him in battle, they cut off his supplies and in a thousand ways obstructed his march. We find it recorded in history that in "September, 1777, five hundred men under Col. Brown were sent from Pawlet to attack Ticonderoga, Mount Defiance and Mount Hope. The work was accomplished by surprise, Sept. 18, not losing a single man." Whether these troops were the same that constituted Col. Herrick's regiment of Rangers does not clearly appear. Capt. Parmalee Allen, son of Timothy Allen, commanded one company of the Rangers, Capt. Ebenezer Allen, the first settler in Poultney, commanded another.

The troops stationed in this town seem to have been under the control of the Continental Congress, but were paid by the Vermont Council of Safety, the then government of the state.

We extract from the records of Bennington the following paper, which shows the sentiment of our fathers on the question of slavery, and which might serve in spirit and substance as a precedent for President Lincoln's emancipation proclamation of Jan. 1, 1863. We give it verbatim.

"HEAD QUARTERS, POLLET,
28th of November, 1777.
To whom it may concern Know ye that whereas Dinah Mattis a negro woman with nancey her Child of two months old was taken Prissnor on Lake Champlain with the British troops Some where near Col. Gilliner's Patten the twelfth day of Instant November by a scout under my command, and according to a Resolve passed by the Honorable Continental Congress that all Prisses belong to the Captivators thereof I being conscientious that it is not right in the sight of god to keep Slaves I therefore obtaining leave of the Detachment under my Command to give her and her child their freedom I do therefore give the said Dinah mattis and Nancey her child there freedom. to pass and repass any where through the United States of America with her behaving as becometh and to Trade and Traffic for her Self and Child as though she was born free, without being Mollested by any Person or Persons. In witness whereunto I have hereunto set my hand or subscribed my name (signed) EBENEZER ALLEN *Capt.*"

To show the spirit of the times, the way our fathers managed before the organization of the state, and the part they took in the stirring events of that period, we annex a few extracts from the

Journal of the "Council of Safety," which commences the day before the battle of Bennington.

"STATE OF VERMONT, BENNINGTON,
In Council of Safety, *Aug.* 15, 1777.
To Mrs. Simonds, Lanesboro :
Madam—Please to send by the bearer, Jedediah Reed, six or seven pounds of Lead by Col. Simonds order.    By order of Council
PAUL SPOONER, *D. Sec.*

In Council of Safety, *Sept.* 6, 1777.
To Capt. William Fitch :
Sir—You are hereby directed to deliver to Capt. Goodnough the bearer two sides of Leather out of Marshs fatts and out of his leather taking his receipt for the same after appraisal.
By order of Council.
IRA ALLEN, *Sec.*

In Council of Safety, 19th of *Sept.* 1777.
To Capt. William Fitch :
Sir—Whereas Mr. Timothy Mead has some days past made application to this Council to take thirteen sheep out of Tory flock in Arlington in lieu of that number which he lost—this Council positively orders that none be delivered uptil further evidence can be had.   I am your humble servant.
By order of Council.   JOS. FAY, *Sec.*

In Council of Safety, *Sept.* 24, 1777.
To Captain Nathan Smith :
Sir—You are hereby required to march with the men under your command, to Paulett on horseback where you will apply to Col. Simonds for a

horse load of flour to each man and horse, you will furnish bags sufficient for such purpose. By order of Council.
      THOMAS CHITTENDEN, *Pres.*

To Capt. Ebenezer Wood:
 Sir — You are hereby required to take the charge of the men, horses and bags, ordered from this town and proceed without one minutes loss of time, to Paulett where you will apply to Col. Benjamin Simonds for a load of flour for each horse, and proceed to Gen. Warner with the same, if Col. Simonds shall think proper. When you return you are to take especial care that the horses and bags be returned to their proper owners.
        JOSEPH FAY, *Secy.*

    In Council of Safety, *Sept.* 24, 1777.
 In consequence of a letter received from Col. Benjamin Simonds, for horses to forward flour to the relief of Gen. Warner at Tyconderoga we have granted warrants to procure them with all expedition. By order of Council. JOS. FAY, *Sec.*

  In Council of Safety, BENNINGTON, *Aug.* 26, 1777.
To Adjutant Elisha Clark:
 You are hereby required to make returns of the names and number of the officers, non-commissioned officers and soldiers belonging to Col. Samuel Herrick's Regiment of Rangers, already raised within this state for the defence thereof, to Ebenezer Walbridge at Arlington at 10 o'clock of the morning of the 28th inst. Of this you are not to fail.
  By order of Council.
      THOMAS CHITTENDEN, *President.*
Attest IRA ALLEN *Sec.*

## PAWLET.

In Council of Safety, 26th *September*, 1777.

To Mr. Wright and other Teams in Company you are to repair from this to Paulet, with your teams, thereto to apply to the commanding officer or Lt. Hyde to be loaded with plunder belonging to Col. Brown, and return with the same, and deliver it safe to this Council. By order of Council. JOSEPH FAY, *Sec.*

In Council, BENNINGTON, *Oct.* 8, 1777.
———. ———, Paulett:

Sir — This Council are informed that you are found, since you passed examination before us with arms and ammunition *secreted* which gives the inhabitants great uneasiness; and nothing short of your making immediate satisfaction to this Council, will prevent your being ordered immediately to remove which must be done forthwith.

By order of Council. Jos. FAY, *Sec.*

P. S. — If you can satisfy the inhabitants and obtain their liberty you may remain until further orders. Jos. FAY.

In Council of Safety, 10th *Feb.* 1778.

This Council having been taken under consideration the complaint of Capt. Zadoc Everest of Paulett, in behalf of the United States of America, against ———. ———, for enemical conduct to the United States having examined the evidence and every attending circumstance relative thereto and after seriously deliberating thereon do judge and order that the said ———. ———, pay thirty pounds lawful money as a fine for the use of this state and pay all reasonable charges of trial, and stand committed until this judgment be complied with. Costs taxed 16 pounds 8 shillings.

By order of Council.

THOMAS CHITTENDEN, *Pres.*

Received Feb. 11, the cost of the above suit 16 pounds 8 shillings, and 21 pounds 14 shillings on the above judgment. Jos. FAY, *Secy.*
18 pounds 6 shillings received by me.
THOMAS CHITTENDEN.

The above extracts will convey an idea of the manner of doing business by this anomalous and most singular body, who exercised all the functions of government, executive, legislative and judicial. Their reference to several prominent early settlers of the town will give additional interest to these extracts.

It will be borne in mind that at this period of our history, the settlers of this town in common with all the other towns in the state, in addition to the war with England — the common enemy — were involved in a bitter quarrel with the state of New York. That state claimed not only *jurisdiction* over the people of this territory but the absolute title to the soil.

Our fathers who had acquired a title to the soil from the royal governor of New Hampshire, and who had cleared much of it, built houses, planted orchards and were beginning to enjoy the fruit of their toils and privations, could not *see* the propriety of being summarily dispossessed of all, and compelled to abandon their homes, or pay for them over again. Hence under the leadership of Ethan Allen and his patriotic compeers, under the general direction of the Council of Safety, they repelled every effort of the New Yorkers to gain a foothold on our soil, and triumphantly maintained their position until 1791, when they were admitted into the Union as an independent state. What thanks do we not owe to our gallant fathers, who persistently refused to become a mere mountain appendage to the empire state. Had Vermont been absorbed in New York the "Star that never sets" would have never risen, and the world would have lost the example of the most chivalrous and patriotic community found in any age or country. While engaged with the common enemy, and with New York, their most dangerous foes, against whom they were the most highly incensed, were the tories within their own midst. While they applied with " Twigs of the wilderness " the " Beech Seal " to the naked backs of intruding New Yorkers, they hung the tories convicted of " enemical " conduct to the nearest tree. We may be pardoned for alluding to one instance. One David Redding had been convicted by a jury of six persons of " enemical" conduct toward the people of the state, and was sentenced to be hung. He applied to the late John Burnham of Middletown, to interfere in his behalf on the ground that according to Blackstone no number of jurors less than twelve, could lawfully convict a criminal. The day of execution came and with it came an order from the Council of Safety to suspend the execution. The people, clamorous for his blood, were about to proceed to hang him, notwithstanding, when Ethan Allen, who had just returned from his captivity suddenly made his appearance, mounted a stump and exclaimed, " Attention ! the whole !" He then informed the people that the execution of Redding was postponed until the next Thursday, and if they would wait peaceably till that time they should see somebody hung. for if Redding was not hung he would be hung himself. During the interim a new trial was had when he was convicted by twelve jurymen, and at the appointed time Redding was placed in a cart with one end of a rope fastened around his neck and the other fastened to the limb of a tree. Redding, then, being allowed to speak, commenced giving good counsel and advice to the crowd, not to war against the state, but conduct themselves as good and loyal citizens, when the impatient assembly cried out, "Go to H—— with your advice,—— drive on the cart."

Notwithstanding our home difficulties, Vermont was ever ready to cooperate with New York and the other states against the common adversary. When Gen. Burgoyne started his first detachment on a raid on the stores at Bennington, they entrenched themselves in a camp a few miles distant and waited for a reinforcement before attacking Gen. Stark. Stark also awaited asistance from Col. Warner who was rallying the Vermonters. Stark hearing of the approach of the Hessians resolved to attack the enemy in his entrenchments before assistance came on either side. After a bloody conflict he succeeded in dislodging and capturing most of the Hessian forces. At this crisis the reinforcements on either side simultaneously appeared on the field when the conflict was renewed with a triumphant victory for our side. Quite a number of our townsmen were in this battle. This was the first effectual check Burgoyne had received, and it led in a few weeks to his complete overthrow at Saratoga.

With the defeat of Burgoyne the war was chiefly ended on the northern frontier, though scouting parties mostly in pursuit of plunder found employment all through the year. This plunder, as we have before seen, was brought to this town, subject to the disposal of the Council of Safety.

The property of the tories was sequestrated, and many of them sent off to Canada.

During the latter years of the war, and at its close there was a large influx of settlers in this town, many of them fresh from the battlefield. Over seventy revolutionary soldiers came to this town, the most of them remaining till their death.

Their longevity shows them to have been men of the highest physical and moral stamina, and the current notion that war demoralizes its votaries is hardly verified in their case. They, as a class, were distinguished for industry, thrift and enterprise, and though the fires of the revolution had consumed their substance and "tried their souls" nearly all of them succeeded in establishing a home and acquiring a competence.

Annexed is a list of revolutionary soldiers who settled in this town, with the rank, and the age and year of decease, of each one so far as we have been able to ascertain. A few of them drew pensions under the act of congress, 1818, and of those who survived until 1832, nearly all drew pensions. A few widows of those deceased also drew pensions, but not generally:

|                          | Age. | Year. |                             | Age. | Year. |
|---|---|---|---|---|---|
| Gideon Adams,            | 84   | 1827  | Silas Jones,                | 68   |       |
| Joseph Adams,            |      |       | Nathan M. Lounsbury,        | 100  |       |
| John Allen,              | 91   | 1852  | James Leach,                | 76   | 1835  |
| Nehemiah Allen,          | 87   | 1852  | Judah Moffitt,              | 92   | 1852  |
| Timothy Allen, jr.,      | 74   | 1834  | Capt. Josiah Monroe,        | 84   | 1846  |
| Gen. Elisha Averill,     | 67   | 1821  | Simeon Pepper,              | 68   | 1821  |
| Lieut. Lemuel Barden,    | 81   | 1839  | Maj. Moses Porter,          | 65   | 1803  |
| Aaron Bennett,           | 96   | 1849  | Capt. William Potter,.      |      |       |
| Roswell Bennett,         |      |       | Capt. James Pratt,          | 92   | 1854  |
| Samuel Bennett,          |      |       | Capt. Samuel Pratt,         | 80   |       |
| Christopher Billings,    |      |       | Josiah Priest,              |      |       |
| Selah Betts,             | 68   | 1826  | Jedediah Reed,              |      |       |
| David Blakely,           | 72   | 1821  | Simeon Reed,                | 84   | 1840  |
| Daniel Branch,           | 86   | 1822  | John Risdon,                |      |       |
| Ebenezer Broughton,      |      |       | George Rush,                | 110  | 1814  |
| Elijah Brown,            | 77   | 1835  | Capt. John Stark,           |      |       |
| Nathaniel Carver,        | 52   | 1804  | Peter Stevens,              | 80   | 1838  |
| Oliver Churchill,        |      |       | Samuel Stratton,            | 69   | 1825  |
| Col. Elisha Clark,       |      |       | Capt. Nath'l Robinson,      | 89   | 1841  |
| Robert Cox,              |      |       | Daniel Risdon,              |      |       |

WAR.    21

|  | Age. | Year. |  | Age. | Year. |
|---|---|---|---|---|---|
| Asa Denison, | 50 | 1810 | Abel Robinson, |  |  |
| Capt. Jedediah Edgerton, | 86 | 1848 | Ephraim Robinson, | 83 | 1833 |
| Jacob Edgerton, | 84 | 1849 | Richard Robinson, | 75 | 1838 |
| Capt. Simeon Edgerton, | 77 | 1809 | Col. John Sargeant, | 82 | 1843 |
| Abiathar Evans, | 89 | 1831 | Jacob Sykes, | 83 | 1843 |
| Col. William Fitch, | 48 | 1785 | Lieut. Eliel Todd, |  |  |
| Gideon Gifford, | 50 |  | James Uran, |  |  |
| Ebenezer Giles, | 78 | 1838 | Seth Viets, | 85 | 1823 |
| —— Gould, |  |  | Isaac Reed, | 83 |  |
| Ezekiel Harmon, | 80 | 1831 | Lieut. Daniel Welch, | 78 | 1827 |
| Nathaniel Hill, | 77 | 1830 | Nathan Williams, | 68 | 1819 |
| Ashbel Hollister, | 81 | 1840 | David Willey, |  |  |
| Lieut. Elijah Hollister, | 85 | 1844 | Andrew Winchester, | 66 | 1827 |
| Serg. Innett Hollister, | 83 | 1844 | John Wiseman, | 60 | 1815 |
| Capt. James Hopkins, | 82 | 1830 | David Wood, | 87 | 1836 |
| Daniel Hulett, | 90 | 1838 | Henry Wooster, | 80 | 1820 |
| Bulkley Hutchins, | 85 | 1850 |  |  |  |

*The War of 1812.*

In 1812, after thirty years of peace and general prosperity, our citizens were again called to confront England, their ancient enemy. True sons of patriotic sires, they did not hesitate to take up arms, to maintain the liberty and independence their fathers had won. We have it by tradition that two companies of uniformed militia, the Light Infantry and Light Artillery, volunteered to take the field, but were not called out.

We annex a list of those who entered the service so far as we can ascertain, with their rank, viz :

Phineas Armstrong, Luther Arnold, Uriah Bennett, Seth Bond, John Brown, John Carver, Col. Augustus Cleveland, Serg. Elisha Clark, Capt. Willard Cobb, John Conant, Lieut. Amos Galusha, Zenas Goodspeed, Capt. Noah Gifford, Serg. Lorin Hamblin, Amasa Hancock, Jarvis Hanks, Maj. Joel Harmon, Lieut. Lebbeus Hascall, Safford Hascall, Nathan Hutchins, Benjamin Hutchins, Timothy Fisher, Hugh Montgomery, Charles Pelton, Serg. Elisha Smith, Lisemore Smith, Simon Smith, Asa Stevens, William Stevens, Lieut. Return Strong,

Festus Thompson, David Wait, Walter Welch,
Aaron Willard, Lemuel Willard, Silas Willard,
Luther B. Wood, Timothy Wood.

### Section 4.

The Mexican war of 1846 made but slight drafts
on our sympathy or military spirit, and we have
only to record the following names of those who
enlisted: Jamon Preston, and Return Strong.

### Section 5, *War of* 1861, *to* 1865.

Come we now to the great civil war of 1861--65,
maintained on our part to preserve the union of the
states, and the national life. To the requisition of
the President of the United States in April, 1861,
for 75,000 men, one regiment of which force was
assigned to this state, George S. Orr, Moses E. Orr,
and Charles Barrett, were the first to respond, who
enlisted in the First Vermont for three months. To
all subsequent calls by the government this town
has promptly responded and left off in 1865, with
an excess of eight men over and above all calls.
We have been represented in nearly every regiment
and battery raised in the state, and in several regiments of other states, and on nearly every battle-
field of the war. Several of our soldiers have been
in over thirty pitched battles, besides innumerable
skirmishes. We give in the annexed tables the
following particulars in reference to all our soldiers
so far as attainable, to wit: name, age at time of
enlistment, company, regiment, state, date of enlistment, rank, term of enlistment, bounties, reen-
listments, those who paid commutations, those who
furnished substitutes and natives of the town, with
their fathers' names who enlisted in other states.

WAR. 23

*Names of Soldiers.*

| Name of Soldier. | Age. | Company. | Regiment. | State. | Date of Enlistment. | Rank. | Term of Enlistment. | Bounty from the Town. |
|---|---|---|---|---|---|---|---|---|
| John Adams, | 22 | E | 7 | Vt. | | | 3 ys | $300 |
| Michael Agan, | 18 | D | 7 | Vt. | Dec. 9, '61 | | 3 ys | |
| Thomas Agan, | | | 20 | Ms. | | Capt. | | |
| Michael Agan, 2d enlistm't | 21 | D | 7 | Vt. | Feb. 19, '64 | | 3 ys | 200 |
| Isaac H. Alexander, | 31 | G | 5 | Vt. | Aug. 13, '62 | | 3 ys | 100 |
| Amos W. Babbitt, | 21 | K | 96 | N. Y. | Nov. 26, '61 | Corp. | 3 ys | |
| 2d enlistment, | 23 | K | 96 | N. Y. | Jan. 1, '64 | | 3 ys | 425 N. Y. |
| John H. Babbitt, | 18 | K | 96 | N. Y. | Nov. 26, '61 | Drum | 3 ys | 425 |
| 2d enlistment, | 20 | K | 96 | N. Y. | Jan. 1, '64 | | 3 ys | N. Y. |
| Charles Barrett, | 25 | K | 1 | Vt. | | | 3mo | |
| 2d enlistment, | 26 | K | 12 | Vt. | Aug. 8, '62 | Corp. | 9mo | 100 |
| Merritt C. Barrett, | 19 | H | 1 | Vt. c. | Sept. 18, '61 | | 3 ys | |
| Harvey C. Beebe, | 43 | D | 7 | Vt. | Dec. 15, '61 | | 3 ys | |
| John H. Black, | 21 | B | 14 | Vt. | Aug. 27, '62 | | 9mo | 115 |
| Robert Black, | 18 | B | 14 | Vt. | Aug. 27, '62 | | 9mo | 600 |
| A. Judson Blakely, | | B | 14 | Vt. | Aug. 27, '62 | 1 Lt. | 9mo | 100 |
| Willis W. Betts, | 32 | D | 4 h. a. | N. Y. | Dec. 21, '63 | | 3 ys | 500 N. Y. |
| Wm. H. Belding, | 22 | G | cav. | Vt. | Oct. 12, '61 | Serj. | 3 ys | |
| 2d enlistment, | | G | cav. | Vt. | Dec. 30, '63 | | 3 ys | 200 |
| Hiram Blossom, | 21 | C | 2 | Vt. | Oct. 8, '61 | | 3 ys | |
| 2d enlistment, | 23 | C | 2 | Vt. | Dec. 21, '63 | Serj. | 3 ys | 200 |
| Andrew J. Blowers, | 25 | B | 14 | Vt. | Aug. 27, '62 | | 9mo | 105 |
| Noble C. Bostwick, | 20 | E | 5 | Vt. | Aug. 15, '61 | Serj. | 3 ys | |
| 2d enlistment, | 22 | E | 5 | Vt. | Dec. 15, '63 | | 3 ys | 200 |
| Royal E. Bostwick, | 18 | H | 1 cav. | Vt. | Oct. 9, '61 | | 3 ys | |
| 2d enlistment, | 20 | H | 1 cav. | Vt. | Dec. 24, '63 | | 3 ys | 200 |
| Charles W. Bourn, | 24 | C | 11 | Vt. | Aug. 12, '62 | Lieut. | 3 ys | 100 |
| Thomas Burroughs, | 24 | H | 1 cav. | Vt. | Dec. 7, '61 | | 3 ys | |
| David M. Buffum, | 18 | B | 9 | Vt. | June 7, '62 | Corp. | 3 ys | |
| Leroy S. Bushee, | 22 | C | 11 | Vt. | July 23, '62 | | 3 ys | 100 |
| Orlando Bushee, | 27 | B | 14 | Vt. | Aug. 27, '62 | Corp. | 9mo | 100 |
| John Burns, | 20 | I | 7 | Vt. | Dec. 27, '64 | | 3 ys | 300 |
| Sylvester Burns, | 19 | I | 7 | Vt. | Dec. 27, '64 | | 3 ys | 300 |
| Willard Comstock, | 26 | D | 7 | Vt. | Dec. 9, '61 | | 3 ys | |
| Abram Capen, | | E | 5 | Vt. | | | | |
| James Cavanaugh, | | B | 9 | Vt. | | | | |
| Peter Castle, | 19 | I | 7 | Vt. | Nov. 22, '64 | | 3 ys | 300 |
| John Conlin, | 22 | B | 7 | Vt. | Sept. 16, '64 | | 1 yr | 725 |
| John Crawford, | 21 | C | 3 | Vt. | Dec. 29, '63 | | 3 ys | 500 |
| Michael Crowley, | 26 | | | Vt. | Jan. 5, '65 | | 3 ys | 825 |
| Simeon E. Cook, | 18 | C | 11 | Vt. | May 12, '62 | | 3 ys | 100 |
| Henry W. Clark, | | H | 5 cav. | N. Y. | | | | |
| Miles H. Delong, | 18 | C | 5 | Vt. | Aug. 18, '62 | | 3 ys | 100 |
| Edward Donnelly, | | F | 169 | N. Y. | | | 3 ys | |
| Edward Durling, | | E | 123 | N. Y. | | | 3 ys | |
| John Fish, | | K | 6 | N. Y. | Nov. 20, '62 | Corp. | 3 ys | |
| 2d enlistment, | | K | 96 | N. Y. | Jan. 1, '64 | Serj. | 3 ys | 425 N. Y. |

## PAWLET.

*Names of Soldiers—Continued.*

| Name of Soldier. | Age. | Company. | Regiment. | State. | Date of Enlistment. | Rank. | Term of Enlistment. | Bounty from the Town. |
|---|---|---|---|---|---|---|---|---|
| John Fogarty, |  | H | 5 cav. | N. Y. |  |  | 3 ys |  |
| Frederick Folger, | 18 | E | 5 | Vt. | Aug. 14, '62 |  | 3 ys | $100 |
| William Duncan, |  |  |  |  |  |  | 3 ys | 825 |
| John M. Frisbee, | 20 | B | 9 | Vt. | June 2, '62 |  | 3 ys |  |
| Robert Gallup, | 29 | D | 7 | Vt. | Dec. 16, '61 |  | 3 ys |  |
| James R. Gibbs, | 22 | A | 2 USSS | Vt. | Aug. 14, '62 | Corp. | 3 ys | 100 |
| James Gibson, |  | F | 9 | Vt. |  |  |  |  |
| Warren Gifford, | 29 | B | 2 | Vt. | May 4, '61 | Serj. | 3 ys |  |
| Joseph Gravlin, |  | H | 30 | N. Y. |  |  |  |  |
| James W. Guild, | 26 | B | 14 | Vt. | Aug. 27, '62 |  | 9mo | 100 |
| Peter Grant, |  |  |  |  |  |  | 3 ys | 825 |
| George Green, |  |  |  |  |  | - | 3 ys | 825 |
| Alonzo V. Guilder, | 24 | B | 14 | Vt. | Aug. 27, '62 |  | 9mo | 100 |
| Wallace V. Guilder, | 21 | B | 14 | Vt. | Aug. 27, '62 |  | 9mo | 100 |
| Selden A. Hall, | 18 | E | 5 | Vt. | Aug. 22, '61 |  | 3 ys |  |
| James L. Hall, | 18 | H | 7 | Vt. | Dec. 1 , '63 |  | 3 ys | 300 |
| Daniel H. Hall, jr., | 19 | G | 11 | Vt. | Nov. 30, '63 |  | 3 ys | 300 |
| Otis W. Harwood, | 18 | 1 ba |  | Vt, | Dec. 23, '63 |  | 3 ys | 500 |
| George G. Hanks, | 18 | I | 7 | Vt. | Feb. 11, '62 |  | 3 ys |  |
| Walter S. Hanks, | 18 | I | 17 | Vt. | April 27, '64 |  | 3 ys |  |
| Frank S. Hanks, |  | B | 124 | Ill. |  |  | 3 ys |  |
| Francis D. Hammond, | 23 | I | 5 | Vt. | Feb. 24, '62 |  | 3 ys |  |
| Justus W. Harwood, | 21 | C | 2 | Vt. | Oct. 6, '61 | Corp. | 3 ys |  |
| 2d enlistment, |  |  |  |  | Dec. 21, '63 |  | 3 ys | 200 |
| Edmund Hicks, | 35 | 2 l.a |  | Vt. | Jan. 1, '64 | Corp. |  | 500 |
| Uriel R. Hayward, |  |  |  |  |  |  | 3 ys | 700 |
| Francis S. Hollister, | 23 | B | 14 | Vt. | Aug. 27, '62 |  | 9mo | 100 |
| Albert E. Hollister, | 20 | B | 14 | Vt. | Aug. 27, '62 |  | 9mo | 100 |
| 2d enlistment, | 22 |  | 5 cav. | N. Y. | Sept. 1864 |  | 1 yr | 900 N. Y. |
| Willis H. Hollister, | 19 | B | 14 | Vt. | Aug. 27, '62 |  | 9mo | 100 |
| Sewell F. Howard, | 33 | K | 14 | Vt. | Sept. 18, '62 |  | 9mo | 110 |
| James Hoy, | 21 | C | 10 | Vt. | July 31,'62 |  | 3 ys |  |
| Warren E. Hulett, | 36 | B | 14 | Vt. | Aug, 27, '62 |  | 9mo | 100 |
| Chester O. Hulett, | 21 | 1 ba |  | Vt. | Dec. 23, '63 |  | 3 ys | 500 |
| Charles B. Hyde, | 22 | H | U.S.SS | Vt. | Oct. 25, '61 |  | 3 ys |  |
| John O. Humphrey, | 18 | H | 9 | Vt. | Jan. 2, '64 |  | 3 ys | 500 |
| George Johnson, | 25 | M | 11 | Vt. | Aug. 3, '63 |  | 3 ys |  |
| John G. Johnson, |  | G | 96 | N. Y. |  | 1 Lt. |  |  |
| Alson L. Kitchel, | 31 | I | 7 | Vt. | March 9, '64 |  | 3 ys | 200 |
| Charles M. Kingeley, | 20 | D | 7 | Vt. | Dec. 9, '61 | Corp. | 3 ys |  |
| 2d enlistment, | 23 | D | 7 | Vt. | Feb. 17, '64 |  | 3 ys | 200 |
| James Lackey, |  | E | 5 | Vt. | Aug. 15, '62 |  | 3 ys | 100 |
| Henry S. Lathe, |  | K | 96 | N. Y. |  |  |  |  |
| Nicholas Lamb, |  | A | 10 | Vt. |  |  |  |  |
| Lorenzo D. Leach, |  | F | 30 | N. Y. |  |  |  |  |
| Eugene Little, | 21 | B | 14 | Vt. | Aug. 27, '62 |  | 9mo | 100 |
| William F. Loomis, | 21 | 1 ba |  | Vt. | Dec. 31, '63 |  | 3 ys | 500 |
| Baptiste Lassor, | 18 | B | 2 | Vt. | Sept. 1, '64 |  | 1 yr | 800 |
| Vital Lassor, | 19 | A | 2 | Vt. | Sept. 1, '64 |  | 1 yr | 800 |
| —— Mason |  |  |  |  |  |  | 3 ys | 300 |

WAR.             25

## Names of Soldiers—Continued.

| Name of Soldier. | Age. | Company. | Regiment. | State. | Date of Enlistment. | Rank. | Term of Enlistment. | Bounty from the Town. |
|---|---|---|---|---|---|---|---|---|
| George Manning, |  | A | 10 | Vt. |  |  |  |  |
| Franklin S. McArthur, |  | I | 7 | Vt. |  |  |  |  |
| Michael McBrinn, |  | K | 169 | N. Y. |  |  |  |  |
| Mark S. Moore, | 25 | cav. |  |  | Aug. 4, '64 |  | 1 yr | $1000 |
| Wyman L. Macomber, | 40 | L | 11 | Vt. | Dec. 31, '63 |  | 3 ys | 500 |
| Joel A. Mason, | 21 | I | 17 | Vt. | May 18, '64 |  |  |  |
| —— Mason, |  |  |  |  |  |  | 3 ys | 900 |
| John McGrath, | 19 | H | 2 USSS |  | Oct. 31, '61 |  | 3 ys |  |
| 2d enlistment, | 22 | ba 1 |  | Vt. | Dec. 17, '63 |  | 3 ys | 500 |
| Patrick McGrath, | 17 | D | 7 | Vt. | Dec. 14, '61 |  | 3 ys |  |
| 2d enlistment, | 20 | D | 7 | Vt. | Feb. 17, '64 |  | 3 ys | 200 |
| James McGrath, |  |  |  |  |  |  |  |  |
| William Kelvia, | 30 | I | 7 | Vt. | March 1, '64 | Corp. | 3 ys | 300 |
| Thomas McKenna, |  | F | 169 | N. Y. |  |  |  |  |
| Edward McKenna, |  | cav. | 5 | N. Y. |  |  |  |  |
| Sylvanus McWain, | 18 | D | 7 | Vt. | Dec. 25, '61 |  | 3 ys |  |
| 2d enlistment, | 21 | D | 7 | Vt. | Feb. 17, '64 |  | 3 ys | 200 |
| Lemuel Moore, |  | I | 7 | Vt. |  |  |  |  |
| Asa L. Monroe, |  | L | 11 | Vt. | June 10, '63 |  | 3 ys | 300 |
| Atherton Monroe, | 44 | H | 2 USSS |  | Dec. 13, '61 |  |  |  |
| Thomas C. Mosher, | 29 | D | 7 | Vt. | Dec. 10, '61 |  | 3 ys | 200 |
| James Murphy, |  | I | 123 | N. Y. |  |  |  |  |
| S. O. A. Magitt, |  |  |  |  |  |  |  | 200 |
| Samuel W. Nelson, | 20 | B | 14 | Vt. | Aug. 27, '62 |  | 9mo | 100 |
| Edward Nye, | 22 | B | 9 | Vt. | June 3, '62 |  | 3 ys |  |
| Calvin S. Nichols, | 26 | E | 5 | Vt. | Aug. 14, '62 |  | 3 ys | 100 |
| George S. Orr, | 24 | E | 1 | Vt. | May 2, '61 |  | 3mo |  |
| 2d enlistment, |  | A | 77 | N. Y. | 1861 | Major | 3 ys |  |
| Moses E. Orr, | 20 | E | 1 | Vt. | May 2, '61 |  | 3mo |  |
| 2d enlistment, | 20 | K | 96 | N. Y. | Nov. 26, '61 | Capt. | 3 ys |  |
| Horace J. Orr, | 16 | H | 5 cav. | N. Y. |  |  |  |  |
| Thomas Newton, |  |  |  |  |  |  |  |  |
| Merritt C. Parris, |  | A | 5 cav. | N. Y. |  |  | 3 ys | 825 |
| Levi Patterson, |  | B | 14 | Vt. | Aug. 27, '62 |  | 9mo | 100 |
| Hubert Perham, | 21 | B | 14 | Vt. | Aug. 27, '62 |  | 9mo | 100 |
| 2d enlistment, | 22 | ba 2 |  | Vt. | Dec. 23, '63 |  | 3 ys | 500 |
| Merritt Perham, | 18 | C | 2 | Vt. | Oct. 2, '61 | Corp. |  |  |
| John Pentony, | 35 | I | 7 | Vt. | May 2, '64 |  | 3 ys | 200 |
| Keyes Potter, | 19 | K | 7 | '. t. | Dec. 14, '63 |  | 3 ys | 500 |
| Calvin Reed, | 18 | K | 7 | Vt. | Dec. 17, '63 |  | 3 ys | 500 |
| Chauncy H. Robinson, | 19 | D | 7 | Vt. | Dec. 10, '61 |  | 3 ys |  |
| 2d enlistment, | 22 | D | 7 | Vt. | Feb. 16, '64 |  | 3 ys | 200 |
| Charles Russell, | 24 |  |  |  | Aug. 27, '64 |  | 1 yr | 1000 |
| Elbridge J. Reed, | 21 | G | 11 | Vt. | Aug. 6, '64 |  | 3 ys | 700 |
| John Scott, | 44 | E | 5 | Vt. | Aug. 30, '62 |  | 3 ys | 100 |
| Charles H. Scott, | 18 | E | 5 | Vt. | Aug. 14, '62 |  | 3 ys | 100 |
| Richard Scott, |  |  |  |  |  |  |  |  |
| Erastus Scovill, |  | E | 123 | N. Y. |  |  |  |  |
| Oliver L. Searle, | 43 | E | 5 | Vt. | Aug. 30, '62 |  | 3 ys | 175 |
| Amyll B. Searle, | 20 | E | 5 | Vt. | Aug. 14, '62 |  | 3 ys | 100 |
| Francis R. Shaw, | 20 | C | 11 | Vt. | Aug. 12, '62 | 2 Lt. | 3 ys | 100 |

3

## PAWLET.

### Names of Soldiers—Continued.

| Name of Soldier. | Age. | Company. | Regiment. | State. | Date of Enlistment. | Rank. | Term of Enlistment. | Bounty from the Town. |
|---|---|---|---|---|---|---|---|---|
| George O. Simonds, | 19 | B | 14 | Vt. | Aug. 27, '62 | | 9mo | $115 |
| Martin Smith, | 27 | B | 14 | Vt. | Aug. 27, '62 | | 9mo | 100 |
| O. Judson Smith, | 24 | B | 14 | Vt. | Aug. 27, '62 | | 9mo | 110 |
| James Sheridan, | 25 | b a 1 | | Vt. | Dec. 23, '63 | | 3 ys | 500 |
| James H. Smith, | 18 | C | 11 | Vt. | Nov. 30, '63 | | 3 ys | 300 |
| John Smith, | 21 | G | 11 | Vt. | Nov. 30, '63 | | 3 ys | 300 |
| Nathan Spaulding, | 18 | B | 9 | Vt. | June 7, '62 | | 3 ys | |
| Benjamin B. Royals, | 33 | I | 7 | Vt. | Mar. 10, '64 | | 3 ys | ?500 |
| Austin Taft, | | | | | | | 3 ys | 700 |
| Charles P. Taylor, | 25 | B | 14 | Vt. | Aug. 27, '62 | Serj. | 9mo | 100 |
| George W. Taylor, | 21 | B | 2 | Vt. | May 9, '61 | | 3 ys | |
| Cyrus P. Taylor, | | G | 8 | Ohio | | | | |
| Chipman I. Toby, | | usss | 2 | | Nov. 15, '61 | Serj. | | |
| Charles W. Towslee, | | B | 14 | Vt. | Aug. 27, '62 | Serj. | 9mo | 100 |
| William Town, | 37 | K | 7 | Vt. | Dec. 30, '63 | | 3 ys | 500 |
| Henry Towslee, | 18 | b a 1 | 7 | Vt. | Dec. 23, '63 | | 3 ys | 500 |
| Henry H. Thompson, | 24 | D | 7 | Vt. | Aug. 27, '64 | | 1 yr | 725 |
| Chester M. Vail, | 26 | D | 7 | Vt. | Dec. 9, '61 | Serj. | 3 ys | |
| 2d enlistment, | | D | 7 | Vt. | Feb. 17, '64 | | 3 ys | 200 |
| George M. Warren, | 28 | usss | 2 | Vt. | Nov. 15, '61 | | 3 ys | |
| Ira C. Warren, | 26 | H | 1 cav. | Vt. | Sept. 13, '61 | | | |
| 2d enlistment, | 28 | H | 1 cav. | Vt. | Dec. 26, '63 | Serj. | 3 ys | 200 |
| Daniel D. Warren, | 25 | H | 1 cav. | Vt. | Nov. 19, '61 | Corp. | 3 ys | |
| John Warren, | | F | 169 | N. Y. | | | 3 ys | |
| Edwin L. Waters, | 27 | C | 11 | Vt. | Aug. 11, '62 | | 3 ys | 100 |
| William C. Weeks, | 27 | B | 14 | Vt. | Aug. 27, '62 | | 9mo | 125 |
| Benjamin P. Wheeler, | 31 | B | 2 | Vt. | Aug. 30, '62 | | 3 ys | 150 |
| John Wheeler, | 19 | C | 5 | Vt. | Aug. 30, '62 | | 3 ys | 150 |
| James W. White, | 20 | H | 1 cav. | Vt. | Sept. 16, '61 | | 3 ys | |
| Ahira E. Wood, | 19 | B | 14 | Vt. | Aug. 27, '62 | | 9mo | 125 |
| William H. Wood, | 27 | B | 14 | Vt. | Aug. 27, '62 | | 9mo | 150 |
| Stephen Wood, | 38 | E | 2 | Vt. | Aug. 30, '62 | | 3 ys | |
| Willard Wood, | 18 | C | 10 | Vt. | Aug. 2, '62 | | | |
| Martin P. Wood, | 26 | B | 2 | Vt. | Aug. 16, '62 | | 3 ys | 100 |
| Henry C. Wood, | 20 | B | 2 | Vt. | May 9, '61 | | 3 ys | |
| Austin E. Woodman, | | I | 7 | Vt. | | Capt. | | |
| Augustus L. Wright, | 22 | C | 5 | Vt. | Aug. 22, '61 | | 3 ys | |
| Reuben H. Williams, | 21 | B | 2 | Vt. | Aug. 28, '62 | | 3 ys | |
| George Williams, | | | | | | | 3 ys | 500 |
| John R. Wilkins, | 19 | E | 5 | Vt. | Aug. 15, '61 | Corp. | 3 ys | |
| 2d enlistment, | | E | 5 | Vt. | Dec. 15, '63 | | 3 ys | 200 |
| Moses E. Wheeler, | 40 | I | 7 | Vt. | Dec. 1, '63 | | 3 ys | |
| John Williams, | | | 7 | Vt. | | | 3 ys | 825 |
| Unknown Man, | | | | Vt. | | | 3 ys | 800 |

The following named persons who were drafted in August, 1863, furnished substitutes usually at the cost of three hundred dollars each: James McD. Andrus, Reuben Dillingham, Jesse C. Gray, Jacob McFadden and Charles H. Russell. Leonard Johnson, who was not drafted put in a substitute at an expense of 175 dollars.

The following persons who were drafted in August, 1863, paid commutation each, 300 dollars: Seth E. Culver,, Ogden Fisher, Levi Hanks, Frederick M. Hollister, Levi Parris, Michael Quinland, Warren Rice and Joel S. Wilcox.

The following persons, natives of the town enlisted in this and other states:

| Name of soldier. | Name of soldier's father. | Remarks. |
|---|---|---|
| Francis Bigart, | James Bigart, | New York. |
| Charles D. Castle, | Tracy Castle, | Wells. |
| Albert Culver, | Erastus Culver, | Pawlet. |
| Capt. William G. Edgerton, | Jacob Edgerton, | Rutland. |
| Lieut. Charles M. Edgerton, | George Edgerton, | Wathingford. |
| Lt. Rollin A. Edgerton, | Marson Edgerton, | Ohio. |
| Ira Foster, | Gilmore Foster, | New York. |
| Milton H. Hanks, | Isaac Hanks, | Wisconsin. |
| Franklin Hollister, | Innis Hollister, | Illinois. |
| Frank Jones, | Ephraim Jones, | Rupert. |
| Owen Loomis, | Gideon A. Loomis, | Minn. |
| Michael Hoy, Jr., | Michael Hoy, | |
| Luther Moffitt, | Alvin Moffitt, | |
| Hiram Moffitt, | Alvin Moffitt, | |
| Ashbel H. Pepper, | Simeon Pepper, | Castleton. |
| James B. Robinson | Denzill F. Robinson, | Illinois. |
| Nathaniel Hollis Robinson, | David Robinson, | Illinois. |
| Edward H. Robinson, | Denzill F. Robinson, | Illinois. |
| Surg. Justin F. Simonds, | Joel Simonds, | Iowa. |
| David H. Smith, | Ephraim Smith, | Illinois. |
| Samuel Snell, | John Snell, | |
| John Stearns, Jr., | John Stearns, | Kansas. |
| James W. Strong, | Martin D. Strong, | Michigan. |
| Thomas J. Strong, | John Strong, | New York. |
| Horace Taylor, | Sylvester Taylor, | Ohio. |
| William Taylor, | Sylvester Taylor, | Ohio. |
| Warren Wickham, | William Wickham, | N. Y. |
| Leroy D. McWain, | Elhanan McWain, | Illinois. |
| Nathaniel McWain, | Elhanan McWain, | Illinois. |

## OBITUARY OF DECEASED SOLDIERS.

As time wears away and the turmoil and excitement engendered by war abates, the thoughtful mind appreciates more and more the sacrifices made by our volunteer soldiers, and laid upon the altar of our country, in leaving their business, their families and homes to endure cold and hunger, disease and fatigue, and to put to extreme peril even their lives. What though the sacrifice of life was not accepted, it detracts not from the merit of the offering, We cannot cancel the obligations we owe them. All we can do is to enshrine them in our hearts and embalm them in our memories. We append a notice of those who gave their lives to their country:

NOBLE C. BOSTWICK, son of Henry Bostwick, enlisted for three years, in Co. E, 5th Vt. regiment, Aug. 15, 1861, and held the position of sergeant. Before the expiration of his term of service he re-enlisted, Dec. 15, 1863, and was killed at the bloody conflict at Cold Harbor, June 1, 1864, aged 23.

CHARLES BARRETT, son of Elijah Barrett, enlisted for 3 months in Co. K, 1st Vt. regiment. After the expiration of his term of service, he again enlisted in Co. K, 12th Vt. regiment, August 8, 1862, and died at Alexandria, Va., May 10, 1863, aged 27.

MERRITT C. BARRETT, son of Elijah Barrett, enlisted Sept., 1861, in Co. H, 1st Vt. cavalry. He was with his regiment in all their daring and perilous campaigns until taken prisoner in August, 1862. He was severely wounded before he was taken prisoner, and died soon after at the age of 20.

## Deceased Soldiers.

Simeon E. Cook, only child of Erasmus D. Cook, enlisted May 12th, 1862, in Co. C, 11th Vt. heavy artillery. While his regiment was stationed at Arlington Heights, Va., he fell a victim to disease, Aug. 3, 1863, aged 19. He was the pride and hope of his patriotic parents, who submitted to their loss with a cheerful acquiescence in the will of Heaven. His remains were brought home for interment.

George G. Hanks, son of Galusha Hanks, enlisted Feb. 7, 1862, in Co. I, 7th Vt. regiment. He went south with his regiment and died at New Orleans, Oct. 2, 1862, aged 17.

Selden A. Hall, son of Daniel H. Hall, enlisted Aug. 22, 1861, in Co. E, 5th Vt. regiment and died Jan. 16, 1862, aged 19. We well remember the joy and satisfaction manifested by his parents, who called at our house on the way to the depot in sending to their soldier boy a choice box of stores prepared by his mother's own hand, which only reached him on the day of his death. His remains were brought home for interment.

George Johnson enlisted Aug. 3, 1863, in Co. M, 11th Vt. regiment, and died in hospital, June 16, 1864, aged 26.

Lieut. John G. Johnson enlisted for three years in Co. G, 96th N. Y. regiment, was killed at Cold Harbor, June 3, 1864. He was a man of uncommon ability and intelligence.

Franklin S. McArthur, step-son of Silas Sheldon, enlisted in Co. I, 7th Vt. regiment. He survived but a few months, falling a victim to the unheathiness of the climate.

Michael McBrinn, son of James McBrinn, enlisted in the 169th N. Y regiment, and was killed at Cold Harbor, June 1, 1864. We are glad to record that his deserving mother receives a pension.

JAMES MCGRATH, son of Daniel McGrath, was in the naval service, and died at Chelsea Hospital, Boston, in 1865. His remains were brought home for interment.

THOMAS C. MOSHER enlisted in Co. D, 7th Vt. regiment, Dec. 10, 1861, and died Nov. 2, 1862, aged 30. He married Clarissa, a daughter of Wm. B. Robinson, who receives a pension.

ASA L. MONROE, son of Atherton Monroe, enlisted for three years in Co. L, 11th Vt. regiment, was taken prisoner, and died at Andersonville, Ga., June 24, 1864, aged 19.

FRANCIS MURRAY, a native of Canada, enlisted Aug. 24, 1862, for three years in Co. E, 5th Vt. regiment. He was instantly killed in a skirmish at Funkstown, Md., July 10, 1863. He was the first soldier killed from this town. He married Maria, daughter of Daniel B. Gould, who receives a pension.

MARTIN P. WOOD, son of Luther B. Wood, enlisted for three years, Aug. 2, 1862, in Co. B, 2d Vt. regiment. He was instantly killed at Spottsylvania, Va., May 12, 1864, aged 27 years. His widow receives a pension.

WILLARD WOOD from Danby, enlisted in Co. C, 10th Vt. regiment, for three years. He was drowned at Whitesford, Md., May 7, 1863, aged 19.

AUGUSTUS L. WRIGHT, son of William Wright, enlisted for three years, Aug. 22, 1861, in Co. E, 5th Vt. regiment. He died November 6, 1861, aged 22.

CHARLES P. TAYLOR, son of Samuel Taylor, Jr., enlisted in Co. B, 14th Vt. regiment, and held the position of sergeant. He died of measles, April 10, 1863, aged 26. He was thorough and energetic in recruiting his company, and was held in the highest esteem. His remains were brought home for interment.

GEORGE W. TAYLOR, son of Samuel Taylor, Jr., enlisted for three years in Co. B, 2d Vt. regiment. He died at Washington city, Sept. 17, 1861, aged 21. He was the first soldier from this town who died in the service.

## REVIEW OF OUR WARS.

During the period of little more than one hundred years, our citizens, in common with those of the state, and in most instances of the nation, have been involved in several bloody and destructive wars. We are not of the class that consider war an unmixed evil. In the present undeveloped stage of human society, it seems a necessary incident. We regard it in the light of a medicine, which, though bitter and repulsive to the taste, is used to remove evils greater than itself. As fever is not disease, but an effort of nature to expel disease from the system, so our wars have been an effort of our people to eradicate evils that could be reached by no other agency. The first war, in which some of our citizens were engaged, was prior to the settlement of the town from 1756 to 1760, and was called the French and Indian war. This war raged with relentless fury on our immediate frontier. As the fruits of it we were released from the debasing thraldom of French Catholic rule; we were saved from becoming a community of Canucks; we were saved from becoming what Canada East now is, and has been for one hundred years. Next in our border war with New York from 1764 to 1790, we saved ourselves from being trodden down by haughty landlords, and being made serfs on the soil we had bought and paid for. This war came right home to our bosoms and pockets, and it was war alone that saved us.

Next, and with it, came the revolutionary struggle from 1775 to 1783. England, instead of fostering our interests and helping us to a fair start in the world, as a kind mother would have done, played the tyrant towards us, and sought to keep us tributary to her, imposing taxation without our consent, and in various ways seeking to degrade and impoverish us. Petitions for redress of grievances and remonstrances against her policy, being alike unavailing we had recourse to war. We fought her; we threw off her shackles and rose to the dignity of an independent nation, a position we have since maintained. Next came the war of 1812 to 1815. England denied us the exercise of the right and duty of every nation — the right to protect and defend our own citizens, including those who had become such by our naturalization laws. We could not stand it; we pitched into our arrogant old mother, and if we did nothing more we showed the world that we could fight.

Next came the war with Mexico in 1846 to 1848. Our citizens did not generally concur in the necessity or propriety of this war. Many of us thought it beneath our dignity to invade a weak and feeble neighbor, cherishing similar institutions to our own. But the government was then controlled by slaveholders, who, envious of the rapid growth of the north, desired the acquisition of more southern territory in which to extend their pet institution, and thus maintain the balance of power.

In this movement, they overshot the mark, for though a large extent of territory was acquired, the larger portion was consecrated to freedom. On the principle, that "the end sanctifies the means," the result of this was most auspicious. An immense territory, rich in the precious metals — rich in its capabilities to sustain a dense population, was added to our national domain. These resources, instead of remaining in the hands of a few roving bands of Indians, undeveloped and unapplied, have been made subservient to the interests of this country and the civilized world. Populous states and cities are springing up as if by magic all over this vast domain. The acquisition and settlement of California, Nevada and the other states is a more momentous event than the discovery of America and its settlement by European nations, and will tell more on the progress of civilization and the good of the human race.

Next, as to the various Indian wars in which we have been involved, though we cannot justify the course of our government towards the natives in all respects, we are not of the school of philanthropists that consider the white man an intruder on this continent. "The earth is the Lord's and the fullness thereof," and mankind can have only a lease of it. When the red man failed to fulfill the conditions of his lease, "to replenish the earth and subdue it," he forfeited his title to it. So in the language of Dr. Watts.

> "Where nothing dwelt, but beasts of prey,
> And men, more fierce and wild than they,
> He bids the poor and oppressed repair,
> And build them towns and cities there."

And in our last crowning effort of arms, from 1861 to 1865, we have vindicated our pretensions to be a nation and not a mere aggregation of states, held together by a rope of sand, and have achieved by force of arms what the philanthropy and Christianity of the nation, for two hundred years had failed to accomplish — the freedom of every human being on this continent. If these millions of freedmen, after a fair opportunity, fail to stand the test of civilization let them too stand aside. We cannot deem it necessary that the Indian or the African, or any other particular race should inhabit the earth, and if they cannot, or will not, come up to the standard of their opportunities let them pass away. So if the master who has lived all his days on the unpaid toil of servants cannot "cut his own fodder" let him stand aside, and if the servant, who has hitherto supported both himself and his master after a fair opportunity granted, cannot sustain himself, let him follow suit. It is not necessary, perhaps, to the world that any man or nation should continue to exist, but it is necessary for the good of the world, that no obstacles be placed in the path of improvement, and no brakes put on the car of progress.

## LOCAL MILITIA.

The revolutionary struggle, our critical relations to New York, the constant apprehensions of invasions from Canada, and the occasional necessity of putting down domestic insurrections, seem to have imbued our fathers with a thorough military spirit from the first settlement of the town. Perhaps no town in the state was more active in organizing uniformed military companies than this. There were organized and maintained for a long period,

## Local Militia.

four uniformed companies besides the standing company.

We propose to notice each of them separately and annex a list of their captains.

### Cavalry.

A cavalry company was in existence here before the close of the revolution, but we have no data from which to determine the precise time of its organization. The larger part of this company belonged to this town, but there were men in it from Wells, Middletown and Danby. Its captains from this town were: William Fitch, Joshua Cobb, Ozias Clark, Cyrus Wells, Joseph Clark, Daniel Welch, Jr., Gideon A. Loomis, Robert H. Smith, Lovine Bromley, George W. Bromley, Isaac Crosby.

### Light Artillery.

This company was formed in 1802, and was furnished with a three-pounder brass-field piece. Its captains were: John Sargeant, James Pratt, Benjamin Fitch, David Cleveland, Willard Cobb, David Whedon, Ralph Sargent, Stephen Reed, Ezekiel Beebe, Thomas Crocker John Conant, John Stearns, Benjamin Sage.

### Light Infantry.

We have no means of fixing the date of the organization of this company, but it was probably before the artillery. Its captains were: Elisha Averill, Joseph Adams, Seth Blossom, Josiah Monroe, Joel Harmon, Jr., Abner Lumbard, James Sloane, Elisha Smith, Joshua D. Cobb, Royal Sargent, Walter Strong, John Fitch, Mahlon Cook, Josiah Toby, Hiram Wickham, George Willard, Jeremiah Bushee, Thomas J. Swallow.

*Infantry.*

This the standing company was in existence, prior to any other and is the basis of all the rest. Its captains were : John Stark, Jonathan Willard, John Cobb, Nathaniel Smith, Jedediah Edgerton, ——— Walden, Simeon Edgerton, Jr., Seth Sheldon, Lyman Reed, David Blakely, Jr., John Cleveland Leonard Utley, David Tryon, Sylvester Pitkin, Harvey Viets, James Johnson, Henry Viets, Joshua Hulett, Jr.

*Pawlet Band.*

Besides the foregoing strictly military companies, the Pawlet Band was organized about 1806. It was handsomely uniformed and was required to muster for duty, at the same time the military companies met. It was under the command of a captain, who ranked as sergeant. This band was got up under the auspices of the lodge of Free-masons who furnished in part the instruments. It is said to have been the first band organized in the state, and was greatly in request to play for masonic celebrations, Fourths of July, college commencements, and various other public occasions. We annex the original muster roll of the company, with such additions as were afterwards made : Lovell Leach, Robert Cox, Daniel Clark, Harvey Cook, Joshua D. Cobb, Philip Clark, Fitch Clark, John M. Clark, Rucard Stoddard, Silas Gregory, Nathan Allen, Harry Griswold, Nathan Stoddard, Robert Wickham, Charles F. Edgerton, Elijah Weeks, David Carver, George H. Purple, James Pratt, Jr. Alva Pratt, Ira Marks, John T. Barden, William Clark, Horace Penfield.

The instruments of this band for a full company of fourteen were as follows : 1 French horn, 1

## LOCAL MILITIA.

bugle, 4 clarionets, 1 clarion, 5 bassoons, 1 violin, 1 drum. Its captains, whom we remember, were Milton Brown, and Asa S. Jones. The ordinary routine of duty for these several companies, was to meet on the first Tuesday of June in each year, for inspection of arms and drill, and on the first Tuesday of October, for drill and exercise to which were sometimes added the performance of mock-fights. They also attended general muster, once in two years, usually at Tinmouth, for review. Occasionally they met for brigade review. The only compensation for all their services, and for keeping themselves uniformed, armed and equipped, was an exemption from poll tax, worth to each one perhaps, seventy-five cents per year.

These companies continued in existence down to about 1840, when they were disbanded.

Under the act of 1864, a military organization was effected in conjunction with Rupert and Wells, consisting of fifty men, thirty of whom are from this town. Its present officers are, Adams L. Bromley, Capt. Phineas Paul, first lieutenant, and Lucius M. Carpenter, second lieutenant. This company meets but once a year, has its uniform, arms and equipments found by the state and besides has pay for its time.

The following field and general officers, belonged to this town: General Elisha Averill, Col. Stephen Pearl, Col. William Fitch, Col. John Sargent, Col. Elisha Clark, Col. Ozias Clark, Col. Samuel Willard, Major Sylvanus Gregory, Major Moses Porter, Major Salmon Weeks.

## LOCAL GOVERNMENT.

For several years after the settlement of this town was commenced, there was no state government, nor other government outside of the town, but the Council of Safety. The Council of Safety appear to have been a self-constituted, irresponsible body, whose decisions and decrees were generally respected. From the fact that the men constituting this body were continued in the highest offices, after a state constitution was framed and had gone into operation, we infer that they held and retained the confidence of the people. Their mode of doing business was summary and prompt, and their decisions and punishments were promptly enforced and executed.

By the laws of 1779, after the state government had gone into operation, a large share of criminal offenses were punishable by whipping on the naked back, from ten to one hundred lashes according to the nature and aggravation of the offense. For several crimes they were required to wear in some conspicious place on their garments the initial letter of the crime they had committed in addition to the whipping. These laws inflicting corporal punishment were continued and modified from time to time until about 1816. We ourselves remember an instance of its infliction on a young lad who was convicted of theft, by Simon Stone, second constable.

In the absence of a common government each town managed its local affairs as best suited itself. Each town elected a board, called at first, townsmen, and afterwards selectmen, who exercised in their respective localities, about the same

LOCAL GOVERNMENT. 39

degree of arbitrary power as did the Council of Safety for the state at large.

*Town Clerks.*

We annex a list of town clerks for this town beginning in 1769, to the present time : Simon Burton, 1769; Parmalee Allen, 1770; Gideon Adams, 1775 to 1813; Gideon A. Loomis, 1813 to 1814, John Edgerton, 1815 to 1826; Elisha Allen, 1827 to 1845; Harry Griswold, 1846 to 1848; Martin D. Strong, 1849 to 1854; Jerome B. Bromley, 1855; Fayette Potter, 1856 to 1857; Hiram Wickham, 1858, to the present time.

*First Constables.*

We annex a list of first constables from 1776 to the present time, with the number of years and first and last years of service.

| Name. | Years in office. | First year in office. | Last year in office. | Name. | Years in office. | First year in office. | Last year in office. |
|---|---|---|---|---|---|---|---|
| Samuel Willard, | 2 | 1776 | 1787 | Ozias Clark, | 2 | 1792 | 1793 |
| Ezekiel Harmon, | 3 | 1777 | 1784 | Sylvanus Gregory, | 1 | 1794 | 1794 |
| Jedediah Reed, | 1 | 1779 | 1779 | Elisha Averill, | 4 | 1795 | 1798 |
| John Cobb, | 4 | 1780 | 1785 | Joel Simonds, Jr., | 1 | 1802 | 1802 |
| Lemuel Clark, | 2 | 1785 | 1786 | John Edgerton, | 2 | 1805 | 1806 |
| Joseph Fitch, | 6 | 1788 | 1804 | Heman Hastings, | 2 | 1807 | 1808 |
| Philip Reed, | 3 | 1789 | 1791 | Ashbel Fitch, | 4 | 1809 | 1812 |
| Phineas Strong, | 2 | 1813 | 1814 | Innis Hollister, | 6 | 1837 | 1842 |
| Safford Hascall, | 3 | 1815 | 1818 | Gerry Brown, | 4 | 1843 | 1846 |
| Willard Cobb, | 1 | 1817 | 1817 | William Root, | 2 | 1847 | 1848 |
| Nathan Allen, | 1 | 1819 | 1819 | Marshall Brown, | 3 | 1849 | 1851 |
| David Anderson, | 1 | 1820 | 1820 | John J. Woodard, | 2 | 1852 | 1853 |
| Return Strong, | 1 | 1821 | 1821 | Orson F. Betts, | 3 | 1854 | 1856 |
| Walter Strong, | 1 | 1822 | 1822 | Charles N. Carver, | 1 | 1857 | 1857 |
| Justin F. Simonds, | 2 | 1823 | 1824 | Fayette Blakely, | 4 | 1858 | 1861 |
| Jacob Edgerton, | 1 | 1825 | 1825 | Casper N. Leach, | 3 | 1862 | 1864 |
| Robert H. Smith, | 8 | 1826 | 1833 | Cyrus P. Taylor, | 1 | 1865 | 1865 |
| Ira Marks, | 3 | 1834 | 1836 | George S. Orr, | 2 | 1866 | 1867 |

## Pawlet.

### Select men from 1775 to 1867.

| Name. | Years in office. | First year in office. | Last year in office. | Name. | Years in office. | First year in office. | Last year in office. |
|---|---|---|---|---|---|---|---|
| David Castle, | 2 | 1775 | 1776 | James Leach, | 9 | 1800 | 1809 |
| William Fitch, | 5 | 1775 | 1782 | Ashbel Hollister, | 1 | 1801 | 1801 |
| John Thompson, | 3 | 1776 | 1783 | Sylvanus Gregory, | 1 | 1801 | 1801 |
| Joel Harmon, | 7 | 1776 | 1796 | Ozias Clark, | 1 | 1801 | 1801 |
| Gideon Adams, | 4 | 1777 | 1780 | Peter Stevens, | 4 | 1802 | 1805 |
| Lemuel Clark, | 3 | 1777 | 1788 | Titus A. Cook, | 1 | 1802 | 1802 |
| Roger Rose, | 1 | 1777 | 1777 | Andrew Henry, | 9 | 1803 | 1812 |
| John Stark, | 1 | 1778 | 1783 | Josiah Toby, | 2 | 1803 | 1804 |
| John Stewart, | 2 | 1778 | 1778 | James Pratt, | 3 | 1805 | 1807 |
| Samuel Willard, | 1 | 1778 | 1778 | Joel Harmon, Jr., | 3 | 1805 | 1807 |
| Jedediah Reed, | 1 | 1779 | 1779 | Iunett Hollister, | 7 | 1806 | 1812 |
| Simeon Edgerton, | 9 | 1781 | 1798 | Joseph Porter, | 3 | 1808 | 1810 |
| Zadoc Everest, | 1 | 1781 | 1781 | Benjamin Fitch, | 5 | 1808 | 1813 |
| John Abbot, | 1 | 1781 | 1781 | John Guild, | 2 | 1810 | 1811 |
| Jonathan Willard, | 8 | 1781 | 1789 | Josiah Monroe, | 2 | 1810 | 1811 |
| Gideon Cobb, | 1 | 1782 | 1782 | Palmer Cleveland, | 3 | 1811 | 1813 |
| Elisha Clark, Jr., | 1 | 1782 | 1782 | Timothy Brewster, | 2 | 1812 | 1813 |
| Lemuel Chipman, | 3 | 1783 | 1785 | Reuben Smith, | 3 | 1813 | 1815 |
| Seth Sheldon, | 7 | 1784 | 1796 | William Wallace, | 2 | 1813 | 1814 |
| Nathaniel Smith, | 1 | 1784 | 1784 | Amos Galusha, | 2 | 1814 | 1815 |
| Benoni Smith, | 2 | 1785 | 1797 | David Cleveland, | 4 | 1814 | 1817 |
| Elkanah Cobb, | 1 | 1785 | 1785 | Reuben Toby, | 3 | 1816 | 1818 |
| Moses Porter, | 2 | 1786 | 1787 | Henry Wooster, | 2 | 1816 | 1817 |
| Elisha Fitch, | 1 | 1786 | 1786 | Phineas Strong, | 1 | 1816 | 1816 |
| Ezekiel Harmon, | 8 | 1786 | 1793 | John Allen, | 2 | 1817 | 1818 |
| Stephen Pearl, | 1 | 1787 | 1787 | Joel Simonds, | 2 | 1817 | 1818 |
| Joseph Hascall, | 8 | 1788 | 1799 | William Marsh, | 1 | 1818 | 1818 |
| James Hopkins, | 1 | 1789 | 1789 | Ervin Hopkins, | 1 | 1818 | 1818 |
| Joseph Fitch, | 6 | 1790 | 1796 | Joel Simonds, Jr., | 10 | 1819 | 1830 |
| Philip Reed, | 3 | 1793 | 1798 | Simeon Edgerton, Jr. | 11 | 1819 | 1829 |
| Abisha Moseley, | 4 | 1793 | 1796 | Joseph P. Upham, | 6 | 1819 | 1829 |
| Findley McNaughton | 2 | 1793 | 1796 | Samuel Wright, Jr., | 2 | 1825 | 1826 |
| John Cobb, | 1 | 1793 | 1793 | Paul Hulett, | 4 | 1826 | 1829 |
| Samuel Wright, | 3 | 1797 | 1799 | Milton Brown, | 6 | 1829 | 1834 |
| John Moseley, | 2 | 1797 | 1798 | Oliver Hanks, | 7 | 1830 | 1836 |
| Edmund Whedon, | 1 | 1797 | 1797 | Return Strong, | 2 | 1831 | 1832 |
| Daniel Fitch, | 6 | 1798 | 1816 | James Leach, Jr., | 9 | 1833 | 1842 |
| Asa Field, | 2 | 1798 | 1800 | Joshua D. Cobb, | 1 | 1834 | 1834 |
| Samuel Rose, | 1 | 1799 | 1799 | Joshua Potter, | 6 | 1835 | 1842 |
| William Potter, | 1 | 1799 | 1799 | Robert H. Smith, | 8 | 1837 | 1855 |
| Jonathan Safford, | 1 | 1800 | 1800 | Nathan Allen, | 2 | 1837 | 1838 |
| John Sargent, | 6 | 1800 | 1805 | Jeremiah Bushee, | 10 | 1839 | 1849 |

LOCAL GOVERNMENT. 41

## Select men from 1775 to 1867.

| Name. | Years in office. | First year in office. | Last year in office. | Name. | Years in office. | First year in office. | Last year in office. |
|---|---|---|---|---|---|---|---|
| Ossian H. Simonds,.. | 1 | 1843 | 1843 | Austin S. Whitcomb, | 7 | 1850 | 1863 |
| Jonathan Staples,... | 2 | 1843 | 1844 | Lucius M. Carpenter, | 6 | 1855 | 1860 |
| David Carver,...... | 3 | 1844 | 1846 | James M. Shaw, .... | 6 | 1856 | 1861 |
| David Blakely,..... | 3 | 1845 | 1847 | Henry R. Hosford, .. | 1 | 1856 | 1856 |
| Jonathan Randall, .. | 1 | 1847 | 1847 | Hewit Blakeley, .... | 4 | 1857 | 1860 |
| Hiel Hollister,...... | 1 | 1847 | 1847 | Norman Winchester, | 6 | 1861 | 1867 |
| Sheldon Edgerton,.. | 2 | 1848 | 1849 | Leonard Johnson,... | 7 | 1861 | 1867 |
| Martin D. Strong,... | 1 | 1848 | 1848 | David G. Blossom,.. | 4 | 1864 | 1867 |
| James Baldrige, .... | 7 | 1849 | 1855 | Elisha B. Cook,..... | 1 | 1864 | 1864 |

## Constitutional Officers.

| Name. | Years. | Last year. |
|---|---|---|
| *Members of the Council of Censors.* | | |
| Jonathan Brace,........................................ .... | 1 | 1785 |
| Nathaniel Harmon,.......................................... | 1 | 1834 |
| *Members of the Constitutional Convention.* | | |
| Lemuel Chipman,........................................... | 1 | 1791 |
| Caleb Allen,................................................ | 1 | 1793 |
| James Leach,........ .. ............................. | 1 | 1814 |
| Benjamin Fitch,............................................ | 1 | 1822 |
| Joel Simonds,.............................................. | 1 | 1828 |
| Nathaniel Harmon,......................................... | 1 | 1836 |
| George W. Harmon, ........................................ | 1 | 1843 |
| Robert H. Smith,........................................... | 1 | 1850 |
| *State Senate.* | | |
| Elisha Allen,............................................... | 2 | 1843 |
| *Representatives to the General Assembly since 1778.* | | |
| Zadoc Everest,............................................. | 1 | 1778 |
| Gideon Adams,............................................. | 6 | 1802 |
| Benjamin Fitch,............................................ | 8 | 1822 |
| William Fitch, ............................................. | 3 | 1784 |
| Simeon Edgerton,........................................... | 2 | 1782 |
| Joel Harmon,.............................................. | 1 | 1783 |
| Lemuel Chipman, ......................................... | 8 | 1793 |
| Joseph Hascall,............................................ | 1 | 1794 |
| Nathaniel Smith,........................................... | 2 | 1796 |
| John Sargent,.............................................. | 1 | 1803 |

42                  Pawlet.

## Constitutional Officers — continued.

| Name. | Years. | Last year. |
|---|---|---|
| Ephraim Fitch, | 3 | 1806 |
| James Leach, | 3 | 1809 |
| Innett Hollister, | 3 | 1819 |
| Phineas Strong, | 2 | 1820 |
| Oliver Hanks, | 4 | 1826 |
| Return Strong, | 3 | 1829 |
| Milton Brown, | 3 | 1832 |
| Elisha Allen, | 2 | 1834 |
| Sheldon Edgerton, | 4 | 1849 |
| Joshua Potter, | 1 | 1837 |
| David Blakely, | 2 | 1839 |
| Horace Wilcox, | 2 | 1841 |
| Hiel Hollister, | 1 | 1842 |
| Ira Marks, | 3 | 1846 |
| Charles F. Edgerton, | 2 | 1845 |
| Robert H. Smith, | 2 | 1851 |
| Daniel H. Bromley, | 2 | 1853 |
| Charles Allen, | 2 | 1855 |
| Asa A. Monroe, | 2 | 1857 |
| James Leach, | 2 | 1860 |
| A. Sidney Houghton, | 2 | 1862 |
| Ervin Pratt, | 2 | 1864 |
| Lucius M. Carpenter, | 2 | 1866 |
| *County Judges.* | | |
| John Stark, | 1 | 1778 |
| Lemuel Chipman, | 6 | 1793 |
| Elisha Allen, | 3 | 1850 |
| *Sheriff.* | | |
| Jacob Edgerton, | 21 | 1861 |
| *Deputy Sheriffs.* | | |
| Return Strong, | | |
| Walter Strong, | | |
| Jacob Edgerton, | | |
| Abraham Edgerton, | | |
| Moses P. Fitch, | | |
| James Rice, | | |
| Fayette Blakely, | | |
| *Post Masters, from* 1808. | | |
| Dorastus Fitch, | 19 | 1827 |
| George H. Purple, | 3 | 1830 |
| Horace Clark, | 4 | 1839 |
| Russell C. Wheeler, | 5 | 1837 |
| Elisha F. Rogers, | 5mo | 1839 |

*Constitutional Officers — continued.*

| Name. | Years. | Last year. |
|---|---|---|
| Daniel P. Taylor, | 2 | 1841 |
| Thomas J. Swallow, | 4 | 1845 |
| Charles W. Potter, | 11 | 1861 |
| Martin D. Strong, | 4 | 1853 |
| Moses P. Fitch, | 1 | 1834 |
| James Rice, | 6 | 1867 |
| At West Pawlet, from 1852. | | |
| Thomas D. Sheldon, | 5mo | 1853 |
| Leonard Johnson, | 1 | 1854 |
| Orson F. Betts, | 1 | 1855 |
| Martin V. B. Pratt, | 6 | 1861 |
| John A. Orr, | 6 | 1867 |

## LOCAL POLITICS.

At the close of the revolution we were all one man's children. The few adherents of monarchy had been cowed into subjection or exiled from the country. Washington was the guiding genius; his name and principles were enshrined in every heart. But the process of reconstructing our government or rather of establishing our federal constitution evoked new issues and raised new questions. Gradually new parties were formed and crystalized by degrees into mutual hostility. Though differing widely in sentiment, they all paid homage to Washington, and called themselves by his name. The parties brought into existence by the new issues, were called instead of whig and tory, federal and republican, or democratic. The federals were for a strong national government and favored long tenures, and even life tenures for some of the principal offices. The democrats jealous of the central government, favored short terms and rotation in office, as involving more responsibility to the people. The ablest statesmen of this, or any country, discussed these questions in the national conventions and in the state legislatures, and the result was a compromise, neither party fully carrying its points. And though both parties substantially acquiesced in the result the foundation was laid for the bitterest political warfare the world had ever known.

It alienated friends, sundered the ties of brotherhood and friendship, broke up churches, and its venomous influence permeated every fibre of society. This town was nearly equally divided, and hence party spirit rose here to its highest pitch.

During the thirty years between the admission of our state into the Union, in 1790 and 1820, this town was represented ten years by federals and twenty years by democrats, the town being all the time nearly evenly balanced. A glance at the leading points of difference may not be in appropriate.

The democrats claimed that the states were sovereign and the general government their agent,—some maintaining that in fact we were no nation at all, only a partnership of states, from which each and every partner might retire at pleasure, the federals maintaining that we were one people, one nation as expressed in our national coat of arms, *e pluribus unum*, which freely translated means : One constituted from many. Here was evolved the germ of that knotty question whose only solvent was the blood of five hundred thousand men. Other questions having reference to our foreign relations became interwoven in the conflict. About the time of our admission into the Union, the French revolution broke out. The French people deposed their king and brought him to the scaffold and a reign of terror engulfed France and threatened to spread over the western continent. Our democrats remembering the signal service of the French, in the trying times of our revolution, favored the cause of the French revolutionists, who were at war with England, while the federals affirmed that England was the bulwark of order and security, and that the French king, whom the masses had dethroned and beheaded, he it was, who had aided us in our extremity and not the bloodthirsty men who had usurped his place.

Thus while the democrats were for " going in " to aid the French, and punish our old enemy, the federals stood aloof, not choosing to mix up in transatlantic controversies and " entangling alliances," and when the French, unable to coax our government into an active support of their cause, demanded of us as the price of our security a *douceur*, it thundered back through the intrepid and heroic Adams, " millions for defense, not one cent for tribute."

Hatred to England, though " bone of our bone and flesh of our flesh," still rankled in the bosoms of the democratic party while the federals favored the things that make for peace, having more confidence in England, than in the revolutionists of France. Meanwhile war raged in Europe; England made aggressions on our commerce, and our rights, as an independent nation claiming as *her* right the services of her native subjects wherever found, even though they had become by our naturalization laws citizens of this country. This aroused still more the anger of this nation, and we declared war against England. After a three years' conflict with varying fortunes, we were willing to make peace without insisting at all for satisfaction for the original grievance.

Our political conflicts for the forty years preceding the last ten, have been mere skirmishes based mainly on questions of expediency in which the struggle has been between the "ins and outs." The slavery propagandism of the south stimulated the north to take a defensive position, and a strong party inscribed on its banners in 1856, " No extension of slave territory." This met with the unanimous disapproval of the south, and of a large minority of the north ; but after two campaigns the candidates nominated on this platform were elected. The south now falling back on their " state rights " of secession, dissolved the old partnership and set up for themselves, taking with them as they went a large amount of furniture, that was common property. Now then comes on the most terrible war of the age or of any other age, which after being waged with varying fortunes for four years resulted in the utter discomfiture of the south. But we have wandered far from our original design, which was merely to give a synopsis of our local politics. The war which closed in 1815, finished the federal party. For some ten years no party lines were drawn. When Gen. Jackson was presented to the people as a candidate for president in 1824, he received but six votes in town, but his friends grew apace and soon became numerous. In 1828, the antimasonic party organized ; then there were three parties in town, the antimasonic the most numerous. It never succeeded in electing its candidates as the other parties would unite against it. In four or five years the antimasons disbanded and were absorbed in the old parties. About 1832, the whig party, many of whose original leaders were democrats, was organized and during its whole existence had a majority in this town, though sometimes defeated on personal grounds. In 1855, the American party was suddenly sprung upon us; but it elected its ticket but one year, and fell back to the old parties. In the last great battle which had to be fought at home as well as in the field, the union party in this town had an immense majority. And let it be here remarked that in all the mutations of party from 1766 to 1867, this town has ever been loyal to the national government, and has paid over its cash and filled its quota, with alacrity and promptness.

## LOCAL LITERATURE.

Whatever the inhabitants of this town for the last hundred years may have been, and whatever they may have done, they are not chargeable with much waste of printer's ink. After diligent inquiry, we were able to find in print, a sermon delivered before the legislature of Vermont, Oct. 8, 1812, by Rev. Isaac Beall; a funeral sermon delivered at the village, Jan. 12, 1813, by Rev. John Griswold, on the occasion of the death of Ephraim Fitch, who was killed instantly in his mill; and a singing manual, by Joel Harmon, Jr. Besides these, we believe a few sermons and controversial pamphlets have been printed. Numerous contributions to the magazine and newspaper press have also been furnished.

Though there is nothing of special interest in the sermons above alluded to, we are tempted to give brief extracts from them out of compliment to our fathers, who deemed them of sufficient value to justify their publication. And first, Elder Beall, whose text is, " When the righteous are in authority, the people rejoice, but when the wicked beareth rule, the people mourn," proceeds to discuss the rather delicate question, whether Christianity is a necessary qualification for a "righteous" ruler. "There are some, who strenuously contend that a person must be possessed of Christianity, or he is not suitably qualified for civil office. Should this be granted, another thing, in order to be consistent, must be granted, viz: that it is the only necessary qualification, for '*when the righteous are in authority, the people rejoice.*' That religion would be of great utility to a civil ruler, will be granted, but that this is the only, or even an essential qualification, cannot so easily be admitted. For, according to this sentiment, any man giving good evidence that he is a Christian, however weak his intellect, might with safety be elected governor of the state, or president of the nation — a sentiment so weak and so glaringly inconsistent, as to need no refutation. As civil government is attended to in the text, it is just and reasonable to conclude that the righteousness there spoken of, is a *political righteousness*, that is, a righteous administration of the government, with which they are intrusted."

We quote from Mr. Griswold's discourse on the character of Ephraim Fitch. "He was a man of great usefulness and extensive connections. Perhaps no man among us did more business of various kinds than he. As to his connections, he had a wife and large family, was himself a member of a large family of his father's, a member of the fraternity of Free-masons, of the Washington Benevolent Society, and of the Cong. Society, so that his relative and social connections were large. As to his usefulness: as a son, he was respectful; as a brother, he was loving; as a husband, kind; as a parent, tender and indulgent; he provided well for his family; as a neighbor, he was obliging; as a magistrate, prompt to do justice. He was a constant attendant on public worship, a friend to good order, and contributed freely for the support of the gospel. He had done much towards the erection of a building for the instruction of the rising generation. Now why should such a man be taken away in the midst of his usefulness? Can we pry into the counsels of God and search out his reasons? No! we can only say, 'Even so, Father, for so it seemed good in thy sight.'"

"*To our view*, numbers could be spared better. We should not feel the loss in society of twenty or more, we could name so much as the loss of him, and we can scarcely think of any but that could be as well spared."

In 1809, Joel Harmon, Jr., published the *Columbian Minstrel*, which contained only fifty-three tunes and anthems. Perhaps not one of these tunes are now in use. It would seem from the preface that they were original compositions. We extract briefly from the preface: "Having been frequently solicited by those who are in the practice of music to publish my compositions for the benefit of those who have entered or may hereafter enter on this delightful and sublime art, I have been induced to offer the public the following work. It is hoped that none will be disappointed that fuging music is in general omitted."

From several sketches of original poetry which have been politely furnished us we select for insertion a few, all our space will admit of.

A word of explanation in reference to the piece entitled, "Oh! to go Home," may not be improper. It was written in commemoration of a beloved twin sister who far away from her childhood's home languished and died, a victim to home-sickness. Who, that has been thrown on a bed of sickness in a land, far away from *home*, however attentively nursed and cared for but will sympathize with the subject of this poem and appreciate the beauty and tenderness of this sisterly tribute.

### THE HAYSTACK MOUNTAIN.

A thousand charms are o'er thee shed,
    Thou ancient rocky pile,
The morning sunbeams on thy head
    Are earliest seen to smile.
And evening's latest purple glow,
Adorns thy venerable brow.

When summer showers their freshning green
    And brilliancy impart,
And crowned with sunset's golden sheen,
    How beautiful thou art!
Thou wearest nature's diadem,
And needest not a costlier gem.

When homeward turned, the searching eye
    First greets thy towering dome,
Who hath not felt the heart beat high
    With tender thoughts of *home?*
Thou beauteous temple — seen afar —
Type of the never-setting star.

And oft in twilight's musing hour,
    Thou seemest to fancy's eye,
The image of some old watch tower,
    Against the evening sky;
How fills the mind, thus fancy free,
With thoughts of thy antiquity.

Yes, ever since the swelling flood
    O'erwhelmed the sinking earth,
There thou immovably hast stood —
    The deluge saw thy birth —
When its receding waters fled,
Thou didst uprear thy lofty head.

> While nations countless as the sand
>   Upon the sea-beat shore,
> Shall pass away — *there wilt thou stand*
>   Till time shall be no more —
> What *beings of an hour are we,*
> Time honored rock — compared with thee.

Pawlet, Vt., May, 1842.

MARY EDGERTON.

## OH! TO GO HOME.

She has lifted the snowy curtain away from the window pane,
And with blue eyes turning eastward, she looks through the dark
    and the rain,
The storm without is fearful, and the drops fall heavy and fast.
But she does not heed the tempest, for she thinks of the beautiful
    Past!
> Like moonlight on ruins streaming,
> Like stars in dark waters gleaming,
> Like bright forms seen in our dreaming,
>   Are memories of Long Ago.

Half smiling, she looks through the darkness, out thro' the mist
    and rain
Forgetting her heart's sad burden, its burden of grief and pain;
For her soul is journeying eastward, to the land where it used to
    rest —
Slowly returning with wounded wing to the beautiful olden nest.
> Her thoughts have gone out Maying,
> 'Mong flowers and buds gone straying,
> On banks of still waters playing,
>   In the forest of Long Ago!

She sees the low white cottage out thro' the night and rain,
The cottage close by the river, and faces at the pane;
She sees the elm and maple and hears the green leaves stir,
And her lips are parted to answer — she thinks they're talking to
    her.
> Oh, the sad soul ceases sighing,
> Hushes its moaning and crying.
> When on thro' dim woods flying
>   It rests in the Long Ago.

She sees the purple lilacs, and the ash-tree close by the door,
And the sunlight streaming in across the snowy kitchen floor —
She hears the clock in the corner, sees the pictures on the wall,
And the old brown barn in the meadow, the grape-vine, the daisies and all.
    She watches the shadows quiver
     Down in the beautiful river,
    And her warm heart thanks the Giver
     For visions of Long Ago!

She has folded the snowy curtain, down o'er the window pane,
Her blue eyes look through tears and her heart takes its burden again;
But ever when darkness gathers, and the wind comes and the rain,
She turns her face to the eastward, and lifts the curtain again!
    For like moonlight on ruins streaming,
     Like stars in dark waters gleaming,
    Like bright forms seen in our dreaming,
     Are memories of Long Ago!
          MARY ROBINSON.

## THOUGHTS ON VIEWING AN ECLIPSE OF THE MOON ON THE EVENING OF FEB. 5, 1841.

  The moon, at her zenith of splendor and might,
  Was dispensing the beams of her pure mellow light,
    Far around her cerulean throne:
The earth became envious while viewing the scene,
And unceremoniously roll'd in between
  That beautiful orb and the sun.
" I will show her," she said, " that her glory shall wane,
And the *borrowed* light of which she's so vain,
  Shall leave her in dusky dishonor,
And 'twill humble her pride as she sits in *my shade*,
Her lustre departed — her beauty decayed,
  That a million of eyes are upon her."
The clouds — she had done them some service it seems,
Had fringed their dark robes with her silvery beams,
  And light on their pathway had cast;
When they saw what was coming — incurtained her throne,
And a mantle drew o'er her — sweet Charity's own —
  Till her transient misfortune was passed.
But the stars felt no sympathy—*this was their day*—
So they burnished their spangles and twinkled away;

Exulting, it seemed, at her fall;
She was subject to *changes*, they knew from her birth—
And should she emerge from the shadow of Earth,
    They feared she might outshine them all.
But there was one thought—not a fanciful one,
That the Moon when thus darkened — shut out from the sun,
    Was an emblem, though feeble and dim;
Of the *Soul*, when estranged from the presence of God,
It has wandered so far from its heaven-ward road,
    That the *World* gets between *it* and *Him*.
O, then, let me count all afflictions as light,
Though the billows of Time in their uttermost might
    Unceasingly over me roll;
But O! may I never the bitterness know
The depth of despair—inexpressible wo,
    Of a total *eclipse of the Soul.*

MARY EDGERTON.

## AFTER BATTLE.

At many a costly entrance, at many a cottage door,
Darkly floats the badge of mourning for those heroes gone before!
Oh the hearts all torn and bleeding — oh the hearts that suffer so,
In the costly stately mansions, and within the cottage low!

Like a dim and shadowy ghost stands a picture in each hall;
Like a fearful horrid phantom, clings it to the lowly wall—
After Battle they have named it, and each mother's heart would break
Did not Jesus, tenderly, more than half the burden take.

Oh the great and ghastly wounds, Oh the bleeding deadly wounds,
Oh the groans and moans and shrieking — how the heart faints at such sounds,
How the soul cries out in anguish, like a dying white-winged dove,
To hear such cries of agony from the lips of those we love.

How those dying eyes look homeward — how those hands reach out for friends,
But a little moment passes and the dreadful suffering ends!
For them no more weary marching, they have *fought the battle well!*
For *us?* the angels know what waits for us — I cannot tell.

Oh the blue eyes full of love! Oh the dark and tender eyes
Whose love and tenderness is gone, to blossom in the skies :

Oh the heads so coldly pillowed, and the feet that march no more,
The quiet feet of the soldier whose battle of life is o'er.

See that throng of weeping sisters, bowed and weeping for their
　　brothers,
Hear the mothers call their dead sons and pale maidens call their
　　lovers!
Oh, the loved that die in battle—how my *soul aches* at the thought,
And I cannot smile at victories with such precious life-blood
　　bought. 　　　　　　　　　　　　　　MARY ROBINSON.

## AGRICULTURE.

Agriculture was the earliest avocation of mankind, and is the basis of all industrial pursuits. It involves a greater diversity of labor than any other calling, and is as much dependent on the mechanical arts for its successful prosecution as that or any other business is on agriculture. The interests of all industrial callings and pursuits are so blended and interwoven that where one suffers, all the others suffer with it.

Our sons who would establish for themselves a home in the west, have immense advantages over our fathers in the first settlement of this town. There the broad prairies invite the plow as the first instrument of cultivation. Here the heavy growth of timber had to be slashed in winrows, burnt over, the trunks gathered together and burnt again, and after all this was done the first crops worked in by hand. But our fathers worked with a will, and in a few years brought under subjection a large portion of the town.

Their leading idea was to grow wheat both for home use and with which to raise money to pay for their land. Brought up on the brown bread of old

## AGRICULTURE. 55

Connecticut, they hoped by coming here to indulge in the wheaten loaf. But their high raised expectations were not fully realized. Most of the newly cleared fields produced wheat in rich luxuriance, and some fields held out for a long series of years. But to speak generally wheat growing was a failure.

The rich and enduring wheat fields of the Holland purchase and the Western Reserve were then hardly explored. Many of our first settlers allured by the splendid reputation for wheat growing of Orwell and other lake towns, emigrated thither, among whom were several families of Clark's, Smith's, Cobb's, Perkins's, etc. Those clay bottoms held out better than our soils.

By degrees our people had to fall back on the brown bread of their fathers. The coarser grains yielded abundant harvests. But they were of small account for distant markets. Hence distilleries were introduced to absorb our surplus grain which was about as valuable for feed after the alcohol was extracted as before.

But in a few years, say from 1820 to 1830, these crops sensibly diminished. A new impetus was given to emigration. The west was now open for settlement; families emigrated as they had never done before. Heavy canvas covered wagons, many of them drawn by oxen, could be seen en route for the west having the words "bound for the Ohio" enblazoned on their sides. This caused a heavy drain on our population which our well-known reputation for "raising" men, could not sustain. Our population rapidly declined. Several considerable settlements in the more remote quarters of the town were abandoned and some highways discontinued.

The introduction of manufactures before, and during this period, partially stayed this tide of emigration, but it has flowed out ever since and there has been no reflux, to the present day. But we have wandered from our subject. When our lands were in some measure worn out by a succession of grain crops, we betook ourselves to the dairy and sheep-fold to recruit our exhausted fields. The effects of this change of business were soon sensibly felt.

Improved breeds of cattle and sheep were introduced and improved processes of cheese making have been constantly going on till they have culminated in the establishment of cheese factories. The cultivation of root crops has been extended, particularly of potatoes which have been raised in large quantities, at first, for starch, and since the rail road was opened for shipment to city markets.

Fruit growing has from the start received great attention. Apple orchards were every where planted in great abundance, and in virgin soil throve well with little care. And as you pass through the town, some parts of which are deserted by its inhabitants, wherever you see a clump of apple trees you may be sure that near that spot some one undertook to establish for himself a home. The smaller fruits were not neglected and plums, cherries, grapes and pears flourished luxuriantly; strenuous but unavailing efforts were made to acclimate the peach. On newly cleared fields the blackberry and raspberry grew in abundance, while the meadows teemed with strawberries and the mountains with whortleberries.

Old age and the severity of our winters are fast destroying our apple-trees and other early planted fruits, and wild spontaneous fruits are growing scarce. But within a few years a new era has opened on our fruit-growing prospects. Improved varieties of apples, pears, plums, grapes, and cherries are being introduced, and the strawberry and other small fruits are being cultivated in gardens. On the whole, the present condition and prospects of the town are highly flattering and though some of our hillsides and badly managed farms may be less productive than formerly, still it is our opinion, endorsed by more competent observers, that the agricultural interests of our town were never in a more flourishing condition than at the present time. Labor is every where munificiently rewarded and though the taxes assessed on real estate are and have been enormous, yet the value of farms has appreciated full twenty-five per cent on the gold standard within the last five years.

## MANUFACTURES.

One of the earliest and not the least important manufactures of the town was the salts of ashes, which by refining processes were made into the pot and pearl ashes of commerce. The process of manufacture was simple and required but little capital. The lye of ashes was boiled down to the requisite consistence, when under an intense heat the salts were produced. This would seem but a small business now, but at that time it was of the greatest consequence, it being almost the only article that would bear shipment to foreign ports.

Along with this, and partly in connection with it, was the manufacture of maple sugar. The same kettles served to boil down the sap which were used to make potash. As the process of sugar making is familiar to every one, we need only remark that sugar makers instead of boring the trees were in the habit of " boxing " them with an ax, and instead of buckets of wood or tin used troughs made of pine, bass, or other soft wood.

As soon as wool and flax could be raised or procured, domestic wheels and looms were set in motion, and for nearly half a century most of the cloth used in families was made at home. The price for a week's work spinning was four shillings (66⅔ cts.) and for housework 4s. 6d. The wool was usually taken in the fleece, carefully picked, oiled, and carded with hand-cards. One person could card about as fast as another could spin. A neighbor at my elbow relates this anecdote. His father had occasion to call on Gov. Thomas Chittenden on public business, who it is well known kept a wayside tavern in Charlotte. After the governor's wife had with her own hands prepared supper and cleared up things, she took her position by the kitchen fire and carded wool till a late hour, while the governor was in the bar-room alternately transacting official business and waiting on customers at the bar.

About 1800 the first carding machine brought on this continent was set up at Middle Granville, N. Y., by James Smith. The price of carding was ten cents per pound. Fulling and cloth-dressing mills were in use at an early day, but how early we can not say. There was one at West Pawlet, run by Walter Jennings, in 1812, and we believe at the village at an earlier date. Jonathan Stevens and John Strong built a woolen factory at West Pawlet in 1812, which was the first in town. About the same time Doct. John Sargent built a woolen factory near the present site of Enoch Colvin's factory. This latter was run several years by Royal Sargent and other parties until it fell into the hands of Asa S. and Joel Jones, who run it until it was burnt, about 1842. Asa S. Jones soon after built the mill on the road, which he sold in 1846 to Robert Blakely, who run it (the latter part of the time in connection with his son William) until 1865, when it was sold to Enoch Colvin.

At an early day Capt. Abner Lumbard run a fulling and cloth-dressing mill at the village and also a woolen factory, part of the time in connection with his son Chester. About 1812, Willard Cobb built a factory on Wells brook near the bridge. Jonathan Stevens run the factory at West Pawlet two or three years, when he went into Cobb's factory, which was soon after burnt. The war with England brought all these factories into existence; at its termination they were all compelled to stop. Jonathan Stevens continued the business in a small way until 1832, when he put up a large factory on Pawlet river near the lower covered bridge, which did a good business until it was burnt in 1852. He then set up the business in Granville, N. Y., which is still continued by his son Robert. A notice of the Pawlet Manufacturing Company and the Flower Brook Company will be found elsewhere.

There have been seven grist-mills in town, all but three on Pawlet river. We name them in the order of their erection as near as we can ascertain. The first was on Wells brook, built by Remember Baker about 1768; the next was built at the village, about the same time, by William Bradford, on Flower brook; the next on the site of the present Red mill, by Col. Samuel Willard, in 1783, which was soon burnt and the present mill erected; the next near the lower covered bridge on Pawlet river, about the same time, by Capt. Benoni Smith; the next, near the Frary bridge, about 1790, by William Hanks; the next near Smith Hitts, by Seth Blossom, Ashbel Hollister and Safford Hascall. There was also a mill at West Pawlet, built by Edmund Whedon. Of these only one, the Red mill, is now in existence, run by Charles F. Edgerton. There have been six or eight saw-mills in town, which are now reduced to the one at the village, run by David Andrus.

Several small establishments were set up in various parts of the town for the manufacture of leather; one on Seely Brown's land, by Wesley Perkins; one near the Frary bridge, by Ebenezer Rollin, and one on our premises, by Ephraim Jones. These were short lived. There were three larger establishments, one at the village, run by Asahel Fitch and others; one south of the village, run by David Weeks and his sons Rich and Seth B., and one on Indian river on the premises of C. S. Bardwell, by Palmer Cleveland & Sons. There is now no tannery in town.

There were trip-hammers on Wells brook, by William Maher; on Flower brook, by Nathaniel Robinson, and on Indian river, by C. S. Bardwell, for the manufacture of edge tools and machinery. The latter is the only one in existence.

There have been five distilleries for the manufacture of whisky from rye and corn, and brandy from cider; one at the village, run by Dorastus Fitch; one at West Pawlet, run last by Theron Norton; one on Alex. Clayton's premises, run by Leonard Utley, one near the centre of the town, by John Edgerton and others; one near Curtis Weeks's, by Mr. Savage, but these were all closed thirty years ago.

A flax-dressing mill was built in 1820, by Ashbel Hollister, which run a few years. A mill for cleaning cloverseed was built in 1807, by Seely Brown, which run fifteen years. A linseed oil mill in 1814, built by Samuel Wright, Jr., and others, run some twenty years. A mill for making potato starch, by Ira Marks on Indian river, was built in 1843. The

## MANUFACTURES. 61

next year one was set up on Pawlet river by ourself and Seth Stearns. Both these did a large business several years. A stave mill for the manufacture of shooks for the southern market was run near the lower covered bridge, by Ebenezer Hayward, which closed in 1865. Lime was burnt in the south part of the town, by James Cook and others, quite a number of years. Provision barrels were made several years on the premises of Stephen McFadden by Samuel Baldwin and Jonathan Monroe, and cheese casks and boxes just above by Nathaniel G. Folger. Cheese boxes were made at North Pawlet two or three years by machinery moved by steam. The only cheese box factory now in existence in town is at the village, by David Andrus. Hats were manufactured at the village by Maj. Sylvanus Gregory and his son Silas Gregory, forty or fifty years. A stocking factory was run at the village several years by Ira Marks. Palmer Cleveland & Sons, about the year 1825, put in extensive machinery for dressing hemp and flax, and constructed a pool for water-rotting them. This business was carried on several years. Florace and Leonard Johnson made cheese boxes at West Pawlet two or three years, and Peter Goodspeed followed the same business near the Frary bridge.

Notwithstanding this rather gloomy record, we take pleasure in noticing two live establishments for making cheese, which will appear elsewhere. We close this chapter by alluding to the prospective erection of works on the farm of Consider S. Bardwell for the preparation of peat for fuel.

## MECHANICS.

Mechanical industry is of high antiquity. Its first development was in the garden of Eden before the expulsion of our first parents. Though the oldest tailors in the world, we are left to infer they were not experts, as soon after God made them "coats of skins." After their expulsion, Cain, their eldest son, "builded a city," and soon after we read of Jubal, the father of such as handle the harp and the organ, and of "Tubal Cain, the instructor of every artificer in brass and iron." After the lapse of a few generations Noah built an ark, which for size, beauty and magnificence has probably never been surpassed. Industrial arts, we may assume, were chiefly lost at the flood, but they revived and perhaps attained the climax of their excellence in the days of David and Solomon. Still later the Greeks and Romans cultivated the arts and sciences to a great extent. Since then the world has undergone many mutations and revolutions, and many of the ancient arts are lost. The last fifty years has witnessed, probably, a greater advance in industrial science than the eighteen hundred that preceded it. Inventive ingenuity is achieving greater and still greater triumphs, and the "Golden Age" of the ancients is being reproduced with additional splendor.

All this, however, may be considered irrelevant in a local history. A large proportion of our early settlers were skilled mechanics, and were trained under the old English law that prescribed seven years' apprenticeship. People in the olden time did not jump at one bound from the plow-tail to the mechanic's shop. But they were ignorant of many inventions that have greatly facilitated the business of the mechanic. By the aid of planing, matching, sawing, mortising and boring machines, it is safe to assume, the manual labor required to build a house has been diminished one-half, and in proportion for most other kinds of mechanical business. We have not space to enumerate the various trades followed by our fathers.

## EMIGRATION.

It has often been made the subject of remark and of regret, that so many of our people should emigrate, and that so many of the old homesteads should be abandoned.

The establishment of manufactures, on a more extended scale has been suggested as a means of keeping our enterprising young men at home. Certainly we have facilities for manufacturing far superior to many of our manufacturing towns. But let us survey the whole ground. Within the last sixty years there has been opened for settlement nearly in our own latitude, the richest and most grandly magnificent territory the sun ever shone upon, reaching from the Hudson across the continent, and embracing a wealth of soil and facilities for settlement unsurpassed in any age of the world.

What an opportunity to spread and perpetuate the principles of our Puritan ancestry! Should this rich domain pass into the hands of foreigners and outsiders and have no "New England" in it? Should we have surrendered to the foreigner of undeveloped liberal tendencies, or to the southerner of thoroughly matured principles of tyranny this rich heritage? And all this that we might immure within the prison walls of factories, our surplus population to rise, eat, work and sleep at the signal of a bell? Would it pay thus to enervate the sinewy limbs and bow down the manly frames of our young men and chase the rose and lily from the cheeks of our fair daughters that a few lords of the loom might get rich? Employees as a class do not lay up money. The man who employs himself goes whistling to his work, while the hireling watcheth the going down of the sun. Westward between the parallels of 40 and 45 there is scarcely a county or even a town that has not a representation from this town. Who can measure the influence exerted by emigrants from New England in moulding and establishing the institutions of these states? Our mission has been to infuse the principles, cherished here, throughout these states. Well may the southern tyrant desire in breaking up our Union to leave us out in the cold. We have few principles in common with him. Will not the benefits resulting from our emigration outweigh any possible advantages we might have secured by staying at home. Though so many has gone, yet a remnant remains. Notwithstanding the decadence of our mechanical and manufacturing interests, involving in its consequences a loss of fifty per cent of our population, we have reason for congratulation at the steady advance of our educational, moral and religious interests. Our primary schools are well sustained and keep step with the spirit of the age. Never before were our religious institutions so liberally sustained. Our people are mainly self-reliant and self-supporting, and fewer instances of destitution now exist than perhaps at any former period. Real estate never before sold higher on the gold standard. What though we have but one small factory and only one mill, a saw mill — stocked mainly from another town, we still live. Our sensibilities are so obtuse that we count ourselves a prosperous people.

## EDUCATION.

Next to providing themselves a shelter and the most common necessaries of life, our fathers, true to the institutions in which they had been reared, directed their attention to the interests of education. Schools were established as soon as a sufficient number of scholars could be gathered in any locality, and the progress of the settlement of the town can be better traced by the *number* of the school district than by any other means. Money being scarce, the better qualified would frequently take turns in teaching with little or no compensation. If nothing better could be had a deserted log cabin would be fitted up for a school-room and made to answer.

Our early schools were limited to the branches of reading, writing, spelling and arithmetic, and it was rare that the latter was extended beyond the rule of three. The education of girls was still more limited and it was not common for them to learn arithmetic. By degrees other branches were introduced, and grammar was taught, perhaps, as early as 1810. Those who first learned grammar were considered prodigies. Other branches have been from time to time introduced, so that our district schools almost rival colleges in the extent of their course of study.

Provision was made in the charter of the town for one share (250 acres) for the benefit of schools, to which was added by state legislation the share reserved for a church glebe, and the share reserved for the Society for Propagating the Gospel in Foreign Parts. This last was, however, taken from the town by a decision of the U. S. supreme court. The legislation of the state has always favored the interests of schools, and step by step the entire expense of their maintenance has been devolved on the property of the town, except the revenue derived from public lands and from the U. S. deposit fund.

There have been seventeen school districts organized in town, which are now reduced to eleven, in only ten of which schools are now kept. Besides, there are two fractional districts in connection with Rupert and Wells. The following statistics are from the report of the town superintendent of schools for the year 1866, see school statistics.

Many of the first settlers were educated men — several of them graduates of college, and were able to appreciate the advantages of a higher standard of education. Hence measures were taken about the beginning of this century for the establishment of an academy or grammar school, as such institutions were then generally called. A commodious brick edifice was erected near the village, in which the higher branches were taught, usually two terms in the year, fall and winter, until its destruction by fire in 1845. We regret that we cannot insert the names of its founders, nor even of its first trustees, and only a few of the names of its preceptors can be given. It is proper to say that most of its preceptors were graduates of college, or members of the senior class. Among its preceptors were Messrs. Barber, Smith, Meeker, Ira M. Allen, Mervin Allen, John Stuart, Lamson Miner.

When the Methodist church on the hill was vacated in 1854 by the society, it was fitted up for an academy under the auspices of Rev. Jason F. Walker,

## EDUCATION.

its first principal. He was assisted and succeeded by Edwin I. Spink. The succession of principals has been about as follows: Henry H. Buxton, Samuel A. Burnham, A. J. Blakely, John L. Edgerton, John Wiseman, Collins Blakely and Mr. Fradenburgh, who have taught the school one or more terms each.

Our citizens have not been unmindful of colleges and other literary institutions, and have contributed to endow Middleburgh College, Troy Conference Academy, Hamilton Theological Seminary and other institutions. The following persons, settlers and natives, have graduated at the several institutions named[1]: *Daniel Hascall, 1806, M.; *Hippocrates Rowe, 1808, M.; Fitch Chipman, 1808, M.; *John Sargent, Jr., 1811, M.; Beriah Green, Jr., 1819, M.; Miner Pratt, 1823, M.; Elijah W. Plumb, 1824, M.; *Ferris Fitch, 1826, M.; *Rollin F. Strong, 1829, M.; Azariah R. Graves, 1833, M.; *Jacob E. Blakely, M.; Merit Harmon, 1825, M.; Job H. Martin, 1825; Azariah Hyde, 1838; Fayette Potter, U.; *Horace Allen, U.; Sheldon Blakely, U.; A. Judson Blakely, U.; Collins Blakely, U.; Quincy Blakely, V. U.; *Festus Hanks, N. J.; Charles Winchester, W. U.; *Lucien B. Wright, T.; *Jonathan Brace, Y.; *Israel Smith, Y.; *Noah Smith, Y.; Warren B. Sargent, C. M.; Nathan Judson, C. M.; Isaac Monroe, C. M.; *William U. Edgerton, C. M.; John Cook, C. M.; Aaron Goodspeed, C. M.; Socrates H. Tryon, C. M.; Nelson Monroe, C. M.; R. G.

---

[1] M. is for Middleburgh College, U. for Union College, W. U. for Wesleyan University, C. M. for Castleton Medical College, C. A. for Castleton Academy, N. G. for North Granville Ladies Seminary, T. C. A. for Troy Conference Academy, G. S. for Glenwood Seminary, D. for Dartmouth College, Y. for Yale College, N. J. for New Jersey College, T. for Trinity College, A. C. C. for Albany Commercial College, U. V. for University of Vermont. A star * prefixed to those known to be deceased.

Monroe, C. M.; Egbert H. Carver, A. C. C.; Sarah Allen, T. C. A.; Mary Allen, T. C. A.; Lucy B. Hurlbert, T. C. A.; Lettie T. Lincoln, T. C. A.; Jane Bromley, T. C. A.; Louise Culver, N. G.; Helen M. Bromley, G. S.; Maria Conant, C. A.; Ann Smith, C. A.; Cornelia Hawkins, C. A. *Honorary* — Ervin Hopkins, 1817, A. M. M.; Jonathan S. Green, A. M. M.; Fayette Shipherd, 1830, A. M. M.; Elijah W. Plumb, D. D. M.; Levi H. Stone, A. M. M.

## LIBRARIES AND PERIODICALS.

About the time the academy was built a library was procured by subscription, which was first kept by Rev. John Griswold, but as far back as we can remember, by Dea. Ezekiel Harmon. It was free only to subscribers. It contained many choice books, the old English classics, religious works, practical and polemic; history, biography, travels, &c., all of standard character. It was used until most of the books were worn out. In 1830 a library of periodicals was established at the village, comprising the *American Encyclopedia* of thirteen volumes, and most of the higher class quarterly and monthly magazines published in this country. This continued a few years when the library was broken up. Soon after a neat and choice library was established at the village on five dollar subscriptions, of which a few avail themselves.

Periodical literature is the great educator of the age. During the earlier years of our town but few periodicals circulated, and those small country papers distributed weekly by post riders. The taste for newspaper and magazine reading has of late years greatly increased and few families are without them. During the excitement of the war a large number of daily papers were taken. The citizens of this town are now receiving through the post-office as follows: Daily papers, 5; semi-weekly, 29; weekly, 283; bi-monthly, 73; monthly, 200, and tri-weekly, 1; embracing in the whole 591 copies.

## MUSIC.

Music is coeval with the creation, "When the morning stars sang together and all the sons of God shouted for joy." The Hebrews in their conflicts with the Egyptians celebrated their victories with songs and dances. In their rejoicings over their enemies it attains its sublimest heights, in their wailings when in captivity its profoundest depths. Perhaps its highest development was in the days of King David.

The birth of the Saviour was heralded with song, and his last act at the institution of the Lord's Supper was the singing of a hymn. St. Paul says, "I will sing with the spirit and with the understanding," as though melody was cultivated at the expense of the sentiment. "Teaching and admonishing one another in psalms and hymns and spiritual songs," is enjoined as a duty. But space fails us to follow out this theme. From the apostolic age to the reformation we only know, generally, that music was cultivated in the Catholic church. Perhaps the oldest piece of music in use among Protestants is the grand and stately Old Hundred. Born of the Reformation and attributed to Martin Luther, its magnificent swell of notes joined to the words set to it, "Be *Thou* O God exalted high," convey a scathing rebuke to the Popish idolatry of that day. This tune outlasting the uses of earth will accompany the song of the angels and be chanted by the " redeemed out of all nations" during the unending cycles of eternity. We cannot give the protestant world much credit for the cultivation of music during the last three hundred years. Music of some kind they must have, but any thing that savored of catholicism they rejected. So their music degenerated into a kind of humdrum psalmody of two parts.

Till within about one hundred years New England music was traditional and not set to notes, the deacon *lining* the hymn, and the whole congregation joining in the song. The first attempt to introduce note-singing encountered the bitterest hostility. The peace of churches was destroyed and in some instances they were broken up. But science prevailed in the end. The revolution which stirred the souls of men developed a new style of music, which was styled fugue music. This was in sympathy with the clash and excitement of the day. New Jerusalem, which will be remembered by all our older citizens, is a representative tune of this class. The parts falling in one after another, each part singing different words at the same time, are thought to represent the clangor and confusion of the battle-field; the base the deep-toned artillery, the tenor the rattling fire of musketry, the counter the crack of the rifle, and the treble the bugle blast heard over all. The fastidious did not relish this medley of sound, and the first effort on record to introduce a different style was made by Joel Harmon, Jr., of this town, who published a singing manual in 1809. The tunes in his book were of his own composition and in express opposition to what he styles "fuging" music. This did not take and his book never got into general use. Fugue music prevailed until about 1820, when it fell into disuse and substantially the style of music now in use was substituted.

The oldest teacher of music in this town, of whom we retain any tradition, was Deacon Seth P. Sheldon of Rupert, who taught music as early as 1782. We next hear of Dea. Benoni Adams, who taught in both parts of the town.

Joel Harmon, Jr., before referred to, taught music classes and attempted to reform the style. Rev. John Griswold and Oliver Hanks also taught music over sixty years ago. About the beginning of this century, Eliakim Doolittle (uncle of Hon. James R. Doolittle, senator in congress from Wisconsin) also published a singing book and taught singing. He was the child of song and no mean composer. In his later years, nervous and sensitive, impulsive and excitable, in tattered garb, with untrimmed locks and beard, in a state bordering on insanity, he wandered through our streets for many a year, the terror of timid women and children, and found rest only when lodged in his grave. We will not undertake to mention the different teachers of music since 1820, when Rev. Lemon Andrus taught. A few good singers and teachers have been developed in this town, none of whom are better known and appreciated than James Whedon and Dr. A. Sidney Houghton.

The prejudice against instrumental church music, cherished by our puritan ancestry, has come down almost to our own time. A base-viol was at first barely tolerated, but now melodeons and cabinet organs are in use in all our churches.

Secular music, which has always been in use, is now much improved and refined, and many tunes belonging to this class have been appropriated for church music. We need only mention "John Brown" as a representative of this class. In the privations and sufferings incident to a war of four years' duration, this song cheered the hearts and nerved the souls of our gallant soldiers until they had achieved a peace that involved in its results the freedom of every slave on this continent. It was this that enlivened the dreariness and monotony of camp-life; it was this that sustained them in their long and weary marches; it was this that nerved their souls to engage in deadly conflict with their country's foes, when they unfurled her banner on a hundred battle-fields and the streams of the sunny south were reddened with their comrades' blood.

And when in the loathsome dungeon, when there was "no eye to pity and no arm to save," it was this that buoyed up their drooping spirits when subjected to a refinement of cruelty unknown to savages. Nor is this song the theme of Americans alone, but of the friends of republican liberty the world throughout.

When two hundred thousand Englishmen met the other day in the interest of the extension of the elective franchise, did they sing God save the Queen? No! Did they sing the republican Marseillaise? No! But it was "John Brown's body lies mouldering in the grave, while his soul goes marching on." And when in the fullness of time "Ethiopia shall stretch forth her hands unto God," and a degree of culture and development unknown to the present age shall be her inheritance, "John Brown's soul goes marching on," shall be the burden of her rich minstrelsy.

Instrumental parlor music is now in vogue, and pianos, cabinet organs, and melodeons are every where met with. Among the teachers of this class of music from this town, we may mention Mrs. Frances Woodfin, Mrs. Betsey (Clark) Everett, Amelia Clark, Cornelia M. Edgerton, Mary Edgerton (deceased), Martha Clark, Helen Sargent, Jennie Culver, and Mrs. Maggie Bardwell.

An instrumental band (noticed elsewhere) was organized in 1802, which continued to play over thirty years. In 1841 a spirited brass band was got up by James Whedon in West Pawlet, which continued several years.

We may remark that most of the new societies that have from time to time arisen among us adopt at first the old style of music, which argues its adaptedness to the childhood of churches. We further observe that the latest phase of church music approximates in some degree to that which so charmed and fascinated us in our early days and whose ringing tones still vibrate in our ears.

## THE OLD SCHOOL HOUSE.

A description of the school house and school in which we received our education from 1811 to 1820, will suffice for most of the schools of that day. A plain plank building of repulsive exterior, having on one end an immense stone chimney, through which there was a grand prospect of the sky, and whose cavernous jaws would hold in their embrace a half cord of wood, a writing table running round next the wall, a row of benches in front made of slabs inverted, supported on pins like carpenters' horses, a few low benches in the centre, a desk in the corner next the chimney on which lay the ferule, the emblem of the school-master's authority, and the establishment was complete.

After the fashion of the day, the teacher would call the school to order and detail one of the scholars and invest him with the rule whose duty was to watch the school and pass the rule to the first transgressor of the rules of school, who relieves guard, and passes it to the next delinquent, and so on, with the comforting assurance that whoever got the rule twice, or had it when the school closed should have it applied to his own palm. The plan served its purpose, and order and stillness prevailed. These ferulings were no joke, especially when the subject was a little spunky.

We have seen ridges raised on both the hands of a delicate girl who would laugh in the face of her tormentor, while the cowardly boy would make a loud outcry and be let off easily. It was a matter of principle with the children not to cry if they could help doing so.

But when flagellations failed, we were sometimes required to extend our arm at a right angle with a heavy rule or book in our hand, the master standing near to rap our knuckles if our arm fell below a horizontal line. Or we would be seated on an andiron or a block of wood near the chimney corner, which would be called a dunce-block and the scholars be required to point the finger of scorn at us. But when wholly incorrigible, as a last resort we would be placed between two girls. This would unseal the fountain of tears and force the perspiration through the hide of a crocodile. We wilted then. But alas! such was the hardening nature of this capital punishment that its frequent repetition reconciled us to it, and as we grew older we even began to relish it.

Arithmetic was taught the boys, and needlework

the girls (in summer), while all learned reading, writing and spelling. Proficiency in spelling was the test of scholarship. We were not distracted with a multiplicity of class-books, but Webster's old spelling book was at our tongues' end and the English Reader learned by heart. The teacher would set our copies and mend our goose quill pens and pay little further attention to our writing. The solution of the problems in Adams's old arithmetic was the work of years. Grammar was studied by the large boys in winter. We remember all our teachers by name. Augustus Frank who was member of congress from Genesee county, N. Y., was our first teacher. Daniel Dana, a veteran old teacher, known all over town, was another. Mary Lee, who married Rev. Allen Graves and went missionary to Burmah, was another. Under these favoring circumstances we were graduated at the old "Braintree" school house at the age of fourteen. The last teacher who gave the finishing touches, we recollect was employed at the extravagant price of seven dollars per month of twenty-six days. This may not seem so extravagant, when we consider that our school only numbered from sixty to eighty scholars.

## FIFTY YEARS AGO.

A comparison between the year 1816 and the present time, exhibits many striking contrasts. Then, as now, we had just emerged from a bloody war, though the loss of life and treasure was twenty times greater in the latter instance than in the former. The close of that war found industry paralyzed, property depreciated, banks broken, even the Vermont

State Bank, founded on the credit of our noble state, and all branches of business, nerveless and drooping. Those who had contracted debts in the flush times of the war could not meet them. The laws then allowed imprisonment for debt. The really poor would go to jail and after a few weeks probation "swear out." Some, who could not do that would give bail and secure the liberty of the yard. All legal devices were employed that would stave off the payment of debts. Doubt and distrust pervaded every circle of society. Mortgage holders would foreclose and acquire the debtor's property at half its value. Capitalists who had ready money could fix their own rates of interest. Creditors then had the long end of the whiffletree, and were not slow to avail themselves of it. Superadded to all these disabilities came the short crops of 1816. It was then not so much the question who should pay his debts, as who should live through it.

The famine and the depletion of the country by the war, were not the only causes of this deplorable state of affairs. At the close of that war the charter of the old U. S. Bank had just expired, which created a monetary crisis, and our tariff was any thing but protective. General Jackson and other heroes of that day had infused into John Bull a thorough respect for us and consequently unlimited confidence. He poured into our markets an avalanche of merchandise which crippled our industry, crushed out our infant manufactories which the necessities of war had created and tried, as he is trying to day, to induce us to adopt the principles of free trade while himself maintains the most stringent protection. The cheap goods thus thrown upon our market proved our undoing. The consumer, the merchant and the importer, were all crushed together. We had few productions that would bear shipment. A

little beef and pork, pot and pearl ashes at the north
and rice and tobacco at the south, the growing of
cotton being then in its infancy.

Following the course of time, fifty years, let us
note the contrast. We have now hundreds of national banks on as stable basis as the nation itself.
We have a tariff on imports altogether, the most
stringent in our history, which yields to our national
treasury, hundreds of millions annually — an internal
revenue, which yields two hundred and eleven millions — a heavy state and local taxation, and yet every
interest of our country is eminently prosperous. The
capitalist is willing to loan money at six per cent;
the mortgage holder will not take his pay unless
compelled; labor is in buoyant demand at three
times the price of fifty years ago; manufacturers and
mechanics are rejoicing in unparalleled profits; merchants were never before doing so well; farmers are
fattening on their rich returns and every interest of
society is in a flourishing condition; rents are doubling in our cities; ladies never before dressed so
richly, and gentlemen were never before so profuse
in their expenditures.

Colleges are being endowed; church building
funds raised; salaries of the clergy greatly enlarged;
contributions for missionary and benevolent purposes
augmented. And but recently we were sending ship-
loads of provisions to feed our enemies, and pouring
millions of dollars into the lap of our Christian and
sanitary commissions. At what period in the history of our race, was the like ever witnessed? And
all this in the face of the heaviest taxation ever im-
posed on any people. The soldiers sent from this
town have received in town bounties and state pay,
over sixty thousand dollars, besides government
bounties, pay, clothing and rations amounting to
double that sum. While we credit protection for a

large share of this prosperity, we are not at liberty to overlook the recently developed sources of wealth within our own borders.

The gold and silver of California, the petroleum of Pennsylvania and more than all the interminable wheat and cornfields of the glorious west are the basis of our national wealth. Fifty years ago we had no canals, the telegraph had not been imagined, nor the rail road even dreamt of, the express which visits nearly every locality in our vast country and conveys untold millions from one place to another had then no existence. Steam was then making its maiden efforts to stem the tides of the Hudson. Mowing and reaping machines which do the work of twenty men with scythe and sickle were then unknown. Drills and cultivators and iron plows had not been invented, but the old wooden Dutch plow, with two yoke of oxen, a driver, and a boy on the beam with a clearing stick, and murdering the soil at the rate of a half acre per day was its principal pulverizer. Then there were not half a dozen carriages in town and those old quillwheel concerns ; but the common farm wagon was the vehicle of pleasure as well as of business.

The power loom, the spinning and sewing machines, and many other labor saving inventions, had not been heard of. Instead of the clumsy iron hoe, shovel and fork, we have the same articles of steel. It may safely be assumed that two-thirds of the labor of farming and nine-tenths of the labor of manufacturing are saved by the implements and machinery in common use.

Fifty years ago water for household and farm use was obtained from a spring or brook, or perhaps from a well, while now almost every house and yard is supplied either through pipes or by the aid of pumps. The well sweep is swept away ; our supplies of water reach us through the principle of gravitation. Instead of the old fire place which engendered an uncertain warmth, our houses are thoroughly heated with stoves and furnaces. Instead of naked walls and floors the former are clothed with paper of every brilliant hue; while the latter are spread with the richest carpets. What has not the last fifty years wrought for us?

## HARD TIMES AND SEASONS.

In order to appreciate fully the blessings showered upon us in the present age, it may not be inappropriate that the *hard times* and *seasons* that our fathers encountered should pass in review before us. The winter of 1780-81 was of unprecedented severity, the snow falling to a great depth. It is handed down to us by tradition that for fifty successive days the snow did not melt on the south side of buildings. This severe weather fell with crushing effect on our settlers, who were poorly supplied with forage for their cattle and with comfortable dwellings for themselves, and added greatly to their privations. In 1789 there were short crops and great destitution. In 1805 there was a drought of great severity, no rain falling from seeding-time in spring to harvest time. The consequence was an almost utter loss of spring-sown crops.

But 1816, which is within our own remembrance, was the great year of famine. It has ever since been referred to as the *cold* summer. There were copious rains in the spring up to May, when a drought set in which lasted till September. There were frosts every

month in the year. Winter grain was a tolerable
crop, but summer grain and grass were almost a
total failure. There was scarcely a bushel of corn
raised in town. There was great destitution and
distress in the following winter and spring. Many
cattle perished and many people reduced to the last
extremity. Benevolent people divided their scanty
stores with the more destitute, but the selfish took
advantage of the opportunity and put on exorbitant
prices. When harvest time came round in 1817,
those who had early crops divided with those who
had none; some of the grain being cut so green that
it had to be kiln dried before it could be ground
into flour). It was not the habit of people to lay up
stores beforehand, and we had then no west to supply us with bread.

For the last fifty years there has been no year of
general failure of crops, though in 1826 the grass-
hoppers made serious havoc, and like the locusts of
Egypt consumed nearly every green thing. They
were different from the ordinary grasshopper and
filled the air in such numbers as almost to cast a
shadow. The next year the caterpillar or army
worm made great devastations and stripped fruit and
forest trees of their foliage. They marched from
west to east in search of fresh fields. In the west
part of the town many fruit trees and most of the
sugar maples were destroyed. Since then the labor
of the husbandman has seldom been unrewarded.
The country did not get over the depression caused
by the war until General Jackson recommended a
protective tariff which was effected in 1832. Since
then the country has passed through the financial
crises of 1836 and 1857, which though many fortunes toppled down had but little influence on the
general prosperity of the country. A cloud of
threatening aspect hangs over our immediate future;

but let us not distrust the providence that has safely carried us through the terrible conflicts of the present decade.

## THE HOMESTEAD.

With many of our fathers the one absorbing sentiment or passion was the establishment of a homestead and its perpetuation in the family. For this they planned, for this they toiled. Other considerations had to yield to this or become subservient to it. Their labors and privations were sweetened by the thought that here they were preparing a home, if not for themselves, for those dearest to them. With pride and complacency they looked upon the fields they had rescued from the domain of nature, upon the buildings and improvements they had made, and exultingly exclaimed with Alexander Selkirk:

"I am monarch of all I survey,
My right there is none to dispute."

Not content with a homestead for themselves, many of them made the greatest exertions to settle all their children around them and become a patriarch in their midst. The land they had redeemed from its wilderness state, which they had cultivated with their own hands, was to them sacred soil. The houses they had built, in which their children had been born and which to some of them had been the gateway to the spirit land, had become associated with their tenderest recollections and sympathies, and no thought was more repulsive to their minds than that they should ever become the abode of strangers. The study of their life, the absorbing thought of their old age, was how to dispose of their paternal acres that they might remain integral and undivided in the family.

Nor was this feeling of attachment to the homestead confined to the parent. How many sweet and pleasant memories cluster around the spot where our childhood was passed. With what rich and undying interest do our minds revert to the scenes of our early life, the streams in which we bathed and angled, the hills on which we gathered nuts and hunted game, the mountains where we picked the luscious berries, the fields and the gardens through which our earliest footsteps roamed, the orchard whose every tree had a name, the school-house where our young ideas learned to shoot and the play-ground where we followed our sports.

But the inexorable logic of events frustrated many of these cherished plans. The children, allured by flattering prospects elsewhere, left the paternal mansion, some of them never to return, and many times drawing after them those very parents who had fondly hoped here to spend their declining years and lay their bones. They had the impressive experience of the lesson that "here we have no abiding place." The fever of emigration pervaded whole families and communities. They gathered up their household gods and followed in the wake of the setting sun.

Where now are the Chipmans, the Fitchs, the Hascalls, the Adams, the Porters, the Harmons, the Strongs, and hundreds of others that occupied these lands and filled our high places. To the solemn and impressive inquiry, Our fathers, where *are* they? we may subjoin, Our children, where are *they?* How few of the loved homes of our fathers are retained by their children! "Westward the star of empire wends its way," and man must fulfill his destiny.

## ANTI-SLAVERY.

The first instance on record of the manumission of slaves by military authority took place in this town in 1777. Capt. Ebenezer Allen, in command of a company of Col. Herrick's regiment of Rangers, while on a scouting expedition within the British lines, captured two slaves. In a rescript dated "Head Quarters, Pollet, 24th Nov. 1777," he sets them free. In the same spirit Judge Harrington demanded of a southern slave-hunter as a condition of the rendition of his victim a "bill of sale from God Almighty." No slave ever entered Vermont without having his shackles broken. William Lloyd Garrison, the great apostle of American emancipation, sojourned long enough in Vermont to become imbued with its spirit when he went to Boston and established the *Liberator*, which more than any other agency has contributed to melt the fetters from every slave in this broad land. It is somewhat singular that while the masses of the state have ever been among the foremost in asserting the principles of liberty and equal rights, we have never sent a Giddings, a Lovejoy, or a Sumner to the halls of congress. Our public men have been followers, not leaders, in this great work. They accepted the result when wrought out by others, but who of them has filled the proud position of leader?

As with the state so with this town. No outspoken abolitionist was allowed to represent us. Among those of our native and adopted citizens who have been conspicuous in their advocacy of equal rights we may mention William Marsh, Rev. Beriah Green, Rev. Fayette Shipherd, Ozias Clark and Paul Hulett. William Marsh lifted his voice, wielded his pen, and emptied his purse in behalf of liberty.

Beriah Green consecrated his splendid gifts of oratory to the promotion of the same great object, and was assiduous and untiring in organizing and concentrating effort to bear on the great question. Fayette Shipherd employed his graceful and impressive powers of elocution to educate the masses and imbue them with the spirit of liberty. Ozias Clark and Paul Hulett were steadfast old "wheel-horses." On one occasion when we were present the trustees of the Congregational church refused to open their doors for an anti-slavery lecture, and when Deacon Clark sent for the key it was refused. "I can get that key said he, and strode off down the road — and he got it. We were not then conscious of the malignant power of slavery, to effect the overthrow of which has cost our country so many thousands of lives and so many millions of treasure. When John Brown left the scaffold at Charlestown, Va., to take his position among the "noble army of martyrs" the ball was set in motion, but it took a four years' war to solve the problem.

## TEMPERANCE.

One of the characteristics of the early inhabitants of this town, and of the state as well, was their addictedness to the use of intoxicating drinks. Their use had so permeated every fibre of society that no enterprise was undertaken without them. They were the symbol of good will, the evidence of friendship. They were potent in settling difficulties which perhaps themselves had caused. No public occasion could dispense with their presence. At weddings and funerals, at courts and elections and in all social circles they were indispensable. In the professional office, in the store, and in the shop, in the field and at the fireside they were always to be found. The food of the unweaned infant was steeped in liquor, and at every stage from the cradle to the grave, its presence was invoked. At trainings and the raisings of buildings they were specially in demand; at auctions were used to obtain the highest bids. It was common for families to have a cask of liquor in their cellars. Apples were diligently cultivated that their juice might be converted into poison, and coarse grains were raised for the same purpose.

Many people were sensible of the great evil, but were so enmeshed in its toils as to be unable to extricate themselves. They would bewail their condition and resolve to abandon the habit and then perhaps go and treat their resolution. It took the thunder of Dr. Lyman Beecher's six sermons on intemperance, published about 1825, to awaken them from their trance. They not only showed up the great evil in glowing colors, but unfolded a way of escape. The simple remedy of total abstinence from the use, and furnishing distilled liquors, was published to the world. It took form by voluntary associations signing a pledge to that effect. A new field of labor in the work of reform was opened and industriously cultivated by those who had faith in its efficacy. The pledge of abstinence was offered to people of all ages and conditions and of both sexes. A large proportion of the youth signed the pledge, and more of them than of the adult class held to their integrity.

It is noteworthy that the greatest opponents of this work of reform were the moderate drinkers. However the leaven spread, the work went on, and a changed public sentiment was the result, and in a short time it become unpopular to drink or furnish liquor to others. A few who signed the pledge indulged in the use of fermented liquors which brought scandal on the cause and made it necessary to reform the pledge, so as to require abstinence from all intoxicating drinks. This last movement led on by John Hawkins at Baltimore, Md., in 1840, spread over the entire country. It was called the Washingtonian plan, and gave a new impulse to the work. Many confirmed drunkards were reformed who were efficient auxiliaries in reforming others.

When the temperance party was in the ascendant in the state, a position it soon attained in this town, restrictive laws on the sale of liquors were enacted by the legislature. The policy and expediency of legislation on this subject is a question hardly settled to this day. Its worst effect was the slackening of moral effort. For the last twenty years temperance men have rested on their oars, leaving to the ministers of law to perfect the reform. The consequence is, as might have been anticipated. The use of liquors is gaining ground with fearful rapidity, and we are sorry to perceive among the young men and boys. Legislation has done all it can for us; moral effort must come to the rescue or we are lost.

Prohibition on the sale of liquor as a beverage has become the settled policy of the state. In all the different phases which the question of legal restriction and prohibition have assumed, the vote of this town has ever been in favor of the strongest and most stringent measures. Among our earliest and foremost advocates of temperance were Rev. Fayette Shipherd, Col. Ozias Clark, Dea. Joseph Porter, Sylvester Pitkin and John Fitch.

Since writing the above, in 1866, a new impulse has been given to the temperance movement. A joint effort is being made by the combined forces of moral and legal effort which promises auspicious results. A staunch temperance friend at my elbow suggests that the picture above given of the state of the cause is rather overdrawn and presents an aspect too gloomy. We hope and trust it may prove so, but have concluded not to alter the text.

## GAME.

Marvellous stories were told by the old settlers of the plentifulness of game when the country was new. The common deer, which still inhabits unsettled portions of the country, was found in great numbers, and was of signal service in the trying times of the first settlement, and in the transition state from the privations of pioneers to the comforts and conveniences which soon surrounded them. Though exceedingly timid they sometimes approached so near the cabins of the settlers as to be within reach of their rifles. Their flesh was capital for food, and their skins were in great request for clothing, moccasins and a great variety of purposes. An anecdote is told of Elisha Pratt, father of Capt. James Pratt, which will bear insertion. In common with other settlers he was sometimes in a state of great destitution. One Sabbath morning, while engaged in reading his Bible, his wife discovered a fine buck in his wheat field near by and handed him his rifle saying, there is a noble buck out there, we are almost starving, had you not better shoot him? No! he replied, the Lord hath sustained us and kept us alive thus far, and if it is His will that we should have that deer to keep us from starving He will cause it to come some other day. The deer *did* make his appearance another day and was secured.

In so high estimation were deer held that before

the organization of a state government regulations were made to protect them from destruction from December to June. Deer-rifts were among the first officers elected in town, whose duty was to enforce these regulations.

The black bear was also common and served much the same purposes; but unlike the deer he was always mischievous and sometimes dangerous.

The abundance of game, as well as the necessities of their situation, led our fathers to cultivate a taste for hunting, trapping, etc., an employment always full of excitement and not unfrequently of danger. On one occasion Ansel Whedon, who was second to none in relish for these sports, went out *cooning* alone and having treed the coon climbed the tree to shoot his game; but the night being very dark he could get no sight at the animal. He came down, built a huge fire at the foot of the tree and watched till daylight revealed a large bear, at which he fired, wounding her severely, when she fell into the bed of coals. Suddenly rising from this uncomfortable spot she made a spring with terrific growls at her enemy, who made good time for the top of a small tree, where he remained closely besieged until his voice echoing through the woods brought timely aid.

The bear is not yet wholly extinct. Solomon Reed, who lives in the southeast corner of the town near Dorset mountain, can tell you capital stories of his encounters with them, even during the last few years.

Beaver meadows, where tradition locates the habitations of these animals, are found in various parts of the town. They have long since disappeared. The last beaver seen in town was killed by Ansel Whedon about 1800, in a corn field, with his hoe. Otters and minks were more plentiful. The latter is found quite frequently now. Dr. Thompson quotes the price of mink skins in 1842 at from 20 to 40 cents, according to quality. Two mink pelts were recently sold, one for ten dollars and the other for eleven dollars. Old hunters say that formerly muskrat pelts were worth more than mink. The former are caught quite often. Within a few years Joshua Potter killed an otter near his residence. Charles Jones killed another measuring five feet eight inches, but none have been recently seen. A few foxes are yet found, though not so plenty as formerly. One of the most exciting sports of the age is to set a hound after a fox, who moves in a circle round his hole, giving the sportsman an opportunity to bring down the game. This mode of hunting is about discontinued and most of the foxes taken now are caught in traps. Once in a few years grey squirrels are plenty and occasionally a black squirrel is found. The raccoon is sometimes started in a corn field. Skunks still infest our poultry yards and woodchucks our meadows. The skins of the former sold a few years ago as high as a dollar and a half a piece; they are worth less now. In our boyhood pigeons were so numerous as almost to darken the air in their annual migrations, but of late years few are seen. The eagle built his nest on the most inaccessible cliffs of our mountains, but is not often seen now. The henhawk and the crow remain and are almost the only legitimate game among birds. A few partridges whirr past us in the forest and occasionally wild ducks flit over our streams. The quack of wild geese is heard periodically from above the clouds. Indian river was the favorite and last fishing ground of the Indians in this part of the country. To this they paid annual visits long after its occupation by the whites. The locomotive is on the trail of the Indian who hunted and fished on what is described in the old deeds as the *Indian river plain*. Trout are still caught here, but the sportsmen do not allow them to attain much growth. As game receded to the northern forests our old hunters and trappers followed on. Some at the present time make an occasional trip and bring home trophies of game and fish.

## USAGES, CUSTOMS AND OBSERVANCES.

Our fathers, tried in the fires of the revolution which had consumed their substance, were men of nerve and great physical power. They came here to make for themselves a home on the fertile slopes and luxuriant valleys of this beautiful town. We have heard and read of their privations, sufferings and destitutions in the first years of their life in the woods. How that many of their rude cabins were without doors and without floors; how the storms beat through their bark roofs and wild beasts howled around their dwellings by night; how that they had no cellars and nothing to put in them; how scanty their wardrobe and still more scanty their furniture; how a kettle or two, a few pewter plates and wooden trenchers, two or three knives and forks, some three-legged stools and a straw bed in the corner constituted their house-keeping articles; how worse than all that, they would have no bread for weeks together and but a scanty supply of meat; how the children would go barefoot the year round and often go supperless to bed; how that they would go thirty or forty miles to mill on horseback and sometimes on their own back.

But amid all these trying circumstances they kept up heart and hope and bravely triumphed. They felled the forest, they cleared the ground, they planted wheat, and corn, and orchards. They soon exchanged their rude cabins for comfortable dwellings. They raised flax and wool, and the music of the spinning wheel and the rattle of the loom were heard in every household. In a new country the better and unselfish traits of human nature are sure to be developed.

They were kind and friendly and ever ready to assist each other. In their recreations they would gather from all parts of the town, and no feeling of exclusiveness would mar their enjoyments.

Steadfastly attached to the institutions of the fatherland they evinced the greatest solicitude to engraft them on their new home. Old Connecticut was reproduced, her laws reenacted, her local festivities observed and Election cake eaten with as keen a relish as when in their own loved down-country home. Cheerful toil was the rule, and more cheerful pastime the exception. The work of the day done they would meet in each other's houses and pass the evening hours.

True to the traditions, superstitions and customs of early New England, they brought with them, with many substantial virtues, a belief in ghosts, respect for dreams and hatred to Indians. These constituted the staple of their conversation. The children with mouth and ears agape drank in these wondrous tales. In their excited imaginations every white object was a sheeted ghost and every dark one a wild beast or Indian. In their work as well as in their play they grouped together. Whether to build a house, clear a fallow, or harvest a crop, they would combine their strength and be sure to get through in season for a game. Athletic exercises, wrestling, ball-playing, etc., were their favorites. Time wears on ; their cabins are exchanged for substantial domiciles, and the homespun age commences. The grand old central fireplace radiant with sparkling flame; the spacious kitchen with its oaken floor; a loom in one corner and spinning wheels all around; its ceiled walls decorated with the products of the spindle, while overhead hung festoons of dried apples and circlets of pumpkins. The shelves of the pantry glisten with burnished pewter and the trusty rifle hangs over the mantel.

The sturdy farmer in his leather apron, and troops of boys in roundabouts are bustling around, while the busy housewife and her bevy of rosy-cheeked daughters clad in the garments their own hands had spun and wove and put together, completed the picture. Without, the well-filled granary, the well-stocked stable, the orchard, the sugar-bush, the golden wheat field, the valleys standing thick with corn, the tapering well-sweep from whose point swings the bucket,

"The old oaken bucket, the iron bound bucket,
The moss-covered bucket that hangs in the well."

Within is heard the clatter of the loom, the hum of the busy spindle, while without is heard the clangor of the flail and the ax, which "redoubling strokes on strokes on all sides round the forest hurls her oaks headlong."

The men and boys have their hunting parties, trainings, raisings and huskings, and the women their quiltings and apple-cuts. By the way, speaking of apple-cuts, did you ever attend an old-fashioned apple-cut? *We have*, and even its memory warms the blood chilled by the frosts of sixty winters. How much of fun and frolic! How many happy hours! Every house and cabin gives up its juveniles who flock to the rendezvous, single, in pairs and groups. The younger strata fill up the corners and vacancies. Amid the wagging of tongues and bursts of laughter the work goes merrily on. Soon the last basketful is reached and disposed of, pans and peelings gathered up and the pie passed round. Then comes a calm, but it is only the stillness that precedes the storm. Some wide-awake girl attacks a fellow and brings him up standing in the middle of the floor, the whole company circle around them, from stairway and chimney-corner they come and round and round they go.

The scene changes and snap and catch-em is the play. How some of those girls would run! What suppleness in their joints! What a spring in their instep! What fox-like doubling on their track! It was all your neck was worth to catch them as they scampered round the ring, over chairs and across the hearth. But when fairly hunted down they *did* turn at bay and with disordered hair, flashing eye, crimsoned cheek and panting breath they fell into your arms; what a glorious surrender!

The ring breaks up and round the chimney to the tune of "The needle's eye, you can't deny," march on the gleeful throng. Little fellows raise their tiny hands that some six-footer may pass under. Kissing and laughing is not done by rule, and lads and lasses run wild with unfettered sport. But apple-cuts must have an end, perhaps among the small hours of the next morning. Then comes the trying time! things are hustled on; the boys stand hat in hand; some have lost their tongues; the bold win and off they go. Hearts are broken, but they will heal and break again.

Old time marriage observances claim a passing notice. Vehicles being scarce, we will mount the aspirant for matrimonial position on his trusty nag. He reins up beside some convenient stump and with one bound the blushing bride is on the pillion. On they speed to old Squire Adams or the minister, who receives them with a genial face and a merry twinkle of the eye. The pair are united, the silver dollar paid and home they go. Perhaps a signal horn sounds on the distant hillside, then the drums rattle, the horns blow, the pans clatter and a motley throng gathers at the matrimonial quarters. If the latch-string is out all goes well; a merry hour they spend and home they go. And then the bundling — but let that pass.

Among the sweet and pleasant gatherings of the old times is the sugar party. Sugar-making is an unromantic business, but when through the openings of the forest you discover a party of young men and maidens, including the girl you love best, coming to enjoy a sugar treat, how your heart bounds in its prison-house! How delicious the repast, as the happy group gather round the smoking kettle and help themselves!

In these homespun times family visits were made in the evening, Instead of the afternoon tea-party both sexes met in the evening when a substantial table was spread, perhaps a turkey or sparerib, at least the best the house afforded. They were great believers in omens, and dreams were of great significance, especially when twice repeated, an event quite likely to happen after late suppers.

With our fathers the Sabbath commenced at sundown on Saturday and closed at the same time on Sunday. Preparations for Sunday living were made on Saturday; the pudding boiled, so that by evening business of all kinds was suspended and the Sabbath was strictly observed. Sunday evening was a season of relaxation (as with the Romanists after Lent the carnival). Families visited; there was a reunion of friends and lovers and a good time generally.

Funeral rites were attended with more solemnity

## USAGES, CUSTOMS AND OBSERVANCES.

and ceremony than they obtain at present. The deceased, borne on men's shoulders, whatever the distance, and attended by pall-bearers, was carried silently and reverently to the last resting place. At the grave, which was always closed before the assembly withdrew, it was expected that the father or husband or next friend would tender the thanks of the mourners.

Ordinations and Quarterly meetings were occasions of great interest and attended by all the country round. Baptismal rites, when performed by immersion, were seasons of special interest. A procession would be formed, preceded by the elder and deacons and followed by the choir, candidates and congregation, would repair to the river side, the choir singing hymns as it moved on.

Church music, though perhaps devoid of the artistic grace and accuracy of its present development, was animating and spirit stirring in the highest degree. In the ear of what old citizen do not the notes of Father Griswold, Benoni Adams and Seth P. Sheldon, still linger?

Our churches were then unprovided with stoves or furnaces which were poorly compensated by foot-stoves. At noon in winter the whole congregation would repair to their homes or some neighboring house to partake of refreshments and replenish their stoves. Our old churches were large structures, cool and airy in summer, and decidedly so in winter. Furs were greatly more in use than at present and served a good purpose. Interesting music, warm hearts and self-denying devotion did the rest, and the churches were well filled.

A few gentlemen of the old school sported the beaver hat, silk stockings and velvet small clothes, while the masses were clad in homespun. Ladies of any pretensions would be arrayed in scarlet cloaks, gold beads and muff and tippet of large dimensions.

It was required of boys to bow on entering a house, or passing a person in the street, while the salutation of the girls was a curious movement involving the falling and rising inflection of the joints.

## MERCHANTS.

Trade and commerce are the great agencies of civilization, and through their medium the treasures of this entire globe are brought within our reach, and made to subserve our comfort and convenience. The furs with which we shield our persons from the rigors of this northern clime are brought, it may be, from Hudson's Bay and the great northwest wilderness; the buffalo robes we wrap around us from the slopes of the Rocky mountains. Our feet are shod with the hide of an ox that run at large on the pampas of South America. Our clothing made from the wool of sheep that roam at will over the interminable plains of Australasia or Central Africa. The tea whose fragrance we inhale grows at our antipodes; our coffee in Java, Arabia, or perhaps Brazil. The rich spices with which our food is seasoned come from the islands of the Pacific and Indian ocean. Our sugar, moistened with the tears and blood of hapless slaves, is brought from Cuba. The sperm with which we light our dwellings and lubricate machinery is procured from among the icebergs of the Arctic ocean. The silks in which we array our persons are the product of the looms of southern Europe. The feathers with which we decorate our hats, the ivory with which we chew our food, from western Africa. The perfumes of our toilet are from central Europe, our delicious fruits from the coasts of the Mediterranean, dainties and delicacies from all parts of the torrid zone. The mahogany and rosewood of our parlors and all our rich colors have their origin in Central America. The medicine that soothes our pain from Turkey, that which gives tone to our enfeebled systems from the slopes of the Andes. Wines and brandies from southern Europe, diamonds from the Amazon and La Plata, pearls from the Indian ocean, and India rubber from southern Asia. Cashmere shawls from the heights of the Himmaleh, our richest carpets from eastern Europe, our finest lace from Belgium, and latest fashions from France. And nearer home: gold from California, silver from Nevada, copper from Superior, lead from Illinois, petroleum, coal and iron from Pennsylvania; beef and flour from the valley of the Mississippi; fish from the mouth of the St. Lawrence; oysters from the Chesapeake, and we have not named half that habit has made necessary. And how do we pay for all these pleasant things and luxuries? By shipping abroad our surplus cheese, butter, wool and potatoes.

To exchange these commodities is the province of the merchant. In the minds of many the name of merchant is associated with fraud, deceit and extortion. *We have been there,* and we do not endorse the charge. We propose to enumerate as consecutively as may be, those who have been engaged in this business in this town for the last century.

At the village we begin with Col. William Fitch, who was a kind of commissary to Col. Herrick's regiment of Rangers in 1777. After him were Joel Harmon, Ephraim Fitch, Dorastus Fitch and Silas Fitch, Phineas and Return Strong, Hart & Judson, Reed Edgerton, George H. Purple, Horace Clark, Russel C. Wheeler, Harvey Baker, William Wallace, Thomas J. Swallow, George Edgerton, Martin D. Strong, David Whedon, Jr., Hiram Wickham, William Sheldon, John Allen, Henry W. Leach, Daniel H. Bromley, Adams L. Bromley, Rollin C. Wickham.

Charles W. Potter, James Rice, Daniel W. Bromley and Collins Blakely are in the business now. At the factory village, the agents of the Pawlet Manufacturing Company, John Guild, Milton Brown, William Sheldon and Marson Edgerton kept store. There was also a Union store here in 1851, Daniel H. Bromley, agent. In the south part of the town, Stephen Pearl, at an early day, and later, Judson & Baker; near the centre, Elkanah Cobb and Andrew Henry; at West Pawlet, Joseph Ackley, Seely Brown, James S. Brown, Ira Goodrich, Theron Norton, Fayette Buckley, Sylvester Norton, Elihu Orvis, Elisha Marks, Ira Marks. Union store, 1851-52, Theodore Stevens, John J. Woodard, William Sheldon, Thaddeus D. Sheldon and Judson R. Harlow, agents; Jeremiah Clark, John J. Woodard, Reuben Marks, Hiel Hollister, Martin V. B. Pratt, James Houghton, Frederick M. Hollister and John A. Orr. Mr. Pratt still follows the business. At North Pawlet a Union store, Division 230, was kept from 1851 to 1861, Lewis Lincoln, agent.

## MARKETS.

As, in all new countries, for several years after the settlement of the town was commenced, there was little produce to go abroad to market. The constant additions to our population required all that was grown for home consumption. Potash, to the manufacture of which our citizens paid early attention, was about the only article that would command the cash, or warrant transportation to markets. Furs and skins to a limited extent may be added. The rich valley of the Mohawk supplied the then sparse population of the cities and villages on the Hudson. In the early years of the revolution wheat was worth only about forty cents per bushel at Albany.

When the town was generally brought under cultivation, and a surplus of produce acquired, Lansingburgh at first and afterwards Troy were our principal markets. Cattle and sheep were mostly driven to Boston.

The expense of transportation to Troy for many years was only twenty-five cents per hundred and coarse grains would hardly admit of transportation even at that low price. The current of trade was changed to some extent when the northern canal was opened about 1820, though many still continued to haul their freight direct to Troy. On the opening of the rail road in 1852, freight business was done almost exclusively through that channel. The occupation of the teamster was gone. Our present principal articles of shipment are cheese, butter, wool and potatoes, to which may be added fruit and poultry to a limited extent.

## PHYSICIANS AND DISEASES.

The noble art of healing has been well represented by its practitioners and disciples in this town. Our early physicians were among the most noted in the state. Dr. Lemuel Chipman being the first president of the Vermont medical society and Dr.

John Sargent, the first president of the Rutland county medical society.

The earliest practitioners of medicine in this town were Eliel Todd and Abishai Moseley in the north part and Lemuel and Cyrus Chipman in the south part of the town. Jonathan Safford succeeded Drs. Todd and Moseley, and John Sargent and Oliver L. Harmon, the Chipmans. Next to these and with them were Samuel Potter, Ithamar Tilden, Warren A. Cowdry, John Sargent, Jr., John L. Chandler, James H. Willard, Alva Paul, Isaac Monroe, Aaron Goodspeed, —— Merrill, John Cleveland, Charles Houghton, Phineas Strong, Jr., and Renselaer G. Monroe, who all practiced medicine for longer or shorter periods in this town. Our present physicians are Warren B. Sargent, and A. Sidney Houghton at the village, and M. H. Streeter at West Pawlet. Sketches of most of these will be found in the chapter on Family Sketches. Annexed is an alphabetical list of all the physicians who have practiced here, or who have received their medical education in whole or in part in this town, so far as known or remembered: Frederic W. Adams, Daty Allen, Allen Andrus, —— Baker, Charles Beman, Joseph Blossom, Charles W. Bourn, George W. Bromley, Simon Burton, John L. Chandler, Lucius M. Carpenter, Lemuel Chipman, Cyrus Chipman, Gilbert Churchill, John Cleveland, John Cleveland, Jr., John Cook, Warren A. Cowdry, Joshua Edgerton, William U. Edgerton, Jonas Fay, Byron Flowers, Alfred Gregory, Aaron Goodspeed, Abel Hannah, Ezekiel Harmon, Jr., Oliver L. Harmon, David A. Hascall, John E. Hitt, Calvin Hollister, Charles Houghton, A. Sidney Houghton, Campbell Johnson, Frank Jones, Nathan Judson, Sylvester Kent, Henry W. Leach, Joseph Loomer, J. W. Marshall, Silas Meacham, —— Merrill, Isaac Monroe, Renselaer G. Monroe, Orville Morrison,

Abishai Moseley, Alva Paul, Elijah Porter, Moses Porter, Jr., Moses Porter, 2d, Robert Porter, Samuel Potter, C. W. Potter, Samuel Potter, Jr., George Potter, Jonathan Safford, ——— Safford, John Sargent, John Sargent, Jr., Warren B. Sargent, Artemas Sheldon, Hiram Sheldon, Justin F. Simonds, Justin Smith, James Smith, Phineas Strong, Jr., Thomas D. Strong, Ithamar Tilden, Philo Tilden, Eliel Todd, Norman Towslee, Socrates H. Tryon, James H. Willard.

At the first settlement of the town fever and ague prevailed to a considerable extent. And since, though no town can boast of a more healthful atmosphere or of purer water, it has been subject to a great variety of diseases. The epidemic of 1812 to 1814, which was so destructive to life in many parts of the state claimed but few victims here. Consumption was more prevalent forty or fifty years ago than of late years. Seventeen young women died of that disease in the north part of the town in the space of two years. It has always prevailed to a greater or less extent. In 1845 the small pox spread to an alarming extent on the mountains in the south part of the town. There were forty persons attacked by the disease, all of whom with the exception of one child recovered. This disease left its impress on the countenance of many of our citizens, and to the skill and faithfulness of our physicians, Doctors Warren B. Sargent and Charles Houghton, together with the prompt sanitary measures of our select men, Jeremiah Bushee, David Blakely and David Carver, may be attributed, under Providence, our singular exemption from fatal results. During the last five or six years diptheria has prevailed to an alarming extent and has proved fatal in many instances. Also the spotted fever this year and the last.

## ATTORNEYS.

The profession of law has been well represented in this town from its earliest infancy. The confident expectation then entertained that this town was destined to become the county seat of the present counties of Bennington and Rutland induced a large number of educated men to settle on the contemplated site of the village in the south part of the town. Among them were three or four attorneys, graduates of colleges. Jonathan Brace, Israel Smith, Noah Smith and Truman Squier, settled here and commenced the practice of law. Disappointed in this, Jonathan Brace returned to Connecticut, Israel Smith removed to Rutland, Noah Smith to Bennington, while Truman Squier remained some twenty years and fell back on Manchester.

The next attorney we hear of was Daniel Church, who practiced law at the village and afterward at Arlington and Bennington, and died near Toronto, C. W. After him came Nathaniel Hunt and Nathaniel Hamblin; the latter remained several years, but they both removed to Ohio. Next we find Nathaniel Harmon who followed the profession some forty years till his death. Leonard Sargent opened an office here when first admitted to the bar, but soon removed to Manchester. George W. Harmon succeeded his father, Nathaniel Harmon, remained a few years and removed to Bennington. Fayette Potter and Jerome B. Bromley are the only practicing attorneys now in town. We subjoin a list of attorneys who have practiced law or originated or received their education here: Horace Allen, Isaac Allen, Merritt Allen, Royal C. Betts, A. Judson Blakely, Sheldon Blakely, Robert S. Blakely, Jonathan Brace, Daniel W. Bromley, Jerome B. Bromley, Aaron Clark, Daniel Church, James Crocker, Joseph K. Edgerton, Chester Edgerton, Fayette S. Fitch, Nathaniel Hamblin, Nathaniel Harmon, Ira Harmon, George W. Harmon, Asa Hascall, Lebbeus Hascall, Ralph Hascall, Galen R. Hitt, Marvin Hollister, James Hopkins, Nathaniel Hunt, Walter Hurlbut, B. Newbury Loomis, Charles Meigs, John K. Porter, Edwin Potter, Fayette Potter, Leonard Sargent, Henry H. Smith, Israel Smith, Noah Smith, Rollin F. Strong, Truman Squier, Augustus Sykes,. John H. Wilcox, Cyrenus M. Willard, Charles Winchester.

## THE MOTHERS OF THE TOWN.

Our history will be glaringly incomplete if we do not devote a chapter to the mothers of the town who stood in their lot and bore their full share of the anxieties and toils, privations and sacrifices incident to laying the foundations of society in a new country. In addition to their domestic and maternal duties they not infrequently assisted their husbands in the field, in clearing land and harvesting crops. Besides the whole labor of carding, spinning, weaving and making up their own and their families' wardrobe, bedding, etc., devolved on them. And in addition to all these labors many of them devoted much of their time to gratuitous attendance on the sick.

Many of them had an intimate knowledge of herbs and roots growing in the woods, and their services in the absence or scarcity of physicians were frequently called in requisition. Besides, we cannot fully appreciate their trials without considering the habits of thought and superstitions of those days.

Implicitly believing in supernatural appearances they had not only to confront real dangers but those that had their origin in a perverted imagination. Hence when left alone, as they frequently were in their solitary huts, they were a prey to all the horrors the mind can conceive of. It is hardly too much to say that our mothers toiled sixteen hours each day besides the frequent interruptions of their hours of rest. It seems almost incredible that they should endure the hardships that fell to their lot, and yet so many of them attain the age of eighty, ninety and even one-hundred years. It is believed that a comparison of longevity would show them to have fallen short of that of the fathers. We give below a list, probably imperfect, of those who attained the age of eighty years and upwards. Were we to include those who attained to three-score and ten the number would be more than trebled: Mrs. Zebadiah Andrus, 94; Mrs. Isaac Beall, 81; Mrs. Selah Betts, 87; Mrs. David Blakely, 85; Mrs. Jonathan Blakely, 85; Mrs. Nathaniel Carver, 80; Mrs. Lemuel Chase, 87; Mrs. Ozias Clark, 96; Mrs. Asahel Clark, 82; Mrs. Luther Cleveland, 86; Mrs. Moses Cleveland, 80; Mrs. Josiah Crocker, 84; Mrs. John Crapo, 81; Mrs. Simeon Edgerton, 85; Mrs. Simeon Edgerton, Jr., 81; Mrs. Abiatha Evans, 103; Mrs. Benjamin Fitch, 83; Mrs. Gideon Gifford, 91; Mrs. Sylvanus Gregory, 82; Miss Minerva Gregory, 80; Mrs. John Griswold, 92; Miss Polly Hall, 88; Mrs. Arunah Hanks, 87; Mrs. Joseph Hascall, 90; Mrs. Ashbel Hollister, 82; Daniel Hulett, 83; Mrs. Joseph Jones, 80; Mrs. James Leach, 87; Mrs. Abner Lumbard, 80; Mrs. Roswell Loomis, 86; Mrs. Cornwall Marks, 87; Mrs. Judah Moffitt, 83; Mrs. Timothy Nye, 84; Mrs. Jacob Perkins, 89; Mrs. Elkanah Phillips, 85; Elisha Pratt, 90; Mrs. Moses Porter, 101; Mrs. Simeon Reed; Mrs. Nathaniel Robinson, 90; Mrs. Jonathan Robinson, 82; Mrs. Joel Simonds, 86; Mrs. Samuel Stratton, 88; Mrs. Reuben Toby, 82; Mrs. Rosabella Tuttle, 96; Mrs. Seth Viets, 80; Mrs. David Weeks, 89; Mrs. Margaret Wheeler, 88; Mrs. Isaac Wickham, 82; Mrs. Joseph Willard, 80;

RAIL ROAD.

The Rutland and Washington rail road was opened in 1851. It passes through the valley of the Indian river from the summit level in Rupert to West Pawlet, and thence nearly on the line of the state to Granville, N. Y. Its whole course in this town is about $2\frac{1}{2}$ miles. Liberal contributions were made by citizens on the line of the road to aid in its construction and no direct return in dividends or otherwise has been received. As an effect of opening the road, real estate greatly appreciated in value, not only in its immediate vicinity but for considerable distance back.

The character of farming operations was changed to some extent, as this road opened direct communication both with Boston and New York, and heavy bulky articles, not before marketable, found a ready sale. Many of our farmers engaged in the cultivation of potatoes, which have usually commanded a remunerating price. As potatoes have always been considered an exhausting crop it was feared the land would wear out and the supply fail. But the contrary appears to be the fact, as potatoes year by year are a more reliable crop, improving in size, quality and yield. The cheese manufacture has also received an impetus and there has been a large increase in its production.

## GEOLOGY.

We cannot discourse learnedly of geology, as we have but scanty knowledge of the terms and definitions used in the science. However, we may say that a great diversity of rocks and soils are found in this town. The exuberant fertility of the soil and its self-recuperating qualities are doubtless owing to the peculiar character of its rocks. By the disintegration of the rocks the soil is supplied with aliment so that almost any exhausted field, if left to itself, will recover its fertility. In the south part of the town are extensive beds of the finest limestone, which were formerly quarried and burned to a considerable extent. And lime is one of the constituents of most of the rocks in town.

In the west part are ranges of slate rock of great extent which yet await development. Experts in the slate business pronounce these beds to be of the finest quality. A beautiful building stone is found in a range parallel to the slate range which breaks into right angled pieces with a precision no joiner can surpass. Though there are no clay-fields of any considerable extent, yet clay of the best quality for brick-making crops out in various parts of the town. Here and there all over the town are deposits of muck, the value of which as a fertilizer we have not yet learned to estimate.

And we are told by Professor Eights that one of the best peat-fields in America is found on the pre-

## GEOLOGY.

mises of Consider S. Bardwell, near the rail road. It is understood that parties from Troy, N. Y., have recently bought of Mr. Bardwell thirty acres of this peat-field for the aggregate sum of thirteen thousand five hundred dollars, which they have paid. It is expected that this peat will be used as fuel on the rail road. It will be lucky for the road as well as for the public if it answers that purpose as wood is growing scarce.

The soil of the town is mostly susceptible of cultivation even to the tops of the mountains, all but two or three of which can be tilled to their summits. And many fields that cannot be plowed make excellent pastures. On the banks of Pawlet and Indian rivers are extensive alluvial meadows enriched by periodical overflows. A large proportion of the soil is a gravelly loam intermingled with slate, and is adapted to the growth of English grain, Indian corn, fruit, tobacco, potatoes, etc. It also yields the sweetest herbage for our flocks and herds. In no part of the world does the sap of the sugar maple yield a larger per centage of sugar.

We notice in Prof. Albert D. Hager's geological map of the state that the western part of this town is of the argillaceous or roofing slate formation, while the eastern part is of the marble and limestone formation, interstratified with silicious and magnesian slate. Prof. John L. Edgerton is our only native geologist who has been conspicuous in this branch of natural history, and we regret our inability to procure an article from his pen to enrich our work.

## ARCHITECTURE.

To observe the progress and development of architecture in our houses, churches and other buildings, is curious and interesting. The pioneer, with no other tool but an ax, before saw mills were built, would construct his rude cabin and make it quite comfortable. To be sure it would have no floor nor roof, but what was made of bark — its door perhaps a blanket; its windows, oiled paper, and its chimney a rude pile of stones topped off with sticks plastered with clay, yet its inmates had strong hands and stout hearts and were probably more exempt from disease than the occupants of princely mansions. However you may be sure that with so enterprising a people as those who settled the country any discomforts attendant on their situation were speedily obviated. On the introduction of saw mills, better log cabins were of course constructed, and, as a general thing, in four or five years they were superseded by one-story plank houses of sufficient size to be partitioned into rooms with an unfinished loft above to serve as dormitories. These in turn soon gave place to the story and a half, the gamble roofed, some with dormer windows, or perhaps the stately two story house with pleasant ventilated chambers and abundance of room. And perhaps it is not too much to say that by the year 1810 the town was better supplied with good roomy convenient dwellings than at the present day. Indeed the people of the town, urged on by the women who had been hampered and cramped in their small houses went to the opposite extreme and built houses not only too large for their comfort but too expensive for their means.

As stoves were not then in use more pains were taken to make the rooms warm by filling in with unburnt brick or plaster than now. In 1800 there were no brick houses in town; the first erected soon after that time was the hotel in the village, built by Ephraim Fitch, and the present residence of Hiram Wickham, built by Sylvanus Gregory. Quite a number of good brick and wooden houses have been built since, mainly to replace those that have decayed, but one leading improvement has been to take out the chimneys and rearrange the rooms.

As with dwellings so with churches and schoolhouses. The first Cong. church, built by Abiathar Evans about 1785, was a plain unpretending structure of one floor, furnished with plain seats, and altogether too small for the growing congregation. This stood some fifteen years when it was turned over to hold town meetings in, and the old Cong. church on the hill was erected, Titus A. Cook, architect. This was a large and imposing structure, with a lofty dome, belfry and steeple, and two tiers of windows. It had a gallery on one end and both sides. Both the ground floor and the gallery, except the singers' seat, were partitioned into square pews, in which one-third of the audience sat with their backs to the speaker and another third had to look over their shoulder. Its inside work was elaborate and in good taste and style, after the fashion of the day, and altogether it took rank among the first churches in the state. The next year, 1800, the church in the west part of the town, on another hill, was built, Titus A. Cook, architect, and its interior arrangements were copied after the Cong. church, but it had no belfry or steeple. The next church built was the Methodist brick church, erected in 1827. This was a substantial plain edifice, fitted up on the ground floor with four tiers of slips. Its gallery, which ran round the house, was also provided with slips. This, about a dozen years ago, was fitted up for a select school under the name of the Mettowee Academy. In 1833 the Prot. Methodists built a church edifice in the southwest part of the town, near John Stearns's. The next church erected was the present Cong. church in the village, in 1841. It was built under the superintendence of Dan Blakely and others, building committee, and Elkanah Danforth, architect. This is an elegant and tasteful structure with a vestry in the basement for occasional meetings. The interior is plainly but chastely arranged and is a model of pleasantness and convenience. The only drawback is the necessity of ascending a flight of stairs, which is perhaps balanced by the convenience of having its furnace in the basement. It has lately been refurnished throughout in beautiful style. In 1853 the new Methodist church in the village, near the Congregational, was erected, Elkanah Danforth, architect, and Jonathan Randall and others, building committee. Its style and general arrangements are similar to the Cong. church.

In 1848 the Church of the Disciples at West Pawlet, Henry Scoville, architect; and in 1852 the Baptist church in the same place, Edmund C. Whiting, architect, were erected. These are neat, plain structures, handsomely arranged in the interior after the modern style. A small but neat and handsome church was erected in 1853, on the site of the old Baptist church. It is used mostly for funerals.

The old school-houses were specimens of inconvenience and all their surroundings were made as repulsive as possible. These have all passed away and our present school-houses are generally pleasant and attractive. All but three or four are of brick, and are being overhauled from time to time and made better to subserve the great purposes for which they were erected.

## HOTELS.

Probably Capt. Jonathan Willard was the first innkeeper in town, on the site of the present homestead of Henry Allen. Here the town and freeman's meetings were held, and most of the public business transacted. His successor was Capt. Timothy Strong, who left in 1816 or 1817. Since then there has been no public house kept here, though it continued for several years to be a place of public resort for trainings, town, officer meetings, etc. At an early day an inn was kept by Col. Stephen Pearl, near the present residence of Daniel Hulett.

We have no precise data from which to show who first kept tavern at the village. The present establishment was erected in 1808, by Ephraim Fitch, who kept it till his death, in 1814. After him Lemuel Barden, and his son, John T., kept it about twenty years when it passed into the hands of Col. Ozias Clark, by whom it was rented to various parties and kept as a temperance house. Harry Griswold, Robert Clark, E. Fitch Clark, and perhaps some others kept it till it passed from the hands of Col. Clark. Since then it has been kept by various parties each for brief periods. We recall the names of Henry Bostwick, Vail, Chapin Andrus, Willam Blossom, Jr., Dewitt Hulett, and probably there have been others. The last named is the present proprietor. At West Pawlet, a tavern and store together was built by Eleazer Lyman, in 1807, which was kept by Joseph Ackley, James S. Brown, etc. The present residence of Capt. James Johnson has been kept as a tavern by himself, Elisha Marks, Innis Hollister, Ira Gibbs and perhaps others. When the rail road was built Ira Gibbs built a public house on the site of the present hotel which he kept several years and sold to David Woodard. This was burnt in 1858 and was replaced by the present commodious house which is called the Indian River Valley Hotel. Connected with this establishment is a spacious and beautiful hall, the best connected with a hotel perhaps in the county. Joseph Armstrong kept tavern twenty-five years in the north-east part of the town.

Reuben Smith kept tavern where B. F. Giles now lives, some twenty years, closing in 1832. At north Pawlet a public house was erected some seventy years ago by Bethel Hurd, whose successors have been Joel Simonds, William Stevens, Willard Cobb, Jeremiah Arnold, James Bigart, and perhaps some others. No tavern has been kept here since 1852.

On inspection of the old town records the names of several appear as having been licensed or approbated to keep tavern, but we cannot determine the location of most of them. The Red house owned by Orla Loomis, has been used as a tavern stand.

## HIGHWAYS AND BRIDGES.

Few of the highways in this town were located on the line of lots, but appear to have been laid where it best suited the nature of the ground or the convenience of the inhabitants. Not one of them, we believe, crosses another at right angles; but they wind through the valleys and run over the hills in every conceivable direction. Many of the highways instead of running at the base of hills run directly over them. The reason of this is obvious. The tops and sides of hills were more easily cleared and put in cultivation than the low grounds at their base; hence the first clearings were made on them and the roads made accordingly. Since the low grounds have been cleared this reason no longer exists and many roads have been changed; improvement in this respect being by no means exhausted.

Originally the main roads were laid four rods wide and the others three rods; but encroachments have generally been made on these limits and the highways have been narrowed down to an inconvenient width. Considerable attention has been given of late to the grading and graveling of roads; the old log causeways removed and replaced with stone and gravel, which, of the best quality, fortunately exists in almost every locality in town. Experience has taught us that it is better and cheaper in the long run to haul on stone and gravel than to throw up the common soil of the road-side.

The extent of water-courses through the town and their peculiar diagonal direction, render a great number of bridges indispensable to the public convenience. Until within about forty years the bridges were built by the voluntary action of the several highway districts, care having been taken so to arrange the districts that the bridges would be fairly apportioned among them. Then the bridges were mostly built on heavy stringers spanning the stream and resting often on wooden abutments. But as timber grew scarce and some were disposed to shirk their proper share of the labor, the people availed themselves of the provisions of law and devolved the entire expense of bridge building on the grand list.

Within the last twenty years great improvements have been made in the construction of bridges. The old wooden abutments have been replaced with stone; the old-fashioned stringers with framed bridges. Within our remembrance there were eight public bridges across Pawlet river, now there are but five, all of them framed and two covered. On Flower brook there are four bridges, three framed, and one at the village of stone. On Wells brook one framed bridge. The smaller bridges, of which there are a great number, are built or being built of stone. Besides these are a large number of private bridges. The substantial construction of most of these bridges, though involving heavy expense, will probably prove economical.

## TOWN FARM.

The state by early legislation made provision for the maintenance of the poor, leaving the particular method of support to the several towns. Each town is required to support its own native poor, unless they have gained a residence elsewhere, all who have gained a residence in town, and all who may chance to come in from other states and from foreign countries. No duty devolves on a civilized and Christian community so sacred and imperative as the proper care and support of those who cannot take care of themselves. Hence a great interest has been taken in the question of the best manner of performing this duty. Some have advocated the establishment of county houses, which must necessarily take the unfortunate away from all those who might be expected to sympathize with them, and who from the ties of old acquaintance might feel an interest in them. Besides the larger the body that has charge of any business involving expense, the less individual interest is felt in making the expense as light as possible.

The course pursued by this town until within a few years was to dispose of the poor to those who would agree to keep them for the least money. By this means they were scattered one, two or more in a place and often fell into the hands of unfit persons.

As those who took them intended to make a profit out of it, it is easy to see that the interests of humanity might be frequently outraged. Awakened to a sense of the impropriety not to say inhumanity of such a course, the town in 1855, appointed Consider S. Bardwell, Lucius M. Carpenter and Adams L. Bromley, a committee to purchase a farm where this class might all be gathered in one family. They purchased the present town farm for $4,500 and in the judgment of a great majority it has proved a decided success. The town has generally been fortunate in its agents to take charge of the farm. It is now managed by John Smith who has leased it for three years expiring in April, 1867, and who provides for all the poor, for the use of the farm and stock. Under the old system it used to cost from ten to fourteen hundred dollars annually.

## CEMETERIES.

There are five or six public cemeteries in town. The oldest is at the village which has been in use since 1776. Margaret Wheeler, aged 88, was the first person interred. It was laid off from the farm of John Cobb, and is almost entirely occupied.

The next oldest is in the north part of the town on land given by Caleb Allen. The first interments were revolutionary soldiers. The third is in the west part of the town on land given by Seely Brown.

Jacob Perkins was the first person interred in 1801. This cemetery has been recently enlarged and handsomely inclosed. A row of maple trees were planted around it in 1857. There is another cemetery near C. S. Bardwell's and another near Andrew Willard's.

There is another small public cemetery near the residence of the late Joshua Hulett, and a family cemetery inclosed with a neat iron fence. In 1866, a new public cemetery was purchased of Lyman Wheeler by the town for two hundred dollars.

It is to be inclosed at the expense of the town. The site is west of the old cemetery at the village and comprises two or three acres.

## BORDER WAR.

As early as 1749, Benning Wentworth, the royal governor of the province of New Hampshire, chartered the town of Bennington, and directly afterwards several other towns. The province of New York entered her protest against it, claiming jurisdiction to the Connecticut river under a grant made by Charles II to his brother, the Duke of York. Nothing daunted Governor Wentworth continued the granting of charters down to 1764, issuing letters patent to as many as one hundred and thirty towns. At this time New York appealed to King George II, who in council of state, June 20, 1764, confirmed the claim of New York. Surprised at this action of the crown, yet the settlers construed it as only extending the jurisdiction of New York in future, while New York construed it as investing it with the title to the soil. This assumption created intense excitement, for the settlers having paid for the land and obtained title to it under grants from the crown, could not imagine by what perversion of justice they could be compelled to abandon the land or repurchase it of New York. It was quite bad enough to be placed under the jurisdiction of the Dutch colony of New York, against whom our fathers cherished an intense dislike, but to repurchase the land they had paid for and improved was more than they could quietly submit to.

New York, however, proceeded to exercise its jurisdiction and issue writs of ejectment against all who refused to comply with her demands. Upon this the settlers banded together, constituted committees of safety and prepared to resist by force the execution of these writs. In these proceedings this town sympathized and participated. When the New York officials crossed the border to execute these legal processes, they were seized, and those who would not respect the great seal of New Hampshire were stamped with the *beech seal*, impressed with twigs of the wilderness on their naked backs. During this period an order was obtained from the crown to stay proceedings until the pleasure of his Majesty should be more fully known.

But New York, in her greed of acquisition, would not stop. Some of our citizens were arrested and sent to Albany jail; one of whom, after enduring a long confinement in a filthy cell, vented his spleen on his Dutch jailers in verse, the last stanza only of which is remembered:

"I beg and pray, both night and day,
The Dutch, with all their gang,
Might swim like smelts in buttermilk
And land at Amsterdam."

The controversy waxed warm; the parties on both sides became greatly exasperated; the American congress refrained from taking decisive action, seeming willing to allow the contending parties to fight it out between themselves. The New York authorities issued proclamations of outlawry against some of our leading citizens. Meanwhile our Green mountain boys procured arms and ammunition, and under Ethan Allen organized in defense of their rights. We cannot give in detail all the events of these stirring times, suffice it to say we stood our ground for twenty-six years and were finally, in 1791, admitted into the Union. Notwithstanding the pendency of this domestic strife at the breaking out of the revolution in 1775, we won the first victory of the war in taking Ticonderoga. On the invasion of Burgoyne in 1777, in his own language, we "hung like a cloud on his flank," and almost unaided achieved the signal victory of Bennington.

In the midst of all these tumults our fathers coolly went to work to establish a state government. A convention met at Dorset in 1776, which adjourned from time to time until Jan. 20, 1777, when it declared the present territory of Vermont a free and independent jurisdiction under the name of New Connecticut or Vermont. Col. William Fitch and Major Roger Rose were our delegates in that convention. It met again in June, 1777, and recommended that each town should be represented in convention, to meet at Windsor, July 2. This convention met, but owing to the invasion of Burgoyne and the unsettled state of the country hurriedly adopted a state constitution, appointed a council of safety to act during the interim, and adjourned. The first election under the constitution was held the first Tuesday in March, 1778, and the first sitting of the assembly the second Thursday of the same month. Zadoc Everest represented this town in that assembly. It met again the next October, when Gideon Adams represented this town.

These border difficulties and the war with Britain greatly retarded the settlement of the town. None but the courageous and adventurous dared enter its inviting fields; the timid and the cowardly kept their distance. It required no ordinary nerve to face the difficulties which encompassed the first settlement of these border towns. Tories and Indians, the British and New Yorkers were all against them. How proud should we feel as descendants from this illustrious ancestry, who have made their mark on the pages of history and will stand forever as the prototypes of all that is brave, chivalrous and daring while earth's records are kept. And how solicitous should we be to gather and transmit to the latest generation the achievements of our gallant fathers. No monument marks the resting place of many of them, and their names even are fast fading from human remembrance. Let us gather up what fragments of knowledge are still within our reach and transmit them to those who are to come after us, as the richest gift and most priceless legacy in our power to bestow.

## UNITED STATES DEPOSIT FUND.

In 1837, congress made provision to deposit with the several states the accumulated surplus money in the treasury. The share of this state was $669,086.74 which was divided among the several towns in proportion to their population. The share of this town was $4,683.59. The towns by a provision of our state legislature were to loan the money on adequate security and apply the income to the support of common schools.

By further provision, this fund was to be redistributed every ten years among the towns in proportion to their then population. As the population of this town has diminished every decade since, with one exception, it follows of course that a considerable sum amounting to about one-quarter of the original sum should be withdrawn.

When the town farm was purchased in 1856, the balance of the fund was appropriated towards its purchase, the interest of which is annually paid into the school fund according to the original provision. The state still holds a lien on this money, whenever it shall be required for a redistribution among the towns or for repayment into the United States treasury.

It might naturally be supposed that the distribution among the people of the United States of so large a sum of money, $28,101,644.97, would make money plenty and easy, but it had precisely the contrary effect and was attended with the most disastrous panic known in our history.

## DONATION FESTIVALS.

These were introduced about 1830, and have become general and very popular. In their inception they were limited to the supply of the pastorate with such necessary articles as each donor could conveniently spare from his own stores. They subserved two principal objects, providing additional aid to the frequently scanty resources of the pastorate and the bringing into social relations the people of the parish so apt to form into cliques and classes having little or no sympathy with each other. We cannot doubt but that their effect has been to create a better feeling in the community, more sympathy among the people, and between the pastor and people, to to say nothing of the material aid furnished the pastor.

These festivals are not now confined to their original object, but are brought into requisition to aid any unfortunate member of society, who, by sickness, or accident, stands in need of help.

They are also used to raise funds for benevolent purposes and special public objects. Through their agency here and elsewhere, churches and parsonages have been furnished; cemeteries bought, inclosed, and improved; hospital stores collected for the army; soldiers' monuments erected, and Sabbath school and other public libraries established. Since money has become the most plentiful article in the community, donations are almost exclusively made in cash, and not infrequently from one hundred to two hundred dollars are raised in an evening. They have become the festival of the day, and whatever the object, seldom fail to call out a crowd.

## BASE BALL.

As if to anticipate and prepare for the dread exigencies of war, then impending, by a simultaneous impulse, all over the country, base ball clubs were organized during the year or two preceding 1861. Perhaps no game or exercise, outside of military drill, was ever practiced, so well calculated as this to harden the muscles and invigorate the physical functions. All the powers of the system were brought into action and subjected to severe discipline.

Three base ball clubs were formed in this town, in 1860 and 1661. The Hickory, at West Pawlet, the Mettowee, at the village, and the Liberty, at North Pawlet. These several clubs engaged in the work with great spirit and earnestness, and had repeated trials of skill with each other and with outside clubs. They were sustained with increasing interest until 1862, when a large portion of each club was summoned to the war. Then, for lack of men to play the game, they were suspended. Since the return of peace, a new impulse has been given to the game, and the old clubs are being revived.

## PAWLET AND WELLS AGRICULTURAL SOCIETY.

This association was formed in September, 1857. Nathan Francis, of Wells, was its first president, and Chipman J. Toby, secretary. Grounds for the fair and a trotting park were laid out on the premises of David G. Blossom. The first annual fair was held on the 6th of October, 1857, and was a decided success. A very creditable display of stock, fruits, vegetables and domestic manufactures was made. No premiums were awarded, but the names of all winning competitors were recorded and published. The annual fair was held on the same ground in 1858; James M. Shaw, president, and Dr. C. C. Nichols of Wells, secretary. The annual fair was held at the same place for the three succeeding years with one exception, when it was held at the village, with undiminished interest, drawing together crowds of people. In 1859, John S. Hulett, of Wells, was president, and Dr. Nichols, secretary. In 1860 and 1861, Allen Whedon was president, and Dr. Nichols, secretary.

The absorbing interest felt in the war which now brooded over our firesides and social circles, and which banished from our hearts and thoughts all interests not connected with itself, induced a suspension, which was then expected to be only temporary. In these days, people toiled, but it was mechanically; their minds and hearts were occupied with events transpiring on the battle-field. Their sympathies were turned towards the field of strife, and expended in efforts to relieve the sick and mangled victims of the war. Our anxieties and solicitude were with the loved ones far away, and we watched the daily papers, expecting each day to hear that some of them had fallen.

These social gatherings are of great service to a community, even when conducted on a limited scale. Through them, we become better acquainted with each other and learn to appreciate our neighbors. Let us hope, as the clouds of war are dispersed, that this peculiar institution of the farmer may be revived.

## THE LYCEUM.

This society grew out of the debating club of the last generation, and in its present development is of recent origin. The usual programme of its exercises is, first, the discussion of some popular question, to which service disputants are assigned at a previous meeting. Volunteers are always allowed a hearing when there is time. Next the reading of a manuscript paper, prepared and read by an editress appointed beforehand. The articles for the paper are prepared and furnished by members of the lyceum or volunteers, and are on almost every conceivable subject, constituting a bill of literary fare of all degrees of merit. This is the most attractive feature of the lyceum, and taxes the wit and wisdom of the contributors to their fullest extent. The more jokes and pleasant personalities there are introduced the better the audience is pleased.

Declamation, the rehearsal of spicy dialogues and glee club music are frequently added to the entertainment. The lyceum is an excellent school in which to train the intellectual faculties, and many an aspiring youth dates his first upward impulses to its influence.

These lyceums have been held at the village, at West Pawlet, and at North Pawlet through nearly every winter season for several years. They commend themselves especially to every young gentleman and lady whose literary advantages are limited to the district school.

## STOCK.

### *Horses.*

Great attention has been given to the rearing of good horses from an early day. The stock of the imported horse Messenger was early introduced, and in so high estimation was it held that all who advertised horses claimed them to be of Messenger extraction. About 1820 Isaac Bishop brought into the vicinity the celebrated Hamiltonian, believed to have been of Messenger blood. From this stock Rattler, one of the best, if not the best horse ever raised in the state, sprung. This horse was bought in 1847, when three years old, of Jacob Burnham, of Middletown, by James Bigart, and, though perhaps inadequately appreciated at home, has won a wide reputation in the western states, in California, and even in South America. One of his colts, second in descent, was sold in Chili, S. A., in 1863, for thirty thousand dollars. When Rattler was four years old, Mr. Bigart offered, for a handsome wager, to trot him against any horse in the state. The offer was not accepted. We are assured by residents of California and Chili, that no stock of horses is held in so high estimation in those countries as his. We believe he is still kept by Mr. Bigart at Sandy Hill, N. Y. Many fine horses are annually sold out of this town, and a handsome revenue derived from their sale. The requirements of the war caused heavy drafts on our stock of horses, and they are now worth, probably, on an average, two hundred dollars each.

*Cattle.*

In early times each farmer kept a herd of native cattle, proportioned to the size of his farm, selling off each year his surplus to the city markets. Some fifty years ago cheese making was introduced, and has been gradually extending to the present time. Fewer cattle, in consequence, are raised for market. The dairy interest has greatly improved, and cheese making almost reduced to a science. The invention by Joel Stevens of a cheese pan and stove combined, furnished greatly improved facilities for its manufacture. The establishment of a cheese factory in 1864, by a dairy association at West Pawlet, and of another at the village in 1865, absorb most of the cheese making interest in town. The statistics of these factories will be given elsewhere. But little attention has ever been given to the fattening of stock for market; those we have usually turned off being mostly grass fed.

English cattle of various breeds have been brought

on from time to time to mix with our native breeds, but we have no systematic stock-breeder in town. The high price of cheese and butter, the former from 18 to 22 cents per pound and the latter from 40 to 50 cents, has created a brisk demand for cows, which now sell for from sixty to one hundred dollars each. Oxen and young stock are proportionably high.

As with cattle so with sheep; our farmers for many years only kept a supply for their domestic wants, and those only of the native breed, selling off yearly a few surplus grass-fed wethers. Before 1812 there were but few, if any, fine wooled sheep in town. About that time Col. Humphreys, of Connecticut, brought here a few choice sheep, descended from his original importation in 1802. The obstructions to commerce during the times of the embargo and the war with England in 1812, had induced the establishment of woolen factories in this town, and throughout the country, and a finer grade of wool was in demand. Merino sheep were soon diffused throughout the town and a new era in sheep breeding was inaugurated. Wool soon became a principal staple. About 1825 Saxony sheep were brought in and crossed with merino grades. This did not prove satisfactory, as tenderer sheep and lighter fleeces were the result. To counteract this the Bakewell breed were soon after introduced, which gave less satisfaction. It will be borne in mind that during all these earlier efforts to improve sheep but few people attempted to raise pure blooded sheep, but our highest ambition was satisfied with grade sheep. During the present decade a new impulse has been given to the sheep interest by the introduction of the improved American merino. The key-note to this last movement has been full bloods.

STOCK. 127

A few prime flocks of this class have been started in town. The wool growing interest has been depressed for the last year or two, and our shepherds have wished themselves out of the business. New encouragement, however, has been afforded them by an act of congress, passed in March, 1867, increasing the tariff on imported wool. By this act the importer of wool pays a duty to government on wool that comes in competition with ours about as follows, duty payable in gold: On wool worth over thirty-two cents at the place whence last exported to the United States, the duty is twelve cents per pound and ten per cent, *ad valorem*, giving us protection on wool worth forty cents per pound to the amount of sixteen cents per pound in gold. On wool worth less than thirty-two cents per pound (say twenty-five cents) the duty will amount to about twelve and three-quarter cents per pound also in gold. On woolen goods, and especially on ready made clothing, the duty is much higher. This act, passed in the last agonies preceding the dissolution of the thirty-ninth congress, will save hundreds of mills from suspension and put new life and hope into the wool-growing interest.

Though swine are raised mainly for home consumption, and are not a leading article, we notice that unwonted interest is taken in their improvement. Perhaps the best, at least the most popular breed, is the Chester county. These are fast supplanting most other breeds. The elephantine ear and the alligator snout have passed away. Our hogs, to a great extent, are grown and fattened on the refuse of the dairy.

*Poultry.*

This important department of husbandry has not been overlooked, but has shared in the general improvement of the age. New varieties of fowls have been introduced, and from their names, Shanghai, Cochin China, etc., we infer that the whole eastern world has been laid under contribution to supply our market. Turkeys, also, which not unfrequently earn their own living, have, by judicious breeding, been raised from twenty-five cents each, by the flock, to two dollars, within our remembrance. Geese are more neglected, but to those favorably situated, it is one of the most profitable branches of business.

## Dogs.

This disinterested friend of man, and but for his sheep-killing propensities, the universal favorite, claims recognition. He has furnished a topic for brilliant forensic display to the assembled "wisdom and virtue" of the state for several years, and surely a subject that occupies so much of the time of our legislature, must not be overlooked by the humble chronicler. The leading question by our local assessors is: Have you a dog? If satisfied on this point, you are let off easily. We hear little of late of the music of the hound, as he follows his prey, guided alone by the sense of smell. The bull-dog, the grey-hound, the spaniel, the terrier and the cur of low degree are fast disappearing. The shepherd dog alone retains his position and is raised almost to the entire exclusion of all other dogs. No dairyman considers his establishment complete without one of them.

## GENERAL CENSUS OF THE TOWN.

The population of the town, according to the United States census, was as follows, to wit:

In the year 1791, population 1458; 1800, 1938; 1810, 2233; 1820, 2155; 1830, 1965; 1840, 1748; 1850, 1843; 1860, 1540.

## GENERAL HISTORY OF THE WAR OF 1861-1865.

Our town was represented in most of the infantry regiments raised in the state; in the cavalry, sharp shooters and batteries. Also, in several New York and other state organizations. Our volunteers were in almost every campaign, expedition and battle of the war, from that at Great Bethel, June, 1861, where the gifted Winthrop gave his young life to his country, to the closing battles around Richmond.

They were in the ill-fated campaign of General McClellan in 1862, in his abortive efforts to take Richmond. They confronted the guerillas and cow-boys of Eastern Virginia under Stuart and Mosby. They were at the siege of Vicksburg and the sanguinary fights in that vicinity; they were in the fruitless campaigns of Generals Pope, Burnside and Hooker, and largely contributed to the triumph of General Mead at Gettysburg; they fought above the clouds on Lookout mountain; they were under General Sherman at Chattanooga, at Dalton, at Atlanta, and accompanied him in his triumphant march to the sea-coast at Savannah, and thence to Charleston, Columbia and Raleigh; they were with the impetuous Sheridan, in his daring and successful march through the Shenandoah valley; they were with General Banks, in his various expeditions, and at the taking of Mobile; they shared in the bloody flanking movements of General Grant, from the Rapidan to the gates of Petersburg; they endured the horrors of Libby, Bellisle and Salisbury; they suffered tortures at Andersonville, which no adjective in any language can fittingly describe. No! Gather all the atrocities noted in the pages of history for all time — the Black hole of Calcutta, the French Bastile, the Spanish inquisition, the New York Sugar house, and the Dartmoor prison, the wholesale slaughter of the Sepoys — put them all in a balance, and for cool, calculating, damning fiendishness, Andersonville outweighs them all!

It was the death throe of slavery, the finale of that most atrocious wrong. And who is in doubt as to the author of these horrible crimes? Shall we hang the miserable subordinate, and honor the guilty principals? Shall we receive back into the councils of the nation the perpetrators of these abominable outrages? Shall we place within their merciless grasp those, who at the hazard of their lives, befriended and assisted us? Those who fed our starving fugitives and guided them to places of safety? And more than all, shall we break our faith to those who trusted us? In short, shall we punish our friends, and reward our enemies? Forbid it, Almighty God! And O! if there be in the armory of heaven one thunderbolt hotter than any other, will it not be hurled against the nation capable of such base ingratitude?

## First Regiment.

This regiment enlisted for three months, was mustered in the service May 2, 1861, and discharged Aug. 6, 1861. Only three from this town were in it; George S. Orr, Moses E. Orr and Charles Barrett, who are noticed elsewhere. It was under Col. J. Wolcott Phelps.

## Second Regiment.

This regiment was mustered in, June 20, 1861, and joined the army of the Potomac. It was in what is distinctively known as the Vermont Brigade, but in its relation to other brigades has been known both as the first and second Vermont Brigades. It commenced its first active campaign at Yorktown, Va., April 6, 1862, and participated in all the engagements before Richmond, up to the final discomfiture of Gen. McClellan in July, 1862. It was in all the battles that followed under Generals Pope, Burnside, Hooker, Mead and Grant, up to the taking of Richmond, April 3, 1865. Probably no regiment in the service, except the 5th Vermont, which was with it, experienced more hardships or suffered greater losses. There were ten volunteers from this town in this regiment. We refer to the Military record for full particulars of the military history of these and all other volunteers from this town. Only three were on the original muster-roll, the others were subsequently added. This regiment, though enlisted for only three years, was in the service over four years, being discharged July 15, 1865. It was under Col. Amasa S. Tracy when mustered out.

### Fifth Regiment.

This regiment enlisted for three years, was mustered in, Sept. 16, 1861, and was in the same brigade with the second regiment. There were sixteen volunteers from this town in this regiment. It was under the command of Col. Lewis A. Grunt, from Sept. 16, 1862, until his promotion as brigadier general, June 29, 1864. It was mustered out, June 29, 1865, under Col. Ronald A. Kennedy. Few regiments were in more sanguinary conflicts, it being in active service from April 6, 1862, till the fall of Richmond, and in all the battles fought by the Army of the Potomac.

### Seventh Regiment.

This regiment was mustered in, February 12, 1862, for three years, and was assigned to duty in the southern department. The names of twenty-five recruits from this town are reported. It was mostly under Col. William C. Holbrook, but was mustered out in the fall of 1865, under Col. David B. Peck.

### Ninth Regiment.

This regiment was mustered into the service, July 9, 1862, for three years, and was assigned to duty, mostly, in unhealthy districts in Virginia and North Carolina, where it suffered greatly from disease; at one time (Oct. 1, 1863) two-thirds of its men being on the sick list. There were seven volunteers from this town in it. It was mustered out, June 13, 1865, under Col. Edward H. Ripley, now brigadier general.

WAR OF 1861–1865. 133

### *Tenth Regiment.*

This regiment was mustered in, for three years, Sept. 1, 1862, and was in the army of the Potomac. It was mustered out under Col. George B. Damon, June 27, 1865. Only three men from this town were in the regiment.

### *Eleventh Regiment.*

This regiment, the first Vermont heavy artillery, was mustered into service for three years, Sept. 1, 1862. This regiment was stationed near Washington city for its defense, until May 15, 1864, when it joined the "Vermont brigade," and bore its full share of the danger and the loss incurred by the brigade during its flanking movements towards Richmond. There were ten volunteers from this town in this regiment. It was mustered out of service August 25, 1865; Col. James M. Warner was in command.

Only one from this town, Charles Barrett, was in the 12th regiment, and two, Joel A. Mason and Walter S. Hanks, in the seventeenth regiment.

### *First Regiment Cavalry.*

This regiment was mustered into service Nov. 19, 1861, and joined the army of the Potomac. There were eight recruits from this town in this regiment. Perhaps no regiment in the service endured more hardships or were in more battles than this. It was mustered out of service under Colonel, now General William Wells, August 9, 1865.

### Second Battery of Light Artillery.

This battery was mustered for three years. It was composed of troops transferred from the first Vermont battery. There were eight recruits from this town. It was assigned to the southern department, and most of the members of the company have been mustered out.

### First Regiment U. S. Sharp Shooters.

This regiment was mustered, in 1861, for three years. There were six recruits from this town. This regiment has been with the army of the Potomac, and has seen hard service. We believe all its members from this town have been mustered out.

Twenty-two other recruits were raised in 1864, and variously assigned; some to the navy, and, of some of them, we have no data to determine where they belonged. Most of them received heavy local bounties, and several deserted.

### Fourteenth Regiment.

This regiment enlisted for nine months, under Col. William T. Nichols, August 27, 1862, and was mustered in at Brattleboro, October 21, 1862. Twenty-four volunteers from this town were in this regiment. During the greater part of its term of service it was stationed near Fairfax Court House, Va., where it frequently came in contact with the guerillas that infested that vicinity. When Gen. Lee invaded Pennsylvania in the latter part of June, 1863, it was ordered by forced marches to join the army of the Potomac, and brought up at Gettysburg on the evening of the first day of

July, 1863. It bore a conspicuous part in the battles of the second and third days of July, and was highly complimented, both by Gen. Stannard, brigade commander, and by Gen. Doubleday, the commandant of the division. Though exposed to the severest fire of the enemy, not a man shirked his duty, but all stood their ground, as our own correspondent wrote us the day after the battle, "as though rooted to the earth." The casualties of the regiment were twenty-five killed and seventy-five wounded. Soon after this (July 30), the regiment was mustered out at Brattleboro.

### Volunteers in New York Regiments.

Situated as we are, on the borders of New York, it was but natural that many of our citizens should enlist in New York regiments. Though if it be true, as some allege, that our boys enlisted from mercenary considerations, they had an odd way of showing it, as invariably, through the war, volunteers in Vermont regiments had seven dollars per month more wages, and, on an average, as high bounties as those who enlisted in other states. The fact probably was, that our boys living near the border were better acquainted with New York boys than with those of our own state, and chose to go where their associations led them, regardless of pecuniary considerations.

Six volunteers from this town enlisted in the 96th N. Y., and were mustered in March 8, 1862. These have all come home, but Lieut. J. G. Johnson, who was killed at Cold Harbor, June 3, 1864. Four men enlisted in the 169th N. Y. regiment. Three enlisted in the 123d N. Y. Six men went into the 5th N. Y. cavalry. Two enlisted in the 30th N. Y., one in the 4th N. Y. heavy artillery, and two in the 77th N. Y. regiment. Besides these, there was one in the 20th Mass., one in the 124th Illinois, and one in the 8th Ohio.

Fifty men have enlisted from this town, most of them for three years, who have received no local bounty, though several of them, by enlisting for another three years, received $200 each. Many of our hired substitutes and men from abroad, who received the highest local bounties, deserted.

But we take pleasure in recording the fact that, so far as our information extends, not one of our native citizens has deserted or been dishonorably discharged.

## CHURCH HISTORY.

One of the earliest wants of the settlers of this town, and one which they took care the first to supply, was the preaching of the gospel. Hence we find provision made in the earliest acts of the town for that object. Money being scarce, subscriptions were taken payable in grain and other produce. The first movement for a church organization was made by the Congregationalists near the centre of the town, in 1781, at about which time the first church edifice was erected, very near the geographical centre of the town.

In 1790 the first Baptist church was formed, in the southwest part of the town, near Hebron, N. Y. In 1790 a Protestant Episcopal church was in existence in the northwest part of the town, near Granville. About 1795 a Methodist class was formed in the southwest part of the town, near Rupert. In 1826 a Methodist Episcopal church was organized at the village. In 1826 the second Baptist church was organized, in the west part of the town. In 1831 the "Disciples" church was organized near the same place. In 1832 the Methodist Protestant church was formed on the mountain, in the southwest part. About 1855 an "independent" society was formed at the village. Besides these, there have been within our limits Universalists, Friends, Mormons, Second Adventists, and perhaps others.

We propose, now, to give a brief history of each one in the order of their organization, including an account of the various church edifices which have, from time to time, been erected.

*First Congregational Church.*

This church was organized August 8, 1781, under the auspices of Rev. David Perry, of Harwinton, Conn. Its first members were Samuel Butt, Jonathan Brace, Joel Harmon, Daniel Welch, Elisha Fitch and Jedediah Reed. Joel Harmon was appointed first church clerk. A sermon was preached on the occasion by Rev. Mr. Perry, from 1 John, ii, 6. For the first three or four years it does not appear that they had any stated supply, though in the records of baptisms the names of Rev. Messrs. Murdock, Sill, Swift, Haynes, Kent, and Perry appear as officiating in that ordinance. We find it recorded that, in 1784, the Rev. James Thompson, of Worthington, was invited to *return* and preach on probation, which implies that he had preached to them before. And, in 1785, the Rev. Zephaniah Hollister Smith, of Glastenburg, Vt., received a call from the church, which call was not accepted, though we have it from tradition that Mr. Smith preached here for some time. We have no date to determine when the first church was erected, but we believe it was about 1785. It stood about 60 rods south of Henry Allen's, and was a plain, small, frame building. Many of its timbers are in the wood house connected with the dwelling of the late Rev. John Griswold.

In 1786, the church gave a call to Dr. Lewis Beebe, then of Arlington, to become their pastor. This was accepted, and, on the 14th of June, 1787, Mr. Beebe was duly ordained to the work of the Gospel ministry." The council convened for the occasion, was composed of ministers and delegates from the following churches, to wit: Stockbridge, Lanesboro, Chesterfield, Lenox, Richmond and Williamstown, in Massachusetts, and Bennington, Dorset and Rupert in this state. Soon after Mr. Beebe entered on his pastorate, serious difficulties arose in the church, which baffled their wisdom to arrange among themselves. Their reference to a mutual council had no better result. It is understood, however, that the difficulties were mostly in relation to Mr. Beebe, one party being dissatisfied with him and the other sustaining him. This quarrel was only brought to a close, by the dismission of Mr. Beebe, in 1791, when the church and society agreed on a unanimous call to Rev. John Griswold. By the way, we may notice the singular method the opposing parties took to close up the controversy, which was, after taking a copy of the proceedings for a year or two, to destroy the original minutes. It is not probable the copy is in existence. Mr. Griswold accepted the call, and on the 23d day of October, 1793, was ordained. The churches called on to assist in his ordination, were Bennington, Sunderland, Sandgate, Benson, Orwell, West Rutland and Thetford, in this state, and Lebanon, in New Hampshire. Rev. Mr. Robbins, of Lebanon, preached the sermon.

## CHURCH HISTORY.

As a relic of the past, and to show how our fathers transacted business, as well as their liberality, we insert a verbatim copy of the first subscription for the support of Rev. John Griswold, obtained from the Rev. Pliny H. White, of Coventry:

We, the subscribers, being sensible of the importance of having a Gospel minister settled among us, Do promis to pay to Mr. John Griswold as an Inducement for him to settle in the worke of the minestre among us, the some that we do enext to our names, one half on the first day of January next, and the other in one yeare from the first payment, to be paid in neet cattle, or wheat and Indian corn.

Witness our hands.
Dated at Pawleet, June 4th, 1793.

|  | £ | s. | d. |  | £ | s. | d. |
|---|---|---|---|---|---|---|---|
| Moses Porter, | 10 | 0 | 0 | Jedediah Edgerton, | 3 | 0 | 0 |
| Samuel Butts, | 5 | 0 | 0 | Cyrus Wells, | 1 | 10 | 0 |
| Joel Harmon, | 10 | 0 | 0 | Stephen Spencer, | 1 | 10 | 0 |
| Lem. Chipman, | 8 | 0 | 0 | Asa Andrus, | 2 | 0 | 0 |
| Ezekiel Harmon, | 6 | 0 | 0 | Daniel Fitch, | 4 | 0 | 0 |
| Jedediah Reed, | 6 | 0 | 0 | Stephen Starkweather, | 5 | 0 | 0 |
| Joel Moffatt, | 2 | 10 | 0 | Samuel Taylor, | 1 | 10 | 0 |
| Abraham Meacham, | 2 | 0 | 0 | Daniel Clark, | 1 | 0 | 0 |
| Ashbel Skinner, | 2 | 0 | 0 | David Carter, | 1 | 0 | 0 |
| Amos Curtis, | 15 | 0 | 0 | John Cobb, | 4 | 0 | 0 |
| Daniel Welch, | 9 | 19 | 9 | Andr. Henry, | 2 | 0 | 0 |
| Joseph Fitch, | 8 | 0 | 0 | Return Strong, | 2 | 0 | 0 |
| Ozias Clark, | 8 | 0 | 0 | Joel Simonds, | 1 | 10 | 0 |
| Philip Reed, | 8 | 0 | 0 | Benajah Bushnell, | 3 | 0 | 0 |
| Sylvanus Gregory, | 1 | 10 | 0 | Isaac Stephens, | 1 | 10 | 0 |
| John Adams, | 4 | 0 | 0 | Rufus Fitch, | 2 | 0 | 0 |
| Isaac Meacham, | 1 | 10 | 0 | John Fuller, | 1 | 0 | 0 |
| Joseph Bradford, | 4 | 0 | 0 | Zeb'd Andrus, | 2 | 0 | 0 |
| Asa Field, | 2 | 0 | 0 |  |  |  |  |
|  |  |  |  |  | £152 | 19 | 9 |

Amounting in dollars and cents to $509.97.

Mr. Griswold entered on his pastorate under the most encouraging circumstances. The troubles in the church had mainly grown out of its connection with Mr. Beebe, and disclosures of his real character made soon after his dismission, convinced his most steadfast adherents of their error, and soon a good understanding prevailed. Mr. Griswold was popular, as well in the society and town, as in the church. His circumspect, thoughtful and yet pleasant manner won the confidence and affection of his contemporaries, and to his prudence and good common sense, rather than to brilliant talent, may be attributed his eminent success.

The church and congregation largely increasing, measures were taken in a few years for the erection of a more commodious church, as well as for its location at a more central point in the society. This, however, was displeasing to the people in the west part of the town, who would have to go one mile further to church. The west part of the town were stimulated, however, to put up a church of its own, which was accomplished the next year.

In 1798, the large, and for the day, splendid church, was erected on the hill north of the village, which stood till about 1842. From all that appears or is known, this church was eminently prosperous and received large accessions up to about 1812, when a serious difficulty, growing out of political differences arose. A portion of the church had become connected with the Washington Benevolent Society, a secret political organization, which gave offense to a large minority of the church. Unavailing efforts were made to adjust the difficulty by a reference to a mutual council, the parties being so evenly divided that it was impracticable to settle it in the church. It was finally referred to the Consociation, whose conclusions left the matter where they found it. The original complainants who had, during the pendency of the question, refrained from participating in the church ordinances, were, in turn, complained of by the adverse party, for breach of their covenant obligations, and, after due course of labor, were most of them excommunicated. Notwithstanding the loss to the church of several of its more prominent members, there were constant accessions, which more than kept the membership good.

Rev. Mr. Griswold continued pastor of the church until 1831, a period of thirty-eight years, being relieved almost entirely from active service after 1824. Rev. Fayette Shipherd was colleague pastor from 1826 to 1830, acting, however, as stated supply from 1824. At his ordination, Rev. Mr. Chester preached the sermon. Rev. Elijah W. Plumb, D.D., succeeded to the pastorate, and was ordained May 18, 1831. Rev. John Hough preached the sermon. He continued pastor until October, 1844. During his pastorate the old church on the hill was taken down, and the present beautiful and convenient church edifice was erected.

Rev. Elijah H. Bonney succeeded to the pastorate, and was ordained February 25th, 1847. Rev. Joseph D. Wickham, of Manchester, preached the sermon. He continued till September 27, 1853. On the first Sabbath in February, 1854, Rev. Samuel M. Wood commenced his labors as a stated supply, and continued until 1858. In 1859, Rev. Azariah Hyde assumed the pastorate as a stated supply, and continued until 1865. He was succeeded, in 1866, by Rev. Levi H. Stone.

The number of members admitted to the church from 1781 to 1800 was 154; from 1800 to 1810, 52; from 1810 to 1820, 152; from 1820 to 1830, 96; from 1830 to 1867, 268; making the whole number, to May 17, 1867, 722. It may be appropriate to remark, that from 1824 to the present time a Sabbath school and bible class have been steadily maintained. This church, too, has been liberal in the support of foreign missions, and has furnished from its membership Rev. Jonathan S. Green, a missionary to the Sandwich islands in 18 , Miss Delight Sargent, missionary to the Cherokees in 18 , who married Rev. Elias Boudinot, a native Cherokee, Mr. Philo P. Stewart, lay missionary to the Cherokees.

The following ministers from its membership have been educated and entered on the ministry: Hippocrates Rowe, Beriah Green, Jr., Jonathan S. Green, Jacob E. Blakely, Quincy Blakely, Judson B. Stoddard, Guy C. Strong, Lemon Andrus, Ferris Fitch, Miner Pratt, Azariah R. Graves.

We may remark, generally, that this church has ever maintained a high position for intelligence and independence. It has not hesitated to subject to criticism the decisions of councils and consociations, and to accept or reject their conclusions.

This church has usually had three deacons in active service. The succession of deacons is about as follows: Moses Porter, Joel Harmon, Ezekiel Harmon, Ozias Clark, Joseph Porter, John Penfield, Joshua D. Cobb, Simeon Edgerton, Dorastus Fitch, David Blakely, Milton Brown, Harry Griswold, George Willard and David Andrus.

*First Baptist Church.*

This was organized on the first Monday in May, 1790, on the present premises of Allen Whedon, then owned by Edmund Whedon. It was organized under the auspices of Elder Brown, of the church in Westfield (a locality in East Fort Ann, N. Y.). Its first members were James Bennett, Thomas Hall, Solomon Brown, Joseph Hascall,

John Crouch, Samuel Sisco, Caleb Agard, Nathaniel Harmon, Samuel Abbott, Alexander Trumbull, Edmund Whedon, Lydia Wilcox, Mary Bennett, Hannah Hanks, Miriam Hopkins, Sibel Sheldon, Lydia Agard and Elizabeth Crouch. For the first ten years, being destitute of a church, its meetings were held in private houses, and not unfrequently in barns. Its preachers were Elders Brown, Skeels, Green, Wait, Cornell, Dodge, Blood and Beall, each for brief periods. These were among the pioneer Baptist ministers of Vermont, and many of them were men of decided talent. In 1800 a church was built on the premises of Seety Brown, by the West Pawlet Meeting House Company, which was used almost exclusively by the Baptists for 24 years. Elder Isaac Beall was called to settle over the church in 1801, and continued with it till its dissolution in 1831. A parsonage was built in 1802, which appears to have been designed for a Baptist minister exclusively. The whole number of members belonging to this church was about two hundred, and it is said to have had one hundred and fifty at one time. A strict, wholesome and orderly discipline was maintained, as the records and files of the church attest. It was the misfortune, perhaps the fault of this church, to be isolated from sister churches during most of its existence.

Its first deacons were Joseph Hascall and Timothy Brewster; after them were Josiah Toby and Jeremiah Arnold. From its membership, Solomon Brown, Timothy Brewster, Daniel Hascall and Lemon Andrus were licensed to preach.

In 1831 the church dissolved; those of its members who desired it being furnished with certificates of their good standing.

A Methodist Episcopal class was formed in 1795,

at the house of John C. Conant, now Stephen McFadden's. It was quite flourishing for several years, and numbered in its membership several of the substantial people of that locality. Among them were Daniel Baldridge, John C. Conant, Jeremy Baldwin and Aaron Bennett, some of whom had been members of the Congregational church. It was supplied with preaching at stated intervals, according to the custom of those days, by two circuit preachers traveling together. They usually traveled on horseback and completed their circuit in four weeks. A few of this class remained as late as 1825, who united with the church at the village.

### Protestant Episcopal Church.

An Episcopal organization existed here as early as 1790, which was represented in the State Episcopal Convention. The names of the delegates to the convention, in order, beginning with 1790, were Ebenezer Cobb, Henry Wooster, Benoni Smith, Jonathan Willard, Seely Brown, Henry Wooster, Jr., Josiah Smith and Asaph Teall. In 1793, the State Episcopal Convention was held in this town at the house of Henry Wooster, when an election was effected of the first bishop of Vermont. This was Rev. Edward Bass, D. D., of Newburyport, Mass., who accepted the position on condition of being allowed to remain in Massachusetts until a sufficient amount should be realized from the church glebe in the state to afford him a maintenance. This did not suit the convention and Dr. Bass was never consecrated. Services were held mostly at the house of Capt. Benoni Smith, during his life, and was continued at the house of his widow.

Among the early Episcopal ministers who officiated here were Rev. Bethuel Chittenden, of Shel-

CHURCH HISTORY. 145

burn, Rev. Daniel Barber, Rev. Amos Pardee and Rev. Abraham Bronson, D. D., of Manchester. About 1810, Rev. Stephen Jewett, from Connecticut, came here and officiated for some time. He afterwards settled in Hampton, N. Y., and continued stated services here. The brick school house, in the northwest part of the town, was built and fitted up, partly at the expense of the church, and services were held here from 1812 to 1815, when Trinity church, Granville, was erected and this church was merged in that. In the early days of the church a small amount was realized from the glebe, which was taken from them about 1803, by the legislature, and appropriated to schools. Litigation was unsuccessful to restore it. About 1823, the church applied for and obtained the lot reserved for the Society for Propagating the Gospel in Foreign Parts, and under the auspices of Rev. Palmer Dyer the church was reorganized by the name of Trinity church. This was little more than nominal, though the organization was kept up several years and was represented in convention. On the removal and death of the principal churchmen, between 1830 and 1840, the church became extinct. The income of the church lands is now appropriated to other churches in the state.

*Methodist Episcopal Church.*

Rev. George Smith, of Hebron, N. Y., then a local elder, was the first minister, at the village, of this church. In 1825 he preached his two first sermons in the hall of the brick tavern. Afterwards he preached at the academy, at the house of Paul Hulett and at the school house, near Elisha Allen's. It was ascertained that there were two hundred hopeful conversions, of all denominations, in town during that season, of whom forty were in the school district last mentioned. The Methodist church was organized in 1826. Paul Hulett, John Crapo, Amos Wooster, Sylvester Pitkin, Nathan Allen, Elisha Allen, Joel Winchester, Fitch Clark, Robert Clark and Chauncy Guild, were among its prominent male members. Samuel Howe and Elias Crawford were the first itinerant ministers in 1826; Daniel Brayton and John Clark in 1827; Roswell Kelly and Laban Clark in 1828, and Roswell Kelly and Seymour Coleman in 1829. The brick church, near the cemetery, was erected in 1826 or 1827, and formally dedicated. Rev. Daniel Brayton and Rev. Lemuel Haynes, of the Congregational church, preached on this occasion. This church has been supplied, mostly, by resident ministers, for whom a parsonage was procured in 1832. For six years after its organization it belonged to the New York conference. In 1832 the Troy conference was organized, and held its fourth annual session here. Rev. Bishop Waugh presided and J. B. Houghtaling was secretary. A camp meeting, very numerously attended, was held on the farm of Joel Simonds, in 1830. Two camp meetings have since been held on the same ground.

In 1853, a new and commodious church edifice was erected in the village and dedicated to the worship of God. Rev. Jason F. Walker preached the sermon. This church has experienced seasons of deep depression and severe trial in the withdrawal of several of its members at different times. Some joined the Protestant Methodist church, others the Wesleyan, and others the independent society. Notwithstanding these adverse influences, the church has been greatly revived within a few years last past, and has nearly recovered its former standing. It has a flourishing Sabbath school, under William Blakely, superintendent, and a membership of ninety on the church records. Since 1829, the following ministers have officiated in this church, though not all in the order named. It is not official, and there may be errors and omissions: Rev. Messrs. Sherman Miner, Jacob Beman, William Gray, Ezra Sprague, Joseph Ames, —— Field, —— Quinland, David Poor, Joseph Ayres, J. B. Houghtaling, William A. Miller, Jacob Leonard, —— Hubbard, Cyrus Prindle, —— Hulbert, —— Shears, Cyrus Meeker, A. A. Farr, C. C. Gilbert, —— Ford, J. F. Walker, Reuben Westcott, —— Perkins, B. S. Burnham, —— Spencer, Sylvester Walker, John Searles, William Earll, John Kiernan.

*Second Baptist Church.*

This church was organized in 1826, and admitted to the Vermont association. It owed its origin to the fact that the first Baptist church, from which all its first members came, was not, and had not been for years, in fellowship with any other body. Isaac Wickham, Seth Blossom, Reuben Toby, Washington Z. Wait and Seth P. Stiles were among its first members. Its ministers were Elders L. P. Reynolds, Wetherell, Abram Woodward, Joseph Packer, Daniel Cobb, E. S. Soullard, Sweet, Mead, Sanders and Archibald Wait, and perhaps some others. Its deacons were Isaac Wickham and Reuben Toby. About the year 1848 this organization was dissolved. In 1852, what is now known as the Baptist church in West Pawlet, was organized under the auspices of Elder A. Wait, who served them as pastor three or four years. The present church edifice was built the same year.

Elder Wait's ministry was attended with considerable success. After him, Elders Combe, Hancock and Mosher were employed, but not until 1859 was this church in fellowship with any other body. In that year, under the auspices of Elder David Beecher, this church was admitted to the Vermont and Shaftsbury association. In 1859 the membership was twenty-four, but under the faithful and zealous labors of Elder Beecher it has increased to one hundred and seventeen members. The need of a larger house is now sometimes seriously felt. Its first deacons were Jeremiah Clark and Samuel Cole. Its present deacons are Samuel Cole, Allen Whedon and B. H. Nelson. It has an interesting Sabbath school of 125 members, which, in 1866, presented to its superintendent, Allen Whedon, an elegant photograph album intended to contain the portraits of all the scholars, together with their teachers and parents.

### *Church of the Disciples.*

In 1831 this church was formed under the guidance of Elder Worden P. Reynolds, then recently of the Baptist church. Deacon Jeremiah Arnold was the first to espouse the peculiar doctrines of this church. Besides him, among its first members, were David Carver, Thomas Laing, Rufus Conant, James T. Bates, Rufus P. Conant, David Hollister and Luther Arnold. Its growth, for awhile, was rapid, meetings being held in the old meeting house and in school houses alternately. In 1847 this society built a church at West Pawlet; Elder Lowell preached on the occasion of its being opened. Since Elder Reynolds left, in 1833, it has been destitute of a pastor a share of the time, though its meetings on "the first day of the week" have been generally sustained. Its only resident ministers have been Elders Worden P. Reynolds, E. T. Wood and Thomas Laing. Elder Clayton, then of Rupert, served the church one-half the time for a year or two. Besides, ministers from abroad have called and held a series of meetings. In 1836, Rev. Alexander Campbell, from Virginia, visited this society, and preached in the old Baptist church. Since the above was written, 1866, Rev. A. W. Olds has supplied the pulpit of this church, and there has been a large increase in its membership, which now numbers eighty. A bible class and Sabbath school are now in successful operation.

*Protestant Methodist Church.*

BY REV. GEORGE SMITH.

"In the year 1832, a Methodist Protestant church was formed on Pawlet mountain, near Aaron Bennett's. Its first principal members were Jesse Monroe, Aaron and Leonard Bennett, Austin Johnson, Joel Baldwin, Amos Wooster and Isaac Roberts. A meeting house was built near John Stearns, in 1833. George Smith, Chandler Walker, Ziba Boynton, William Gone, Daniel Vaughn, Eldridge G. Drake and John Croker, supplied the church with preaching about 23 years. Then, as the most prominent members moved out of the state, the church run down. The meeting house was sold, taken down and converted into a dwelling house."

An independent religious society was formed at the village in 1855, under the auspices of Rev. Jason F. Walker, then late of the Methodist church. For some years, while Mr. Walker was statedly with them, their meetings were largely attended, being held mostly at the Academy. For some time, their meetings have been wholly discontinued.

Besides the churches and societies already named, the Universalists have been numerous, particularly in the north part of the town, and have affiliated with those of like faith in Wells. Joseph P. Upham, Ephraim Jones, Innett Hollister, Reuben Smith, Elijah Brown and Daty Allen, 2d, were among its more prominent members. Their meetings were generally held in Wells, though sometimes at the old Baptist church, a considerable part of which was owned by them.

The peaceful and exemplary Friends, have not been without their representatives. Many of our older citizens will remember the genial and hospitable William Boyce, who lived on the Lyon place, and Lemuel Chase, who lived quite retired, in the west part. Other Friends have, from time to time, lived in various parts of the town.

*Mormonism.*

Soon after the rise of Mormonism in western New York, its missionaries found their way to this town, and held stated meetings for several weeks. Among them, came Brigham Young, then young and unnoted, who visited this town and held his meetings at the old Red school house, not ten rods from where we now write. Joseph Smith, Sen., also visited the town, preached and baptized Mrs. Cornwell Marks. A few adherents were obtained, mostly from families educated in the Congregational church, who followed the fortunes of the party to Kirtland, Ohio, thence to Nauvoo, Illinois, and thence, some of them, to Great Salt Lake City.

In 1833, Capt. William Miller, the founder of the Second Advent church, visited this town on the invitation of the writer, and made his first oral effort in advocacy of his peculiar views. His mission here was followed by slender results. About 1850, one Mr. Lyon promulgated the same views, substantially, of the Disciples' church, and baptized a few converts. Notwithstanding the limited success in this place, the doctrines first preached here have enlisted in their advocacy, some of the ablest intellects in New England, and are clung to, somewhat modified, with great pertinacity to this day.

## FREE MASONRY.

#### BY JONATHAN RANDALL.

Hiram Lodge, No. 8, was organized March 22, 1796, and met, for the first time, at Samuel Rose's, in the south part of the town. At that meeting William Cooley was appointed master, Zadock Higgins, senior warden, and George Clark, junior warden.

The 24th of June, this year, the lodge celebrated the nativity of St. John the Baptist. The Rev. John Griswold preached a sermon before the lodge at the meeting house.

In February, 1799, the lodge met at the hall of Ephraim Fitch, and continued to hold the meetings there until the house was burned, in October, 1806; in that fire some of the records were destroyed. At that time the lodge numbered about seventy members.

Social Royal Arch Chapter, No. 10, was chartered and met for the first time at the hall of

Lemuel Barden, in Pawlet village, the 9th of February, 1819. The three principal officers were Titus A. Cook, Jonathan Robinson and Phineas Strong. A public installation was held at the Congregational meeting house the same year, the Rev. Jonathan Nye, of Newfane, preached a sermon on the occasion, before one of the largest assemblies ever convened in Pawlet.

At present, the Free masons in Pawlet are members of lodges in the vicinity, some belong to the lodge at Poultney, others to the Manchester and Rupert lodges.

The masonic institution suspended their meetings in 1834, and they have not been resumed.

## INCORPORATED MANUFACTURING COMPANIES.

#### BY JONATHAN RANDALL.

In November, 1814, the legislature passed an act incorporating the Pawlet Manufacturing Company. The corporators were John Guild, Ozias Clark, John Penfield, Jr., Jonathan Robinson, Nathaniel Robinson, Jr., William C. Robinson, Napthali Guild, David Richardson, Dan. Wilmarth, Daniel Fitch, and their associates, successors and assigns.

The first meeting of the corporation was held at the dwelling house of John Guild, in Pawlet, the first Monday in January, 1815. John Guild was chosen agent.

The company, that year, erected their factory building. It was built of brick, 70 feet long and 36 feet wide, and three stories high. It was situated about half a mile east of Pawlet village. It made a good article of cotton sheeting and cotton warp or twist for market. There was in the building 860 spindles and 16 looms. They employed about 25 hands.

The company did a very good business for many years, or during the time that Milton Brown was the agent. There was a store connected with the manufacturing business.

This was about one of the first cotton factories built in this state. There was a machine shop connected with the factory, where much of the machinery was made by Nathaniel Robinson and others.

A few years after Mr. Brown retired from the agency, the company failed; the machinery was sold, the building taken down, so that now nothing marks the spot where the factory stood except some of the foundation stones.

The Flower Brook Manufacturing Company was incorporated in November, 1836, by act of the legislature. The persons incorporated were Sheldon Edgerton, Jacob Edgerton, Jr., Jonathan Randall, John M. Clark, John T. Barden and William Wallace, for the manufacturing cotton and wool.

The first meeting of the company was held at the house of John T. Barden, in Pawlet, on the first Tuesday of January, 1837. At that meeting Jonathan Randall was chosen agent of the company, and Jacob Edgerton, Jr., clerk.

The factory building was built at Pawlet village. It was 80 feet long and 36 feet wide; was built of wood. It was five stories high on the west end and three on the east end.

There were 3 set of carding machines, or 9 machines, 720 spindles and 10 broad looms. When the machinery was all running they worked 300 pounds of wool a day.

There were two water wheels, one above the other, in the mill, one wheel of 18 feet diameter, the other wheel was 11 feet; the water was used over twice. There was about 34 feet fall of the water; the wheels were overshot. Mr. Randall was agent three years, William Wallace two or three years, when John M. Clark bought out all the stock holders, and run the factory a year or two, when it finally failed. The machinery was sold at auction, the building taken down, and the site forms a part of the yard used in connection with R. C. Wickham's cheese factory.

When the machinery was all in operation, it gave employment to 24 or 25 persons.

The establishment cost about twenty thousand dollars.

### *Washington Benevolent Society.*

This was a secret political organization which spread over New England, and, to some extent, in other northern states. A branch was established in this town about the breaking out of the war of 1812. Its friends claimed that it was merely a protective institution, to preserve the interests of the north against the obnoxious acts of the federal administration. Its enemies charged it with treasonable proclivities. At the conclusion of a treaty of peace with Great Britain, in 1815, the organization was dissolved, and all that has been heard of it since is an occasional fling at its friends by the opposing party.

# FAMILY SKETCHES.

## INTRODUCTION.

It was said by Edmund Burke, that: "Those who never look back to their ancestors will never look forward to their posterity." When we first undertook to prepare a history of this town, our thought was only to follow the pattern set by writers of local histories elsewhere, and notice a few, perhaps a dozen, of our early leading families. But after making a beginning, with that view, we were not satisfied, and have continued to enlarge this section until the number of separate articles reaches nearly five hundred, embracing in their collaterals and connections not less than two thousand families. Our chief regret in this undertaking is our inability to ascertain all the leading facts in the history of each family. Many old families will be omitted, as hundreds have lived in town who have passed away from the recollection of its present inhabitants.

If it is asked why we introduce the names and history of the humble and obscure, it is sufficient to answer, that in the changes continually going on in society, the high and the low are incessantly changing places. The grub of to-day is the butterfly to-morrow. The *sans-culotte* of yesterday wears breeches to-day. Whence were the large array of professional men who have gone out from this town recruited? We say mainly from the ranks of the lowly and obscure. No one obtains positions of honor and influence but through personal exertions. And this is the crowning glory of our free institutions.

So far as we can ascertain we have given the town and state from which those of our citizens, who are not natives, came, and also the place to which, those who have left town, have removed. Also we have given generally a record of marriages and deaths, which is imperfect, and will doubtless contain many errors. We have also given, in many instances, brief sketches of character, interesting incidents and anecdotes.

ADAMS, GIDEON, from Canterbury, Conn., 1770, m. Jude Leach, a sister of James Leach, Sen., who died in 1819, aged 75, leaving three children, Jude, Margaret, who married Joseph Keigwin, and Mary, who married John Kirby, Middlebury. He settled where Henry S. Lathe now lives. He at once took a leading position in the town, which then contained only nine families. He was in the legislature in 1778, and served, in the whole, six years. He was town clerk and justice 39 years. He was a man of ready wit and genial temper, of strong sense and sound judgment, and won and retained through his whole career, the confidence and esteem of his fellow citizens in an eminent degree. He died in 1827, aged 84.

ADAMS, JESSE, from New Lebanon, Conn., 1786, settled on the present farm of N. W. Bourn. After his death, in 1812, aged 55, his numerous family removed to Nunda, N. Y.

ADAMS, BENONI, claims commemoration as one of the earliest singing masters in town. He sung the old fugue tunes, which, on being reproduced in recent times, are found to be immensely popular. His home was in New Milford, N. Y.

ALEXANDER, BENJAMIN, from England, 1837, m. Mary Thorn, who died in 1844, leaving four children; Elizabeth, Mary Ann, Susan and John. Mary Ann married Marshall Brown, and died in 1862.

Elizabeth married Marshall Brown; John married Ellen Howe. Next he married Sylvia, daughter of Isaac Harlow, of Whitehall, N. Y., who has three children, Henry and Henrietta (twins), and Harriet, who married Andrew Dunton.

ALLEN, TIMOTHY, from Woodbury, Conn., 1768. He was a cousin of Ethan Allen, and the first settler in the northwest quarter of the town. He evinced great sagacity in the selection of a home, it being the present homestead of David G. Blossom. He was moderator of the town meeting in 1770. He is well remembered by many of our older citizens as a man of singular piety and eminent gifts. The detachment of troops that surprised Ticonderoga in 1775, halted for the night at his house on their march to that place. He died in 1810, aged 96. His son, Parmelee, was town clerk in 1770, and a captain in Col. Herrick's famous regiment of Rangers, organized in this town in 1777. Another son, Daty, was a physician and an emigrant to Mt. Clemens, Mich., in 1800.

ALLEN, TIMOTHY, Jr., was in the battle of Bennington in 1777, at the age of 17. He was an early settler of Bristol, and deacon of the Baptist church in that place. In 1814 he removed to Hartford, N. Y., where he died, 1834, aged 74. Of Deacon Allen's children, Rev. Barna Allen is Baptist minister in Hubbardton, and Hon. Alanson Allen, of Fairhaven, has been county judge and state senator, and is now assistant assessor of internal revenue.

ALLEN, CALEB, came with his father, Timothy Allen, in 1768. He was a land jobber, a vocation which the peculiar condition of real estate in the early years of the settlement of the state demanded. Most of the land was owned by non-residents, many of whom took little interest in it. Hence business men looked them up, bought their claims, many times at a nominal price, and then sold the land in parcels to actual settlers. The cemetery in the north part of the town was given by him to the school district in which it lies. Its first occupants were revolutionary soldiers. He died in 1804, aged 56. His son, Daty, succeeded to the homestead, which he held till 1816, being followed by David C. Blossom. He removed to Whitehall, N. Y., where he died some years ago, leaving numerous descendants.

ALLEN, NEHEMIAH, was an early settler from Worcester, Mass., living alternately in this town and in Granville, N. Y. He was in Rochester, N. Y., when the present site of that city was offered him for one shilling per acre. He died in 1852, aged 87; his wife in 1841, aged 73. His oldest daughter married David Whedon; his youngest daughter, Jane, Ansel Whedon, who died in 1831, aged 36. She then married William Clark, of Whitehall, N. Y., and died in 1850, aged 50.

ALLEN, JOHN, from Danby, 1815; settled with his sons, Nathan and Elisha, on the Jonathan Willard place. He was a substantial, thrifty farmer, and held in high esteem. He died in 1852, aged 91; his wife in 1851, aged 71.

ALLEN, NATHAN, m. Julia, da. of Jeremiah Leffingwell, of Middletown. He was one of the earliest and most influential members of the Methodist church. He was one of the directors of the Poultney bank several years. He died in 1863, aged 72. His children were, John, m. Ellen, da. of Joel Winchester; Charles, m. Anna, da. of James Rice. He was in the legislature two years, and lives in Darien, Wis. Isaac, m. Eliza Allen, has been attorney general of Iowa. Henry, m. Sarah Shedd, of Pittstown, N. Y., and succeeded to the homestead. Sarah, m. Lewis F. Jones, of California. She was a graduate of Troy Conference Academy, and its female principal two years. Lucy, m. Richard H. Winter, of Whitehall, N. Y.

ALLEN, ELISHA, m. Annis, da. of Dr. Jonathan Safford; settled on the place and built the brick house now owned by Albert A. Boynton. He was also a leading member of the Methodist church. He was in the legislature four years, two of them in the senate, judge of the county court three years, town clerk, nineteen years, and director of the Poultney bank several years. He died in 1856, aged 62. His oldest son, Horace, m. Kate, da. of Jacob Edgerton, Jr., and d. in St. Paul, Minn., in 1865, aged 43. He was a graduate of Union College, and an attorney. He represented Rutland in the legislature two years, and was state senator one year. His youngest son, Merritt, was an attorney, and died at St. Paul in 1855, aged 24.

ANDRUS, Hon. JOHN H., from Danby, 1820; settled on the present Town farm. He was a representative in the legislature from Danby several years, and was a man of note and influence. He was a judge of the county court. He d. in 1841, aged 73; his wife in 1821, aged 50.

ANDRUS, EZRA, son of Judge Andrus, m. Nancy, da. of James McDaniels, and settled near his father's homestead in Danby, on the Timothy Brewster place. He died in 1864, aged 65, leaving a family of three sons and six daughters; James McD., who occupies the homestead, John H., Merritt, Sarah Ann, Eliza Ann, Nancy, Julia, Esther and Cordelia. Sarah Ann m. Mark Wooster, Manchester; Eliza Ann m. Dr. Phineas Strong; Julia m. Parker Jones.

ANDRUS, Capt. ZEBADIAH, Sen., from Norwich, Conn., 1784; settled on the present homestead of

David R. Smith. He died in 1804, aged 86; his wife in 1789, aged 74.

ANDRUS, ZEBADIAH, Jr., came with his father from Norwich, Conn., and settled with him. He d. in 1830, aged 86; his widow d. in Mt. Tabor in 1850, aged 94. Her death was caused by her clothes taking fire.

ANDRUS, ASA, Sen., son of Zebadiah, Sen., settled on the present homestead of Asa A. Monroe. He died in 1821, aged 79.

ANDRUS, ASA, Jr., succeeded to his father's place; sold out in 1821, to Josiah Monroe, and removed to Lockport, N. Y., where he died in 1863, aged 90.

ANDRUS, Rev. LEMON, son of Asa Andrus, Jr., was licensed to preach in 1821, by the Baptist church in West Pawlet. He was pastor of the church in Low Hampton, N. Y., several years, but left about 1830, for western New York. His wife is a daughter of Capt. Joshua Cobb.

ANDRUS, ALLEN, son of William Andrus, m. Betsey, da. of Rev. John Griswold, and settled as a physician in Pulaski, N. Y. He died in this town.

ANDRUS, BENJAMIN, son of Zebadiah Andrus, Jr., m. Emily Chapin, and settled on the mountain, near Rupert. He died in 1864, aged 81; his wife in 1852, aged 64. His family consists of four sons and one daughter, all of whom live in the vicinity. Sylvester, m. Paulina ———; Chapin, m. Harriet, da. of Capt. Moses Whitcomb; David, m. Ann, da. of Guild Willis; Benjamin, m. Ann, da. of Henry Belden, and Almeda C.

ANDRUS, DAVID, m. a da. of Daniel Welch, and settled near the Town farm. His son, Fayette, m. Harriet, da. of Samuel Thompson, and owns the Simeon Edgerton, Sen., farm. Mr. Andrus died in 1826, aged 45; his widow in 1859, aged 69.

## Family Sketches.

ANDREWS, REUBEN, from Connecticut, at an early day; settled near the old Baptist church. He was an ingenious mechanic, and made the old fashioned eight day clock, which was in common use fifty years ago.

ARMSTRONG, JOSEPH, from Bennington, 1776; settled in the northeast part of the town, and kept tavern some 25 years. His wife died in 1810, aged 62. Their sons were Jasper, Jesse and Phineas; their daughters Sally, Clarissa, Polly and Nancy.

ARMSTRONG, PHINEAS, m. Eunice, da. of Zebadiah Andrus, Jr., and settled at the village, where his widow and daughter Harriet, the only survivors in town of the Armstrong family, still reside. He died in 1836, aged 50.

ARNOLD, JONATHAN, from Connecticut, settled at an early day on the present homestead of Oliver Williams. He was an intelligent, exemplary citizen. He died in Granville, N. Y., in 1838, aged 83.

ARNOLD, JEREMIAH, son of Jonathan, m. Mary Ellsworth, and settled on the late homestead of Harvey R. Weeks. He struggled manfully against the adverse influences of chronic ill health and slender means and educated his numerous family well.

For several years he was engaged in riding post, delivering newspapers at the door of subscribers. He was a deacon of the Baptist church, and the first in this vicinity to embrace the peculiar views of the Church of the Disciples. He removed to Wisconsin, where he recently died, aged about 70.

AVERILL, Gen. ELISHA, from New Milford, Conn., 1787, was among the most prominent of the early settlers. He was the first captain of the light infantry. He removed west in 1803, and died at Manchester, N. Y., in 1821, aged 67; his widow in 1823, aged 63.

ACKLEY, JOSEPH, was the successor of Edmund Whedon in the mercantile business about the beginning of this century. He removed to North Granville, N. Y,, about 1812, where, in connection with Capt. Oliphant, he established an extensive brewery on the site of the ladies' seminary.

ADAMS, GEORGE JONES, from Maine, 1857, occupied the pulpit of the Disciple's church at West Pawlet, six or eight months. He had been an extensive traveler on the Eastern continent. He exerted a magnetic and fascinating influence over most persons with whom he came in contact. In his religious history he had "swung around the circle," having been, it is understood, a Methodist, Mormon, Freewill Baptist and Spiritualist before he joined the Disciples. He was also professor of elocution and a theatrical performer. He is now the founder of a colony of 160 persons at Jaffa in Palestine. Newspaper reports, during the last winter, have represented this colony as on the point of breaking up; but the latest accounts (April, 1867), show it to be in a thriving condition. They took the timber for their houses from the state of Maine, and are said to have 300 acres under cultivation and plenty of provisions.

BAKER, REMEMBER, whose career makes so prominent a part of early Vermont history, was a proprietor and temporary resident of this town as early as 1768. He built the first grist mill erected in town on land now owned by George Toby. Not long after he was killed by Indians near St. Johns, Canada, at the age of 35.

BAKER, ELIJAH, from Canterbury, Conn., 1786, settled in the south part of the town with three sons,

FAMILY SKETCHES. 163

Ebenezer, Rufus and Ichabod, who all raised large families. Few of their descendants remain in the vicinity. He died in 1811, aged 86.

BAKER, HARVEY, from Arlington, about 1826, m. Mariettea, da. of Col. Ozias Clark. He kept store awhile with Dr. Nathan Judson, south of the village, and afterwards, a short time, at the village. He was held in high esteem, He removed about 1833 to Oswego Co., N. Y., thence to Whitewater, Wis., where he died in 1864, aged 63.

BALDRIGE, DANIEL, from Rhode Island, about 1785, settled on the present homestead of Henry Smith. He was one of the first Methodists in town. His sons, Daniel, Jr., and Edward succeeded him and raised large families, all but one of whom, Catharine Jones, have left town.

BALDRIGE, JAMES, son of Edward, m. Fanny, da. of Nehemiah Bourn, and succeeded to the homestead. He died in 1862, aged 48. He raised a large family, most of whom, after his death, removed to Rupert. His son, Edwin S., was educated at Union College; James, Jr., is a physician in Rupert; Mary married David R. Smith.

BALDWIN, JEREMY, from Townsend, Mass., 1785, settled with his brother Samuel, near Stephen McFadden's, whence they removed to Chautauque Co., N. Y. Jeremy died in 1850, aged 84; his widow, who was the widow of Daniel Baldridge, Jr., died in 1852.

BARDEN, LEMUEL, from Dighton, Mass., 1814, succeeded Ephraim Fitch, in the brick hotel at the village, which he kept until about 1830. Though of a rather rough exterior, he was a kind hearted, benevolent man, and would not serve his customers with liquor after he thought they had enough. He died in 1839, aged 81; his wife in 1839, aged 79. His son, John T. Barden, kept the tavern a few years and removed, about 1840, to Chautauque Co., N. Y., where he died some years ago. He married Clara, da. of Nathaniel Harmon, who died in 1830. Next he married Amorette, da. of John Penfield.

BEALL, Rev. ISAAC, from Clarendon, 1800, was the first settled pastor of the First Baptist church, which position he held until 1831. He was a man of great shrewdness and strong intellect, which compensated, in part, for deficiencies in his early education. He was a gentleman of the old school, courteous and affable in his deportment. He built up a thriving church which numbered, at one time, 150 members. The large house in which they worshiped was wont to be well filled. He died in Clarendon in 1833, aged 82; his wife did not long survive.

BARDWELL, CONSIDER S., from Shelburn, Mass., 1834, m. Mahala, da. of Allen Willis, and settled on the Palmer Cleveland farm. His wife dying in 1841, aged 34, leaving one son, Merritt W. Bardwell; he next married Sally, another daughter of Allen Willis, who died in 1863, aged 57. Next he married Minerva, da. of Lyman Kinney, of Rupert. His farm buildings and surroundings are models of taste and convenience. He has an artificial pond fed by springs gushing from its own bosom, which supplies motive power for machinery and is well stocked with trout. It is a favorite resort for sportsmen from the city. He carries on the edge tool manufacture, and, with his strong right arm, has hammered out a handsome property. He built in 1864, the first cheese factory in the state, which is now run by a dairy association, incorporated in 1865. Peat, said by experts to be of the best quality, is found on his premises, contiguous to the rail road.

BARDWELL, MERRITT W., m. Maggie E., da. of Benjamin Wilson, of Hebron, and occupies the farm of his late grandfather Willis.

## Family Sketches.

BATES, JAMES T., from England when a child. His father settled in Rush Hollow. He has long been known as a merchant, traveling and local. He is an independent thinker, and an earnest advocate of all the moral reforms of the day. He passes through our streets in his accustomed rounds, but not so frequently as of old, as the weight of 76 years has bowed his frame and impaired his energies.

BARRETT, ELISHA, came to this town in 1804. He married Sally Uran, and raised a family of four sons, Charles, Elijah, Elisha and Levi. He died in 1828, aged 60; his widow in 1854, aged 79.

BARRETT, ELIJAH, the only one of his father's family remaining in town, m. Emily McWain, and raised a family of six sons and five daughters. Two of his sons, Charles and Merritt C., enlisted and died in the service.

BEEBE, Rev. LEWIS, from Arlington, 1787, was the first settled minister, and obtained the lot of land reserved for that purpose in the charter. He was ordained June 14, 1787, and dismissed May 6, 1791. While living in Arlington, he was a member of the first council of censors, convened in 1785. This council was the most important ever convened in the state, as the task devolved on it of reviewing and recommending the repeal of much of the crude legislation of the seven preceding years. He removed hence to Lansingburgh, N. Y., and abandoned the clerical profession.

BENNETT, AARON, from Canterbury, Conn., about 1784; settled near the present residence of Charles Phillips. He raised a numerous family, many of whose descendants remain in town. His sons, Leonard and Ahira, were well known and respected citizens. The former removed to the west; the latter was drowned in Lake Champlain He died in 1849, aged 88; his wife in 1842, aged 76.

BENNETT, SAMUEL, from Canterbury, Conn., 1784; settled near his brother Aaron. His only daughter married Benjamin Sage, and raised a family of three sons and one daughter, Samuel, Wesley, who was killed by the premature explosion of a gun on independence day, 1816, and Benjamin, Jr.

BENNETT, BANKS, from Halifax, 1790; settled near Capt. Pratt's. He suffered acutely from a rheumatic affection, which drew his head down so that it rested on his breast. He died in 1829, aged 88.

BEECHER, Rev. DAVID, a native of Granville, entered on the ministry in the Baptist church over twenty years since. He first settled in Collins, N. Y., thence removed to western Pennsylvania, thence to Harmony, N.Y., and thence in 1859, to West Pawlet, where he assumed the pastorate of the Baptist church, in which his labors have been eminently successful. He married a daughter of Dea. George Hill. His oldest son, Charles, married Althea Congdon, who died in 1866.

BETTS, SELAH, from Norfolk. Conn., 1783; settled on the present homestead of John Betts. He was in the battle of Danbury, Conn., under Gen. Wooster. During the battle, the lock of his gun was shot away, when he coolly remarked, "They have shot off the lock of my gun," seized another musket and continued the fight. He died in 1826, aged 68; his wife, Sibel, in 1849, aged 87.

BETTS, JOHN, m. Lydia, da. of Hosea Loveland, and, with his brother Selah, Jr., succeeded to the homestead. He raised a family of six sons and two daughters: Orson F., d. in 1858, aged 34; Marshal, d. in 1856, aged 27; Willis W., Royal C., m. Melissa E. Holmes, and is an attorney at Granville and special judge of Washington county, N. Y.;

Sidney, who lives in Fort Miller; Franklin, who lives in Poultney; Sibel and Laura.

BIGART, JAMES, a native of Scotland, whence he came when a lad, with his father, to this town. He married Lola, da. of Alvin Goodspeed, of Wells, and kept the Vermont Hotel, at North Pawlet, for several years, closing in 1852, when he removed to Sandy Hill, N. Y. His wife died soon after, when he married a second wife, who recently died. He brought out in 1847, the celebrated horse Rattler, which is noticed in the chapter on Stock.

BIDWELL, JONATHAN, from Glastenbury, Conn., 1810; settled on the John Stark farm. His wife's name was Betsy Strong. They raised a family of one son and five daughters. Anson, who was instantly killed by falling from a staging, aged about 30; Caroline, m. William Lamb of Wells; Lucy Ann, m. Seth Barton, of Dorset; Harriet, m. Joseph Gilbert, of Cambridge, and died in early life; Emily, m. Russell Pember, of Wells, and Laura, m. Gerry Brown. Mr. Bidwell died in 1852, aged 74; his wife died in 1839, aged 59.

BLAKELY, DAVID, from Woodbury, Conn., 1782, settled on the late homestead of his son, Dan Blakely. He was noted for industry, frugality and thrift. He died in 1821, aged 72; his widow, who was an aunt of Gov. Hiland Hall, died in 1831, aged 85.

BLAKELY, Capt. DAVID, Jr., m. Esther, da. of Jacob Edgerton, and settled in the northeast part of the town. He was in the legislature two years, and has been deacon of the Congregational church since 18 . Their family consists of six sons and four daughters: Jacob E., Quincy, Hewitt, Martin, Walton and Marshal; Cythera, Maria, Phebe and Ann. Maria m. Silas Moore, who died in La Crosse, Wis; Phebe m. —— Norton, of Tinmouth: Ann, m. John Horr, of Brookline, Mass.

BLAKELY, Rev. JACOB E., Pastor of the Congregational church in Poultney, died in 1854, aged 34; Rev. Quincy Blakely, pastor of the Congregational church in Hampton, N. H.; Hewitt, m. Mary, da. of John Harwood, is a merchant at Northville, N. Y.; Martin m. Philinda Branch, and died in 1849, aged 30; his widow in 1860, aged 40; Walton m. Angenette Horr, of Castleton; Marshal m. Mary Aikin, da. of Dr. Aikin, and removed to Rutland.

BLAKELY, DAN, succeeded to the homestead, m. Hannah, da. of Jacob Edgerton, and raised a family of five sons and two daughters : Fayette, who married Abby H. Lasell, Hiland H., Sheldon, A. Judson, Collins, Franklin; Almira, who married Curtis Reed, and Mary. He died in 1862, aged 69. He was a public spirited and influential citizen, and for many years took a leading part in the business and religious interests of the town.

BLAKELY, JONATHAN, from Conn., 1785, m. Margaret, da. of Christopher Billings, and settled at the village. He died in 1845, aged 70; his widow, who was a woman of rare worth and devoted to deeds of kindness, died in 1863, aged 85. Their son, Billings Blakely, was favorably known as hotel keeper at Troy, Saratoga and Union Village, N. Y., at which latter place he died in 1864, aged 66. Anna, who married Jonathan Randall, is the only survivor of the family.

BLAKELY, ROBERT, from Ireland, 1832, came to this town with no capital and a dependent family. By close application to the woolen manufacturing business he has secured a handsome competency. His wife died in 1862, aged 58. He raised a family of four children: William, m. Abigail Eldred, and settled at the village; Robert, who was educated at Union College, died in 1863, aged 30; Mary, who married Enoch Colvin, and Margaret, who married Seth B. Pepper, of Castleton.

BLOSSOM, Capt. SETH, from Falmouth, Mass., 1783, m. Elizabeth Henshaw, and settled on the present homestead of Smith Hitt. He was an active and worthy citizen. He removed with his large family to Batavia, N. Y., in 1829, and died in 1845, aged 82. Dea. Benjamin Blossom, of ——, Mich., and Abigail, wife of Arthur Toby, of Pittsford, N. Y., are his only surviving children.

BLOSSOM, DAVID C., from Wells, 1816, m. Lucy, da. of Daniel Goodrich, and settled on the Timothy Allen farm, where he lives, retired from business, at the age of 83. His wife died in 1852, aged 65. They raised a family of seven children: Pauline, Anna, Laura, David G., Hiram S., Henry and Bethiah. Pauline m. John Upham, Winooski; Anna m. Orson Goodrich, Richmond, and died in 1839, aged 48; Laura m. Col. Lee T. Rowley, of Granville, N. Y., died in 1855, aged 41; Hiram, m. Jane Woodward and died in 1852, aged 32; Henry m. Sarah Stevens and removed to Chicago; Bethiah m. Orson Goodrich, Richmond. David G. Blossom, the only one remaining in town, m. Fidelia Goodrich, and succeeded to the homestead, on which he has just erected an elegant and convenient house.

BLOSSOM, WILLIAM, from Wells, 1844, m. Phebe, da. of David Lewis, and settled on the Samuel Wright place. They raised a family of four children: Benoni, who married Lucia, da. of Gideon A. Loomis; William, who married Paulina, da. of Paul Hulett, who died in 1852, aged 32; next married Mary I., da. of Charles Lamb, of Middletown; Joseph, who married Paulina, da. of Orlin Hulett, and died in 1863, aged 43, and Rebecca, who married Pomroy Wells, of Poultney.

BRACE, Hon. JONATHAN, from Glastenbury, Conn., 1780. He was probably the first attorney in town; a man of commanding talents and contributed largely to set the machinery of society in order. He settled near the present residence of James Leach, the contemplated site at that day of the county buildings. He was a member of the council of censors in 1785. In a few years he returned to Connecticut, where he became distinguished in his profession and in public life.

BRANCH, DANIEL, from Norwich, Conn., 1784, settled in the northeast part of the town, on the present homestead of Samuel Thompson; his numerous descendants have mostly left town. He died in 1822, aged 86; his wife in 1812, aged 73.

BRANCH, JOSEPH, son of Daniel, was an active business man and for several years ran a line of stages from Burlington to New York and also from Albany to Buffalo. He died in 1853, aged 73.

BRANCH, MINER, son of Daniel, m. a sister of Rev. Dr. Nathaniel Colver, of Boston. She was an aunt of Hon. Erastus D. Colver, late minister to Venezuela. The family left town many years since.

BONNEY, Rev. ELIJAH, from Hadley, Mass., 1844, succeeded Rev. Dr. Plumb in the pastorate of the Congregational church. Reserved and circumspect in his deportment, his public efforts evinced careful preparation. In his private and pastoral relations he was highly esteemed. He married Jane, da. of Asa S. Jones. He is now in Vernon, N. Y.

BREWSTER, Rev. TIMOTHY, from Norwich, Conn., settled on the Ezra Andrus homestead, in 1784. He was licensed to preach by the Baptist church in 1791. He removed to Ellisburg, N. Y., in 1813, and became pastor of the Baptist church in that place. He lived to a great age and frequently visited this town.

## FAMILY SKETCHES. 171

BROMLEY, Capt. LOVINE, from Danby, 1811, m. Nancy, da. of Daniel Hulett, and settled on the Joseph Fitch farm. He died in 1842, aged 49. He raised a family of ten children: Daniel H., who married Lucy Thompson and is a merchant at the village and was two years in the legislature; Amos W., m. Laura B. Robinson; George W., a physician, m. Angenette, da. of Philip Clark, and lives in Huntington; Jerome B., m. Laura B., da. of Fitch Clark, was state's attorney for the county in 1865 and 1866; Adams L., m. Harriet, da. of Fitch Clark, who died in 1861, aged 38; next m. Mrs. Mary Phelps, da. of Dorastus Fitch, who is the only representative of the families of Moses Porter and Joseph Fitch, left in town; Fayette m. Alta, da. of Edward Herrick, and occupies the homestead; Henry, the youngest son is blind, has received an education at the asylum for the blind in Boston.

BOYNTON, ALBERT A., from Manchester, 1843, m. Hannah D., da. of Jacob Lyon, and settled in 1865, on the Elisha Allen farm.

BOSTWICK, HENRY, kept the village hotel several years. Of late he is well and favorably known as stage driver and express man, from Pawlet to Granville, N. Y.

BROWN, Capt. MILTON, from Attleboro, Mass., 1815, m. Eunice, da. of John Guild, and settled near the cotton factory, of which he was agent some 30 years. He was in the legislature three years and a director of the bank of Manchester 25 years and for several years its president. He was deacon of the Congregational church from 1844 until he left for Potsdam, N. Y., in 1853.

BROWN, ELIJAH, from Stamford, Conn., 1783, settled on the late homestead of his son Gerry Brown. He was an industrious and useful citizen. He died in 1835, aged 77; his first wife, Phebe, who was the mother of his children, died in 1817, aged 57; his second wife, Esther, da. of Elijah Stevens, died in 1832, aged 55. He raised a family of seven children: Seth, who married —— Shepherd, removed to Clyde, N. Y.; Russell, Seely, David, who died in 1830, aged 33; Polly, died in 1836, aged 42; Amanda, married Gideon A. Loomis, and died in 1835, aged 42, and Gerry, noticed below.

BROWN, GERRY, m. Laura, da. of Jonathan Bidwell and succeeded to the homestead. He died in 1864, aged 63. They raised three children: Selden S., who married Densia, da. of Washington G. Wait and succeeded to the homestead; Celestia, who married Dewitt C. Wait, and died in 1858, aged 22, and Castera.

BROWN, RUSSELL, m. Betsey, da. of Jared Wilcox, who died in 1821, aged 33, leaving three children: Marshal, Maria and Jane. Next he married Laura Loveland, and died in 1825, aged 39. Maria m. Samuel G. Guilford, of Middle Granville; Jane m. Sidney Wright, now of Cambridge, N. Y.

BROWN, SEELY, 2d, m. Lydia, da. of Jared Wilcox, and died in 1836, aged 47; his wife in 1817, aged 27. Their only daughter, Lydia, m. Horace Crofoot, and died 1841, aged 25.

BROWN, SEELY, from Stamford, Conn., 1780; m. Jemima, da. of Capt. Benoni Smith, and settled just north of the old Baptist church. He was an enterprising and liberal citizen, and gave to the West Pawlet meeting house company the site for the church, parsonage and cemetery. He built, at the Falls near by, a saw mill and clover mill. He died in 1809, aged 50; his widow, who married Capt. Ephraim Robinson, died in 1834, aged 66. None of the family remain in town.

BURCH, PORTER, from Granville, 1866; settled on

the Abraham Woodard place, near the depot, West Pawlet.

BURT, GEORGE W., from Northumberland, N. Y., 1855, m. Cordelia, da. of David F. Hammond, and settled in 1867, on the Isaac Wickham place.

BURTON, Dr. SIMON, after assisting in the organization of Arlington, became the first settler of this town. On account of his being the first settler, the proprietors voted him fifty acres of land, though tradition has it that it was given to his wife, as the first white woman who ever set foot in town. He was town or rather proprietor's clerk in 1769, the oldest record in existence. He lived to a good old age, at North Pawlet, and died about 1810. He was interred in the village cemetery, but no stone marks the spot.

BUSBEE, Capt. JEREMIAH, from Danby, m. Dorcas, daughter of James Bassford, and has been village tailor some forty years. He was selectman ten years, only one man, Simeon Edgerton, Jr., holding the office longer than he.

BUSHNELL, Dea. BENAJAH, was an early settler on the farm now owned by Jacob Lyon. He was an honored member of society and held in high esteem. He died in 1814, aged 71; his wife in 1814, aged 73.

CARPENTER, LUCIUS M., a native of Kirby, from Rupert, 1850, m. Phebe, da. of Jonathan Staples, and succeeded him on the Daniel Fitch, Jr., farm. He was a medical graduate, but never practiced the profession; was in the legislature in 1865-6.

CARVER, NATHANIEL, from Canterbury, Conn., 1780, m. Lydia, da. of Simeon Edgerton, and settled on the farm now owned by George Barker. They raised a family of seven children, John, Betsey, David, Chester L., Lucy, Lydia and Ahiva. He died in 1805, aged 52; his widow in 1842, aged 80.

CARVER, JOHN, m. Anna Beebe, who died in 1823, aged 35. Next he married Martha Gifford, who died in 1861, aged 76. He died in 1864, aged 78. His children were Mary, who married John Scott, and Lydia, who died in 1865.

CARVER, DAVID, m. Betsey, da. of Dea. Josiah Toby, who died in 1866, aged 69. He occupies the Peter Stevens place. His children are Charles N., m. Catharine, da. of Artemus Wilcox; James A., m. Jane Clark, and was mortally wounded by a stone thrown by an unknown party, at the state fair at Rutland, in 1860, aged 35; Helen m. James M. Shaw, and Maria. His age is 71.

CARVER, CHESTER L., m. Lucy M., da. of Ransom Harlow, of Whitehall, who died in 1847, aged 39, leaving four children, Joseph H., Ransom H., Nancy M., and Egbert. Joseph H. was educated at Bethany College, West Virginia, and Antioch College, Ohio, and settled in Missouri as teacher, where he died in 1859, aged 26. Ransom H. was a soldier in the border war in Kansas, and died in Whitehall, in 1861, aged 27. Nancy M. was tenderly reared in the family of Robert Wickham; coming of age, she completed her education in Oberlin and Antioch colleges, Ohio, and is now engaged in teaching in St. Louis, Mo. Egbert, left an orphan, was cared for by his aunt, Mrs. Elon Clark, of Shaftsbury; coming of age, he graduated at the Commercial College, Albany, and is now in receipt of a salary of two thousand dollars per annum, as cashier of the Otego, N. Y., bank. Boys! do you hear that? Mr. Carver, in 1849, m. Emeline George, and died in the asylum for the Insane at Brattleboro, in 1863, aged 65.

CHIPMAN, Dr. LEMUEL, from Connecticut, 1780, m. Sina, da. of Col. William Fitch, and settled near the present residence of James Leach. He was one

FAMILY SKETCHES. 175

of a distinguished family who have shed an enduring lustre on the early history of the state. He was the first president of the State Medical Society, organized in 1796. He was in the legislature eight years. He removed to Richmond, N. Y., in 1798, where he became distinguished as a judge as well as physician. He lived to an advanced age.

CHIPMAN, Dr. CYRUS, brother of Lemuel, married Anna, da. of Col. William Fitch. He left for the west with his brother and settled in Rochester, Mich., about 1820. He died in 1840, aged about 80.

CLARK, ELISHA, from Suffield, Conn., 1784, settled next south of the town farm. He removed to Orwell, 1795, and lived to a great age. His sons, who remained in town, were Ozias, Daniel, Joseph and Asahel.

CLARK, Col. OZIAS, m. Rachel, da. of Col. William Fitch, and settled nearly opposite Austin S. Whitcomb's; his mansion, one of the best in town, being burned in 1840. He was a man of great force and energy, and a liberal and influential member of society. He was deacon of the Congregational church forty-seven years. He was one of the corporators of the Pawlet Manufacturing Company, which ran the first cotton mill in the county. He died in 1855, aged 91; his widow in 1864, aged 97. They raised a family of eight children: Fitch, John M., Robert, Irene, Nancy, Alta, Betsey and Mariette.

CLARK, FITCH, m. Laura Baker, and settled on the Joshua Cobb farm. They raised a family of ten children: Ozias, Lucretia, m. George Willard, Annis m. Johnson Loomis, and after his death, Henry Remington, of Castleton; Sheldon, Harriet, m. Adams L. Bromley, and died in 1861, aged 38; Jonathan B., m. N. M. Bromley, Laura B., m. Jerome B. Bromley, Sarah, m. Fayette Guilford and died in 1862, aged 28; Harry G., m. Flora Sherman, and Horace A., m. Addie Stevens. He celebrated his golden wedding in 1864, at which five generations were present. His age is 75.

CLARK, JOHN M., m. Julia, da. of Harry Beckwith, of West Granville; succeeded to his father's homestead, but removed in 1845 to Whitewater, where he died in 1864, aged 61.

CLARK, ROBERT, m. Calista Brown, and resides in the village. For several years he kept the village hotel. They have raised a family of six daughters: Betsey, who graduated at the Troy Female Seminary, and married Harrison Everett, of Chicago, Ill.; Mariette, who married James B. Robinson and died in 1860, aged 31; Lemira, who married Franklin Penfield, of Rockford, Ill.; Amelia, teacher of music, Fanny and Kittie.

CLARK, DANIEL, m. Sibel, da. of Col. William Fitch and settled on the present homestead of Allen Cook. They raised a family of eleven children: Elisha, William, Philip, Wheeler, John, Cyrus, Darius, Corilla, Cornelia, Sina and Daniel. Philip married Lucy Swallow, who died in 1865, aged 67. He was a member of the Pawlet band, and widely known for his proficiency as a bugler. He died in 1842, aged 74; his widow in 1850, aged 78.

CLARK, Capt. JOSEPH, m. Elizabeth, da. of Zebadiah Andrus, and settled on the present homestead of William Monroe. None of his family remain in town. He died in 1820, aged 43.

CLARK, ASAHEL, m. Polly B., da. of Daniel Welch, and settled on his father's place. He died in 1859, aged 79: his widow in 1864, aged 82. Their children were Ephraim F., who married Jane, a daughter of Capt. Joshua D. Cobb; Caroline, who married Daniel F. Cushman, and died in 1851, aged 43, and Catharine, who married Rich Weeks.

CLARK, Hon. AARON, son of David Clark, was a

native of this town, born in 1791. The family removed to Whiting. He graduated at Union College and was admitted to the bar at Albany, N. Y. He was private secretary of Gov. Daniel D. Tompkins during his term of service. Afterwards he was clerk of the assembly. In 1826 he removed to New York city where he became wealthy. He was mayor of the city in 1840–41.

CLEVELAND, MOSES, from Connecticut, at an early day, m. Zuba Kendall and settled where the widow of his son, Asa, now lives. He was public spirited and benevolent. He raised a family of five children: Calvin, Luther, Augustus, Asa and Olive. He died in 1820, aged 75; his wife in 1830, aged 80. Luther m. Joanna Brewster; he died in 1866, aged 93. He came to this town when eight years of age and probably lived longer in town than any other person has. His wife died in 1861, aged 86. Augustus was a colonel in the war of 1812; Asa succeeded to the homestead and m. Lydia, da. of Eleazur Crosby; he died in 1864, aged 73. His widow removed west in 1867.

CLEVELAND, PALMER, from Salem, N. Y., settled on the present homestead of Consider S. Bardwell, first occupied by John Fitch. He was a deacon of the Presbyterian church in Hebron, N. Y. Besides being a large farmer he carried on the tanning business. He removed to Indiana with his family about 1832, where died at an advanced age.

CLEVELAND, Capt. DAVID, from Salem, settled on the farm next above Palmer's, now occupied by Merritt W. Bardwell. He married a daughter of Seth Viets, Sen., and raised a large family, all of whom, with himself, removed west some thirty years ago.

CLARK, HORACE, son of Gen. Jonas Clark, of Middletown, married a daughter of Hiram Wait, of

Tinmouth, and settled in the mercantile business at the village, in 1829, which he continued with a short interval of five or six years. He was post master four years. He was a thorough and efficient business man, and was mainly instrumental in procuring the charter, and effecting the construction of the Rutland and Washington rail road. Just as the road was completed, he was attacked with a malignant fever at Salem, N.Y., and was taken on almost the first train that passed over the road to his home in Poultney, to die.

CLARK, WILSON, from Danby, 1848; raised a family of three sons, Merritt, Horace and John. Merritt m. Martha Hanks, and lives in Poultney; Horace m. Sarah J. Robertson, who died in 1866, aged 35; John m. Josephine Gray, of Middletown.

CLEVELAND, DAVID A., from Salem, N. Y., a relative of the preceding, settled on the Rev. John Griswold place, in 1866.

COBB, GIDEON, was one of the earliest settlers from Connecticut, and brought a large family with him. John and Joshua Cobb were his sons. He died 1798, aged 81.

COBB, JOHN, was a prominent man in the early days of the town, as the records show. He settled on the hill, near the old cemetery. The old church grounds and cemetery were on his premises. He removed to Orwell, and died in 1815, aged 73.

COBB, Capt. JOSHUA, m. Hannah, da. of Simeon Edgerton, Sen., and settled on the present homestead of Josiah R. Sherman. He removed to Vernon, N. Y.

COBB, Capt. JOSHUA D., m. Nancy, da. of Col. Ozias Clark, and settled on the homestead of Alonzo Smith. He was deacon of the Congregational church, from 1835 till his removal to Whitewater, Wis., in 1847. He died in this town, while on a visit, in 1866, aged 74; his wife in 1845, aged 50.

COBB, ELKANAH, from Connecticut, 1770; married Mary, da. of Jonathan Willard, and settled on the late homestead of Elisha Allen. He died in 1795, aged 49. His son, Capt. Willard Cobb, was an officer in the war of 1812, married a daughter of Caleb Allen. He built the store house at Polley's landing, in Fort Ann. Thence he went west. Another son, James, was in the war of 1812, and, at its close, entered West Point Military Academy. He removed to the state of Georgia. It is understood that Howell Cobb, conspicuous in the late rebellion, is his son.

COLE, Dea. SAMUEL, from Hebron, N. Y., 1858; married his second wife, Electa Smith, and succeeded to the homestead of Rufus Perkins. His son, David D. Cole, is a merchant in Granville, N.Y.; another son, Whitman, is a commission merchant in New York city.

COLVIN, ENOCH, from Danby, 1845, m. Mary, da. of Robert Blakeley, who died in 1856, aged 30; next m. ———. He succeeded Robert Blakely in the woolen mill in 1865.

COOK, TITUS A., son of Samuel and Chloe Cook, was the first person born in town, July 22, 1768. He settled near Granville, N. Y., where Mrs. Amanda Culver now lives. He was master builder in the construction of churches and the better class of dwellings. The old Congregational church, the Baptist church, the old Episcopal church at Granville were erected by him. He was justice over thirty years and esteemed a pure and upright magistrate. He died in 1827, aged 60. None of his family remain.

COOK, JAMES, from Sandisfield, Mass., settled near

Sherman Weed's. He was an exemplary and worthy citizen and universally beloved. For several years he manufactured lime from an excellent quarry on his premises. He raised a family of three sons: Mahlon, John and Erasmus D. Mahlon m. Cornelia, da. of Joel Sheldon, and lives in Manchester; John is a physician and now resides in New Jersey; Erasmus D. m. Charlotte, da. of Simeon Edgerton, Jr., and succeeded to his homestead. Mr. Cook removed to Manchester in 1835, and died in 1850, aged 75; his wife in 1849, aged 76.

COOK, EPHRAIM, settled at an early day in the east part of the town. He was an intelligent, active man. He, with his family, removed west over thirty years since. His son, Ephraim F. Cook, who married a daughter of David Andrus, was for many years city superintendent of schools in Buffalo.

COOK, ALLEN, from Danby, 1865, m. Hannah, da. of Caleb Parris, and settled on the Daniel Clark farm.

CONANT, Capt. JOHN, son of John G. Conant, who died in Wells in 1830, aged 60; m. Martha da. of Findley McNaughton, and settled at West Pawlet. His wife died in 1859, leaving four children: Daniel, who recently died in Little Falls, N. Y.; Orlando, rail road engineer; Charlotte, who married Harvey Pratt, of White Creek, N. Y., and Maria, a graduate of Castleton academy and teacher of drawing, painting, etc.

CONANT, RUFUS P., from Enfield, N. H., 1811, settled at West Pawlet in the cloth dressing business. He married Fanny Lathe, who died in 1829, aged 41; next he married Nancy Goodrich. He removed with most of his family to Wisconsin, about 1847, where he recently died.

COWDREY, Dr. WARREN A., from Wells, married Patience, da. of Joel Simonds, and taught school

FAMILY SKETCHES. 181

and practiced medicine in this town in 1815. He removed to Le Roy, N. Y. He and his wife embraced Mormonism, but did not follow on to Utah. He was a brother of Oliver Cowdrey, one of Joseph Smith's "Witnesses."

CRAPO, JOHN, from Deighton, Mass., about 1814, m. Polly, da. of Lemuel Barden, and settled on the present homestead of his son, Alden B. Crapo. He was of quiet and industrious habits, and died in 1862, aged 87; his widow in 1862, aged 81.

CROCKER, JOSIAH, from Falmouth, Mass., 1783; married a sister of Josiah Toby, and settled on the present homestead of David Farrar. He raised a family of six sons and several daughters: Benjamin, James, John, Thomas, Timothy and Ezra. James was an attorney, and died recently at Buffalo. John settled in Warsaw, N. Y. Thomas m. —— Hooker, and succeeded to the homestead, but removed to Poultney, where he recently died. The other sons went west, but none of them are living. Mr. Crocker took special pride in his family, and gave them unusual advantages for education. He died in 1846, aged 86; his widow in 1847, aged 84.

CROSBY, ELEAZAR, from Brattleboro, 1806; married Margaret Toby, and raised a family of nine children, all but one of whom have removed west. The exception is Isaac, who married Eliza, a daughter of Guild Willis, who died in 1865.

CROUCH, ITHAMAR, from Brimfield, Mass., 1794; settled near Capt. Pratt's, and raised a numerous family, most of whom died in early life. He removed to Chautauque county, N. Y., about 30 years since. We saw him in 1856, when, though able to walk about, he had nearly lost all consciousness, and could not remember his old neighbors. He was then about 90.

CROUCH, PHINEAS, a brother of Ithamar, settled near by, and also raised a numerous family, all but one of whom (David Crouch, of East Rupert), with their father, removed to the west. He was a prominent member of Elder Beall's church.

CULVER, SAMUEL, from Wells; m. Betsey, da. of Joshua Potter, and settled on the Jesse Tryon place. He has raised a family of six daughters: Louise is a graduate of the North Granville Ladies' Seminary; Jenny is in Lycoming county, Pa., a teacher of music; Nellie m. Frederick Baldwin, of Fort Edward, N. Y.

CULVER, ERASTUS, m. Amanda, da. of Joshua Potter, and settled on the Titus A. Cook place. He died in 1865.

CURTIS, ELDAD, from Connecticut; settled at a very early day on the place now owned by Robert Stevens. He was uncommonly intelligent and very fond of music. When compelled, by the improvidence of others, to leave his home when nearly 90, he composed a farewell hymn, which he sung on crossing the state line. When he had finished the hymn, he reverently lifted his hat and bade Pawlet *farewell.*

CURTIS, AARON, son of Eldad, succeeded to the homestead, on which he had an extensive rope walk, during the war of 1812. Two of his children were instantly killed, by being thrown from a wagon, in 1813. He removed to Ithaca, N. Y., about 1818, where he established an extensive rope walk. He was deacon of the church in that town. He died a few years since, aged about 80.

CUSHMAN, DANIEL F., was the son of Rowland Cushman, from Attleboro, Mass., 1811, who settled near the town farm and died in 1825, aged 78; his widow in 1828, aged 70. He m. Caroline, da. of Asahel Clark, who died in 1851, aged 43; next he

m. Huldah, da. of Jonathan Morgan, of Middletown. He owns the farm first settled by Elkanah Cobb, in 1782.

DAY, CHARLES, settled some fifty years since on the premises of Galusha Hanks. His daughter, who is the widow of John Brown, of Osawatimie, is understood to be a native of this town; she is now in California.

DEAN, DANFORTH, from Wethersfield, about 1812, m. Narcissa, d. of Simeon Pepper, and settled near West Pawlet. He carried on the brick making business. He raised a numerous family, most of whom have left town. Their names follow: Simeon, Phipps, Danforth, Seth, Jane and Catalina. He died in 1856, aged 72.

DENISON, ASA, settled on the late premises of Samuel Taylor, Jr., and built the house now standing. He died in 1800, aged 50.

DERBY, BENJAMIN, was an early settler at West Pawlet, near which place he died some years since at an advanced age. He raised a large family, of whom we knew only Benjamin, Hiram, Warren and Seba, who married Chauncey P. Pepper, all of whom are dead.

DERBY, JAMES C., son of Benjamin, Jr., is of the firm of Derby & Miller, book publishers, New York, and U. S. commissioner to the Paris Exposition.

DILLINGHAM, STEPHEN, from Granville, N. Y., settled on the James Hopkins place, which he sold in 1865 to Merritt C. Phelps. He married a daughter of Deliverance Rogers, and is noted for the excellent quality of his butter and cheese. He removed to Granville, N. Y., in 1866. Of his children, Judith m. James W. Gray; Amy m. Lawson Bardwell, of Poultney; Dilla m. William Pierce and died in 1865; Mary m. Jesse C. Gray, and Reuben m. a daughter of James Norton, of Wells.

DYER, Rev. PALMER, from Rutland, was a graduate of Union College in the same class with the late Hon. Isaac W. Bishop, of Granville, N. Y. He became rector of Trinity church, Granville, and Trinity parish in this town in 1823. He was a man of refined scholarly tastes and earnest and eloquent in his public efforts. These societies prospered greatly under his ministry and the old brick church was wont to be well filled. He removed hence to Whitehall about 1831. He was precipitated from a narrow bridge over the Au Sable river while escorting some timid ladies and was drowned in 1844, at the age of 46.

EDGERTON, Capt. SIMEON, from Norwich, Conn., 1781, son of Capt. Joseph Edgerton, who, with his ship, just before the revolution, was foundered at sea and never heard from. He was literally one of the fathers of the town, his descendants numbering 95 at his death in 1809, aged 77. At the death of his widow, Abiah, in 1821, aged 85, her descendants numbered 209. They brought with them five sons: Jedediah, Jacob, John, Simeon and David, and eight daughters: Betsey, m. Elijah Hyde; Abiah m. Joseph Adams; Lydia m. Nathaniel Carver; Hannah m. Joshua Cobb; Sally m. Joel Sheldon; Philena m. Seth Sheldon; Polly m. Calvin Dutton, and Esther m. Ezra Reed. Capt. Edgerton was a man of few words, but noted for his energy and uprightness of character. He was at the capture of New London and the massacre of Fort Griswold. He was in the legislature two years and was intrusted with many responsible offices.

EDGERTON, Capt. JEDEDIAH, settled on the Silas Reed farm. Thence, in 1803, removed to Moriah, N. Y., and was deacon of the Congregational church in that place. He raised a numerous family, none of whom settled in this town. Losing his wife, he married the widow of Enos Clark, of Middletown, and lived in that town until her death. In extreme old age, he went to live with his son, Dr. Joshua Edgerton, in western New York, where he closed his exemplary life in 1848, aged 86. His son, John L. Edgerton, is well and widely known as a teacher and lecturer on natural science. One of his grandsons, William U., was a physician in Caldwell, N. Y., where he died in early life. Another grandson, Joseph R., was in the 38th congress from Indiana.

EDGERTON, JACOB, settled on the present homestead of his son, Sheldon. He married Esther Reed, who died in 1792, aged 26, leaving two children, Reed and Esther. Next he married Hannah Sheldon, who died in 1840, aged 69, leaving eight children, Sheldon, Hannah, Jacob, Hiram, Abraham, George, David and Alta. Jacob m. Narcissa Gregory, and settled in Rutland. He was sheriff of the county 22 years, and now assistant assessor of internal revenue. Abraham m. Rachel, da. of Joshua D. Cobb, and removed to Wisconsin, where he died in 1864, aged 57. George m. Amanda Lasell, and removed to Wallingford.

EDGERTON, JOHN, m. Mary, da. of Gen. Elisha Averill, and settled on the present homestead of his son, Charles F. He was town clerk from 1815 to 1826. He died in 1827, aged 50; his widow in 1846, aged 64, leaving five children, Charles F., Louisa, Sophia, Betsey and Frances. Louisa m. Robert Wickham, and died in 1867, aged 62. Sophia m. Rev. Nehemiah Nelson, of Granville, N. Y., who died in 18  . Next, she married George White, who is also dead. Frances m. John Woodfin, of Tennessee, who died in 18  . She was teacher of music in Troy Conference Academy several years, and also in Tennessee. After Mr.

Woodfin's death, she was matron of Sing Sing Prison, N. Y. Betsey m. Rev. Mr. Sprague, of Schenectady.

EDGERTON, Capt. SIMEON, Jr., m. Elisabeth, sister of Rev. John Griswold, and succeeded to the homestead. He was deacon of the Congregational church 22 years. He held many responsible offices, and was beloved by all who knew him. He died in 1862, aged 88; his wife 1861, aged 81. They left six children, Porter, John G., Betsey, Charlotte, Henrietta and Elizabeth. Porter m. Sylvania, da. of David Andrus, who died in 1863, aged 53. He removed to Castile, N. Y., in 1864. John G. m. Charlotte Wyman, and removed to Fort Ann, N. Y. Betsey m. Silas Gregory. Charlotte m. Erasmus D. Cook, who succeeded to the homestead. Henrietta m. Philo Sheldon, and Elizabeth, Willis Felch, both of Castile, N. Y.

EDGERTON, REED, m. —— Lyon, and settled in the mercantile business at the village. His wife died in 1821, leaving three sons: Marson, Chester and Henry. He next m. Harriet, da. of Rev. John Griswold; he died in 1829, aged 40. Marson m. Betsey, da. of Capt. Milton Brown, who died in 1847, aged 28; next he m. Lucy, da. of Silas Gregory, who died in 1861, aged 32. He was agent of the cotton factory several years, and is now a tea merchant in New York city. Chester removed to Fremont, Ohio, is an attorney and has been mayor of that city.

EDGERTON, SHELDON, m. Fanny, da. of Rev. John Griswold. Their children are: Charles, David, Augustus, Delia, Sophia and Fanny. Delia m. —— Johnson; Sophia m. Grove Wright, now of Sterling, Illinois. He was in the legislature four years and succeeded to the homestead, which he sold in 1867.

EDGERTON, CHARLES F., m. Corilla, da. of Daniel

Clark, and raised four children: Helen, Horace, Cornelia M. and Mary. Helen m. James Hayes, of Oriskany, N. Y., and died in 1855, aged 23; Horace m. Matilda Taylor; Mary died in 1865, aged 25. He was in the legislature in 1844 and 1845. Cornelia M. is a graduate of Philadelphia Medical College.

EVANS, ABIATHAR, from Connecticut, served through nearly the whole of the revolutionary war. Many of his descendants to the fifth generation remain in town. He died in 1831, aged 89; his widow in 1847, aged 103. She drew a pension from 1832.

EVANS, ABIATHAR, Jr., m. Sally Train, and raised a large family of children: Elijah, Osborn, Truesdell, Henry and Mary. Elijah m. —— Bourn; Truesdell m. Sally, da. of Asahel Clark.

EVEREST, ZADOC, was a patriot of the revolution and representative to the first legislature of this state in 1778. We find him a trusted and confidential agent of the council of safety, and employed in enforcing their edicts of sequestration. He was representative of Panton in 1789, and of Addison in 1785.

FAIRFIELD, WILLIAM, was the second settler in town, and, as such, received a gratuity of thirty acres of land. Personally, for aught we know, he was a worthy man, but having adhered to the royal cause his property was confiscated and himself sought a refuge in Canada West, where his descendants still remain.

FARRAR, DAVID, from Rupert, m. Esther M., da. of Maj. Sylvester Smith, and settled on the Josiah Crocker farm.

FAY, Dr. JONAS, m. the mother of Dr. Jonathan Safford, and in his old age came to this town to spend the evening of his days. We remember him well in our young days when his venerable form, bent with the weight of four-score years, went tottering towards the grave. He was one of the most efficient founders of the state; a compeer of Ethan Allen, Chittenden, and a host of worthies. He was clerk of the council of safety, clerk of the convention, that in 1777 declared Vermont a free and independent state, and was also a supreme court judge.

FINNEY, LYMAN, m. Mary, da. of Abiathar Evans, Jr., and raised a family of six children: Lucetta, Mary, Angelia, Helen, Harriet and Abiathar E. Helen m. Dr. John W. Marshall, and Harriet m. Merrick Knapp, both of Granville.

FITCH, Col. WILLIAM, from Lebanon, Conn., was one of the earliest settlers and most prominent citizens of the town. He was employed by the council of safety to furnish supplies to the troops raised to repel the invasion of Burgoyne in 1777. When the settlers north of this town fled, panic struck before Burgoyne, his wife with three small daughters, all mounted on one horse, started south for a place of refuge, but being reassured they soon returned. He owned the first saw and grist mill built at the village, by William Bradford, and kept the first store in town. The village was known on our early maps as Fitch's Mills. He died in 1798, aged 48. His children were: John, Sina, Anna, Rachel, Sibel, Abial and Margaret.

FITCH, JOHN, settled on the homestead of C. S. Bardwell and died in 1799, aged 34.

FITCH, DANIEL, Sen., from Norwich, Conn., 1784, settled in the east part of the town. He raised a family of nine children: Daniel, Isaac, Benjamin, Return, Jared, Prosper, Lucy, Salina and Philene. All of these, except Daniel, settled abroad. He died in 1801, aged 58; his widow in 1814, aged 65.

FITCH, DANIEL, Jr., m. Candace, da. of Judge Armstrong, of Dorset, and settled on the present

## Family Sketches.

homestead of Lucius M. Carpenter. They raised a family of five children: Hiram, Cyrus, Daniel H., Cynthia and Jane. Hiram entered college, but did not graduate, becoming partially insane; Cyrus m. Camilla Garrett and moved west; Daniel H. was a classmate of Hon. John K. Porter in Union College in 1837, who furnishes the following account of him: "He was a young man of brilliant talents and high promise. He removed to Texas and became the editor of the *Houston Star*, which he conducted with marked ability. He is said to have fallen soon after in a duel which he did not feel at liberty to decline, though he refused to fire at the party by whom he was challenged and slain." Cynthia m. Adolphus F. Hitchcock, of Kingsbury, N. Y., who is now member of the assembly for Washington county; Jane m. Alpheus Baldwin, of Westfield, N. Y., who recently died. Mr. Fitch removed hence to Westfield, N. Y., some thirty years ago, where he and his wife have recently died at a very advanced age.

FITCH, JOSEPH, from Norwich, Conn., 1776, settled on the present homestead of Fayette Bromley. He was among the foremost and most substantial men of the town and contributed largely to the general welfare, His large family of children mostly settled in town, though now there is but one representative of the family, Mrs. Adams L. Bromley, left in town. His children's names were as follows: Ephraim, Benjamin, Asahel, Stephen, Silas, Mary and Sally. His wife died in 1822, aged 76, when he married widow Hannah Wood, who survived him. He died in 1830, aged 84.

FITCH, EPHRAIM, m. Sally, da. of Deacon Moses Porter, who died in 1790, aged 21, leaving one son, Dorastus; next he married Rhoda Sears. He was one of our most enterprising and public spirited citizens.

He was in the legislature three years. He built the brick tavern at the village, which he kept and conducted the mercantile and milling business. He was instantly killed, while cutting ice from the water-wheel, in 1813, aged 45. His other children were: Nancy, who married Dr. James H. Willard, and recently died; Ferris, and Moses P., who married Chloe, daughter of Titus A. Cook.

FITCH, Capt. BENJAMIN, lived on the farm with his father. He was an influential leader of the democratic party during the early years of this century, and probably no more popular man ever lived in town. He was kind and charitable to a fault, and in his private relations greatly beloved. He was in the legislature eight years. He had three sons: Braman, John and Appleton. Braman m. Dorcas, da. of Capt. James Pratt, and moved west; John is noticed below; Appleton m. Mary, da. of Gen. Thomas Davis, of Montpelier, where he resides. She died in 1839, aged 35. Capt. Fitch died in 1823, aged 58; his widow in 1846, aged 83.

FITCH, Rev. JOHN, m. Sophia, da. of Maj. Sylvanus Gregory, and succeeded to the homestead of his father, which he held but a few years. He was one of the pioneers of the temperance reform. He was a preacher of the Methodist church, mostly local. He died in Middletown in 1859, aged 59, after a protracted and most painful illness.

FITCH, ASAHEL, settled at the village in the tanning business. He raised a large family, who, with him, moved to the west in 1824.

FITCH, SILAS, was long a merchant at the village and an accomplished salesman. He m. Martha Barnes, who died in 1821, aged 25; next he married Sarah, da. of Lemuel Barden, who died in 1832, aged 43. He removed to Detroit, Mich., about 1840, where he soon after died.

FITCH, DORASTUS, m. Julia Bright, who died in 1823, aged 36, leaving five children, Ann, Betsey, Julia, Delia and Sarah. Ann is the only one living. Next, he married Anna Hubbard, and raised a family of four children, Mary, Fayette S., Helen and Lucy. He was long an active business man at the village, and was mainly instrumental in erecting the Pawlet Academy. He was post master 19 years, and deacon of the Congregational church several years. He died in 1860, aged 78.

FLOWER, ANSON, from Chazy, N. Y., 1829; m. Mary Bassford, who died in 1843, aged 35. Next m. Vesta, da. of Nathaniel Hill. His son, James T., m. Mary Michael.

FITCH, Rev. FERRIS, was a graduate of Middlebury in 1826. He married Sally, youngest daughter of Rev. John Griswold, and was first settled over a Congregational church in Elliott, Me. Thence, in 1830, he removed to Ohio, where he died.

FOLGER, DANIEL, from Easton, N. Y.; m. Susan Herring, and settled on the Amos Wooster place. Though they have raised no children of their own, they have done the next best thing, in carefully bringing up several children of other families.

GIBBS, ZEBULON, from Connecticut; settled near West Pawlet. He raised a family of three sons, Clemons, Spencer and Ira. Clemons's second wife is aunt to Col. Ellsworth, who was assassinated at Alexandria the first year of the war, and lives in Saratoga. Spencer kept tavern near Troy, N. Y., where he died recently. Ira m. Betsey, da. of James Roach, of Hebron; kept the hotel at West Pawlet several years, and now resides in the northeast part of the town. Mr. Gibbs died in 1855, aged 78; his wife in 1842, aged 76.

GIFFORD, GIDEON, from Ponaganset, Mass., 1792;

was by trade a blacksmith, and served through the war of the revolution. He married Ruth Butts, of Rhode Island, who died in 1796, leaving eight children. Next, he m. Betsey, da. of Asa Willey, and raised another family of ten children. The only survivors are Noah and Mrs. Kelley.

GIFFORD, Capt. NOAH, is one of the few surviving veterans of the war of 1812. He deserves special mention for hi zeal, fidelity and efficiency in collecting and reporting much of the material of this chapter. He has attained the age of 74. We may be permitted to relate a war anecdote, in which his son, Warren, was a party concerned. At the battle of Spottsylvania C. H., Va., May 12, 1864, while desperately engaged in close contact with the enemy, Sergeant Gifford took a stand of colors belonging to the second North Carolina regiment, which were planted directly in front of his position. He despatched the color bearer with his bayonet, seized the colors and bore them off in triumph, amid the cheers of his comrades. He has the colors now in his possession.

GOODSPEED, SAMUEL, from Barnstable, Mass., 1790; m. Sylvia, da. of Josiah Goodspeed, of Wells, and raised a numerous family, most of whom left town. Names of children follow: Zenas, Heman, Josiah, Jemima m. Col. Asa Thompson, Granville, N. Y.; Chloe, Susan m. Silas Shepherd; Mercy, Rebecca m. Roswell Clark, of Hampton, and died in 1851, aged 51, and Hannah m. Levi Stratton. He died in 1816, aged 58; his widow in 1844 aged 77.

GOODSPEED, ZENAS, m. Anna, da. of Selah Betts, and succeeded to the homestead. He raised a family of eight children: Lucius, Arthur, Harry, Peter, Samuel, Phebe, Polly and Hannah. Arthur m. Sibel, da. of John Betts, and owns the Samuel Weeks place; Harry m. Esther, da. of John Pepper, who died in 1862, aged 43; Phebe m. Warren Thompson and moved to Missouri, where she died in 1861, aged 40. Mr. Goodspeed died in 1863, aged 78; his wife in 1845, aged 47.

GILES, EBENEZER, from Townsend, Mass., 1807, settled near West Pawlet. At the breaking out of the war of the revolution he was among the first to volunteer for his country. While in the service, near New York city, he was severely wounded and taken prisoner. He was confined in the Sugar House, a specimen, on a small scale, of Andersonville. He died in 1838, aged 78. His children mostly moved to the west. His youngest daughter, Lucy, who sent the above particulars, died in 1865, aged 49.

GILES, BRAMAN F., son of Ephraim Giles, and grandson of the preceding, is the only representative of the family left in town. He married Eunice Folger, and lives on the Reuben Smith place. His oldest daughter, Mary, is a graduate of the state normal school of New Jersey.

GRAVES, AMOS, from Rupert, 1815, settled just above Capt. Pratt's. He raised a numerous family, some of whom were educated at college. His son, Rev. Azariah R. Graves, graduated at Middlebury in 1833, and settled as a Congregational minister in the state of Florida. The family removed hence to Northumberland, N. Y., in 1842, where Mr. Graves soon after died.

GREEN, BERIAH, from Randolph, about 1810, settled in the east part of the town, and was conspicuous for his zeal and forwardness in religious concerns. He removed to Ohio about 1830, and lived to a great age. His only sons known to us are Beriah and Jonathan S.

GREEN, Rev. BERIAH, Jr., was a graduate of Middlebury, 1820. In 1822 he became the pastor of the Congregational church at Brandon. We next find him at Whitesboro, N. Y., principal of the Oneida Institute and an able and a zealous champion of the anti-slavery cause. He was the first secretary of the American Anti-Slavery Society, formed in Philadelphia in 1831. That society, hunted from city to city, and unable at times to find a place in which to hold its anniversaries, steadfastly maintained its existence till the accomplishment of the purposes for which it was formed. The abolition of slavery was not accomplished directly in the way contemplated by this society, who hoped to effect it by moral appeals. But, doubtless, the flood of light poured on the American mind at its anniversaries, where were wont to convene the strongest men of the country, aided by the press, hastened its accomplishment. When the history of American emancipation is written the name of Beriah Green will stand high on its roll of fame.

GREEN, Rev. JONATHAN S., enlisted in the missionary service some forty years since. His field of labor was the Sandwich Islands, which by missionary effort has been transformed from heathenism into Christian communities. He has also held high office in the civil service of those islands.

GREGORY, Maj. SYLVANUS, from Suffield, Conn., 1790, settled at the village in the hat making business. He took a lively interest in public concerns, and about 1806 took a census of the inhabitants of the town, which exceeded three thousand, a larger number by seven hundred than were ever reported by the U. S. marshals. He raised a family of eight children: Silas, Alfred, Simeon, Minerva, Clarissa, Polly, Sophia and Elmira. Alfred became a physician and settled in Fort Ann, N. Y.; Simeon removed to the west; Minerva died single in 1865, aged 80; Clarissa also died single in 1849; Polly m. Allen Vail, of Middletown, and died in 1866, aged 74: Elmira m. David Savage, of Champlain, N. Y. Maj. Gregory and his wife both died in 1848, each at the age of 82.

GREGORY, SILAS, is now the oldest inhabitant of the village. He m. Lucy, da. of Nathaniel Carver, who died in 1824, aged 32; next he m. Lydia, sister of the first, who died in 1857, aged 57, leaving two children, Lucy and Betsey; next he m. Betsey, da. of Simeon Edgerton, Jr. He has long been known as an active, industrious citizen, and has attained the age of 77.

GRISWOLD, Rev. JOHN, from Lebanon, N. H., 1792, succeeded Rev. Lewis Beebe in the pastorate of the Congregational church, and was ordained Oct. 23, 1793. He was successful in building up a large and influential church, over which he was pastor until 1831, a period of thirty-eight years. He was highly esteemed by his cotemporaries in the church, society and town, and was in good repute among neighboring churches. His reputation as a peacemaker was great and he was frequently called on to aid in council, over which he frequently presided. He was a graduate of Dartmouth, N. H. He m. Betsey Lay, who died in 1808, leaving six children: Harry, Harriet, Betsey, Fanny, Sophia and Sally. Next he m. Sarah, widow of Dr. Meigs, of Bethlehem, Conn. He died in 1852, aged 87; his widow at New York city in 1857, aged 92.

GRISWOLD, HARRY, m. Alta, da. of Col. Ozias Clark, and settled on the present homestead of Charles Hulett. He was an amiable and worthy citizen, and deservedly held in the highest esteem. He was deacon of the Congregational church several years and was town clerk from 1846 to his death in 1848, aged 52.

GUILD, JOHN, from Attleboro, Mass., 1802, settled near the cotton factory, of which he was agent several years. He was an upright and thorough business man and safely conducted the cotton business through the trying times that succeeded the war of 1812. His children were: Chauncy, Plina, Milton, Eunice, Lucy and Abigail. He died in 1850, aged 87; his wife in 1830, aged 63. His sister, Lucy, married Nathaniel Wilmarth, of Ira, and was killed by falling out of a wagon in Ira, at which spot a stone is erected, marked L. W. Chauncy Guild m. Celinda, da. of Nehemiah Bourn, who died in 1839. He is the only survivor of his father's family in town and is well and favorably known as land surveyor and tinsmith. His age is 78.

HALL, DANIEL H., married a daughter of Amasa Vail. He had three sons in the service; the oldest of whom, Seldon A., died of disease.

HANKS, WILLIAM, from Suffield, Conn., settled on the present homestead of Alex. Clayton. He was an enterprising though eccentric man. He planted a vineyard north of his house, which, for a while, was promising, but the boys would steal his grapes, which so vexed him that he let it run down. On many places in West Pawlet a vine derived from this vineyard still flourishes. He built a grist mill on Pawlet river just below the Frary bridge. He died in 1807, aged 79; his widow was burned to death in 1809, aged 73. His sons, who settled in this town, were Oliver, Joseph and Arunah.

HANKS, OLIVER, settled at West Pawlet. He held the position of magistrate fifty-one years, and secured and retained the confidence of the community through this long period. His decisions, seldom appealed from, were never reversed. His knowledge of legal forms enabled him to perform much of the law business required by the people.

He was in the legislature four years and solemnized 93 marriages. He married Deidamia Porter, who died in 1840, aged 63, leaving eight children, Marcia, Romeo, William, Camillus, Isaac, Galusha, Safford and Ermina. Camillus m. Jane Nelson, and moved to Ohio; Isaac m. Lucinda Whedon, Wisconsin; Galusha m. Lovina, da. of Simeon Pepper, Jr. Next, Mr. Hanks m. Rebecca Ross, and died in 1859, aged 82.

HANKS, GALUSHA, m. Lovina, da. of Simeon Pepper, and settled at West Pawlet. They have a family of twelve children, three of whom were in the service. Of their daughters, Martha m. Merritt W. Clark, of Poultney, and Olive J. m. Walter S. Warner.

HANKS, JOSEPH, ran the grist mill his father built. He raised a numerous family, and with most of them removed to West Virginia, in 1816. His eldest son, Jarvis, was a drummer boy, at the age of 14, in the war of 1812. He afterwards became noted as a landscape and portrait painter, at Cleveland, Ohio. His next son, Festus, became a Presbyterian minister in New Jersey, where he died in early life.

HANKS, ARUNAH, m. Lucy, da. of Jacob Perkins, and succeeded to the homestead. Of his seventeen children, but few survive, and only one, Arunah, Jr., remains in town, who married a daughter of Abel Robinson. Mr. Hanks died in 1830, aged 60; his wife in 1860, aged 88.

HARMON, EZEKIEL, from Suffield, Conn., 1774; settled on the present homestead of David Andrus. He married Lydia Harmon, Jan. 10, 1775, they being the first couple married in town. He was a man of integrity, and commanded the confidence of his townsmen. He was a magistrate a great number of years, and was deacon of the Congregational church over forty years. He had a numerous family, but scarce one of his descendants remain in town. He had three sons who were professional men: Nathaniel; Ira, who suffered from chronic poor health, and died in middle life, at Benson, and Ezekiel, who was a physician and died young. Deacon Harmon d. in 1831, aged 80.

HARMON, NATHANIEL, m. Alice, da. of Dea. Joseph Hascall, and settled as attorney at the village. He practiced law over forty years, being most of the time the only practitioner in town. He was held in the highest esteem by his professional brethren, and deemed one of the ablest jurists in the state. Though a man of decided political views, his tastes did not lead him into the arena of public and political life, and he seldom attended the polls. He was a member of the Council of censors in 1834, and of the Constitutional Convention in 1836. His mind was a rich store house of knowledge, especially of historic lore, which (when off duty) he took great pleasure in communicating to others. He died in 1845, aged 65; his widow in 1853, aged 73. They raised three children: Proserpine m. Willard Meacham, and died in 1832, aged 29; Clara m. John T. Barden, and died in 1830; and George W. m. Mary Ann Penfield, and removed to Bennington, where he is an attorney and cashier of the Stark bank. He was a member of the Constitutional Convention from this town, in 1843.

HARMAN, Capt. NATHANIEL, from New Lebanon, Conn., 1768, married a daughter of Col. William Fitch, and settled on the present homestead of William Monroe. He was one of the first members of the Baptist church in West Pawlet. He removed west in 1798, since which we know nothing of him.

HARMON, Dr. OLIVER L., from Suffield, Conn., commenced the practice of medicine in this town in 1798, and continued in it till his death in 1852, aged 82; his widow died in 1853, aged 78. He settled at the village. He was an extremely modest and amiable man, and was held in high repute as a family physician. Only one daughter, Berintha Hulett, of a large family, remains in town.

HARMON, JOEL, m. Abial, da. of Col. William Fitch, and settled on lands now owned by Alden B. Crapo. The town records show him to have been a leading man. He was deacon of the Congregational church several years.

HARMON, Maj. JOEL, Jr., m. Clara, da. of Deacon Joseph Hascall, who died in 1795, aged 22. He was a teacher of music, and published a manual of music which was a pecuniary loss. He was one of the earliest merchants and an officer in the war of 1812. He removed to Richland, N. Y., in 1804, where he followed the profession of music teacher many years.

HARWOOD, Capt. JOHN, from Rupert, which town he had represented in the legislature, married a daughter of Hon. Grove Moore, who died in 18—; next he married Sophia, widow of Ezra Reed. He settled at the village.

HARWOOD, ROLLIN J., son of Capt. John Harwood, married Sarah, daughter of Silas Reed. He owns the land in the extreme northeast corner of the town.

HASCALL, JOSEPH, from Bennington, 1787, married Alice Fitch, and settled on the present homestead of James N. Mason. He was deacon of the first Baptist church twenty-four years. He was a man of great energy and perseverance and contributed more than most men in the construction and building up of society. He raised a family of ten children, to whom he gave all the educational advantages compatible with his limited means; their names follow: Ralph, Asa, David A., Daniel, Safford, Lebbeus, Alice, Clara, Nancy and Philene. Ralph was an attorney and settled in Essex, N. Y. He represented his county in the senate and assembly; Asa was an attorney, settled in Malone, N. Y.; he also was in the senate and assembly and in congress; Dr. David A. settled in Kentucky. Rev. Daniel Hascall settled in Hamilton, N. Y.; Safford m. Betsey, da. of Nath. Carver, and succeeded to the homestead, but removed to Kentucky about 1818; Lebbeus was an attorney and settled at Ticonderoga, N. Y. Clara married Joel Harmon, Jr.; Alice, Nathaniel Harmon; Nancy, Dr. Stearns, of Pompey, N. Y., and Philene, Mr. Baker, of the same place. It is a somewhat singular fact that all these brothers lost their wives and married a second time. Three of the sisters died before their husbands. All of them are now dead. Deacon Hascall died in 1814, aged 73; his widow died at Pompey, N. Y., about 1845, over 90. Their descendants are widely scattered in the northern and western states.

HASCALL, Rev. DANIEL, graduated at Middlebury in 1806, and was soon after licensed to preach by the Baptist church in this town. He was a man of great industry and ability and was mainly instrumental in establishing the theological seminary at Hamilton, N. Y., where he was settled as pastor. He was the first principal of that institution and continued in that position for several years. He spent a few of the last years of his life in West Rutland, where he had married the widow Moses.

HAWKINS, RILEY, from Castleton, married Maria Stearns and settled at West Pawlet as village tailor. His family consists of one son and one daughter: Don, who married Hattie Taylor, and Cornelia, who is a graduate of Castleton seminary, and has for many years followed the profession of teaching.

FAMILY SKETCHES.  201

HASTINGS, HEMAN, m. Lucy Pomroy and settled near the centre of the town. He was among the first in town to engage in wool-growing. He raised a large family, most of whom have left for the far west. He removed to Milwaukie some thirty years since. Several of his sons settled in this and adjoining town and were men of property and standing.

HENRY, ANDREW, from Ireland, married a daughter of Abiathar Evans, and settled on the present premises of Albert A. Boynton in the mercantile business. He was a man of note and influence in his day. He removed to Hector, N. Y., about 1820 and lived to a great age. He left one memento, the "Henry" apple, of most exquisite flavor.

HENRY, JEFFREY J., from Brattleboro, 1840, settled at the village at the harness-making business.

HILL, NATHANIEL, from New York city, lived mostly at the village, where he died in 1830, aged 77. Two of his daughters married Bassfords, who settled in town leaving many descendants.

HILL, NATHANIEL, Jr., married Diantha Harmon, and now lives at the village at the age of 78. Several of his sons removed to the state of Georgia; only one son, Charles K., remains in town.

HITT, SMITH, from Danby, 1841, m. Maria, da. of Caleb Randall, of Danby, and settled on the Seth Blossom farm. They have raised a family of seven children: William H., Caleb S., John E., Anson, Galen R., Mary and Sophia. William died in Atlanta, Geo., 1858, aged 27; John E. m. Mary Danforth, and is a physician at Wallingford; Caleb S. m. Mary Whedon, and is settled at Rutland; Anson m. Caroline License; Galen R. m. Sarah, da. of Dr. Crowley, of Mt. Holly, and is an attorney at Albany, N. Y.; Mary m. John Stearns, Jr., and removed to Kansas.

HOLLISTER, ASHBEL, from Glastenbury, Conn., 1781, m. Mary Pepper, from New Braintree, Mass. He was in the revolutionary service under the immediate command of the renowned Polish general, Kosciusko. He raised seven sons and one daughter: Ashbel W., Orange, David, A. Sidney, Horace, Harvey, Hiel and Mary, who married Eleazer Lyman, of Oswayo, Pa. Ashbel W. m. —— George, who died in 18  ; he died 1864, aged 74; Orange m. Penelope, da. of Josiah Smith, and died in 1862, aged 70, in Starkey, N. Y.; David m. Zilpha Brooks and died in Truxton, N. Y., in 1854, aged 60; Horace m. Julia, da. of Josiah Smith, who died in 1838; next he m. Caroline, da. of Samuel McWhorter, and settled last at Warsaw, N. Y.; Harvey died in 1820, aged 21. Our father was an early settler and knew nearly all the old families in town. On the stock of anecdotal lore, acquired from him, our most liberal drafts are duly honored.

We may be indulged in a brief history and genealogy of our family. Our earliest known ancestor was John Hollister, born in Glastonbury, England. Here is the genealogical tree: 1. John Hollister, born 1612, m. Joan Treat, in Glastenbury, Conn. He died 1665, aged 53; she died 1694. 2. John Hollister, Jr., born 1642, m. Sarah Goodrich, 1667, died 1711, aged 69. 3. Thomas Hollister, born 1672, m. Dorothy Hill, 1696, died 1742, aged 70. 4. Josiah Hollister, born 1696, m. Martha Miller, 1718, died 1766, aged 70. 5. Amos Hollister, born 1724, m. 1750, died 1779. 6. Ashbel Hollister, born 1759, m. Mary Pepper, 1790, died 1840, aged 81. 7. Hiel Hollister, born 1806, in Pawlet, Vt.

HOLLISTER, Rev. A. SIDNEY, received a collegiate education at Fairfield, N. Y.; m. Anna, da. of Joseph Teall, and entered on the Episcopal ministry in 1821. He served as a home missionary in Oneida and Onondaga counties, N. Y., until 1840, when he removed to Michigan, and acted in the same capacity. He was chaplain of the Michigan State prison one or two years. He died in 1856, aged 60.

HOLLISTER, HIEL. It may possibly be interesting to some, to have our autobiography. This town has always been our home, and we feel proud of her record, and a deep interest in her prosperity and well being. Our main occupation through life has been farming, though we kept district school seven winters, and were engaged in mercantile business, at West Pawlet, seven years, from 1854. We were married in 1830, to Sarah M. Sage, of Sandisfield, Mass., who died in 1832, aged 24. Next m. Caroline C. Harlow, of Whitehall, N. Y. Our family consists of six children, Frederic M., Francis S., Albert E., Willis H., Orange S. and Augusta C. Frederic M. m. Estelle Wells of Glastenbury, Conn.; Francis S. m. Julia, da. of Mark Warner, Jr., and Willis H. m. Emeroy, da. of Daniel D. Nelson, of Granville, N. Y.

HOLLISTER, INNETT, from Glastenbury, Conn., 1781; took part in the revolution, and was present at the execution of Major André, whom, we have frequently heard him say, was the handsomest man he ever saw. He was a man of singular mildness and gentleness of disposition. He was intrusted with several responsible town offices, and was in the legislature three years from 1816. He married Mary Kendall, who died in 1831, aged 72; he died in 1844, aged 83. He raised a family of six children: Amos, Hartley, Laura, Mary, Innis and Calvin. Amos m. Catharine Hurlbut, who died ——, aged 65, leaving two children, Horatio and Jane, who, with their father, occupy the homestead. Hartley m. Lucy Miller, and died in 1843, aged 48. His widow is the wife of William Clark, of Whitehall, N. Y. His only son, Marvin, is an attorney in Wisconsin. Laura m. Ashbel Stevens, and died in 1808, aged 19, leaving one son, William H. Stevens, of Whitehall. Mary m. William R. Huggins, of Michigan. Innis m. Martha Page, of East Rupert, and removed to Illinois. Calvin m. Lois Moon, of Granville, N. Y., and resides near Fairfax C. H., Va.

HOLLISTER, ELIJAH, from Glastenbury, Conn., 1782, settled in the northwest part of the town near the brick school house. He was a lieutenant in the revolution and was at Bunker Hill. He removed to Allegany county, N. Y., where he died about 1840, over 80 years of age.

HOPKINS, JAMES, from Rhode Island at a very early day, settled in the southwest part of the town on the Governor's right. He commanded a company in Gen. Ethan Allen's expedition to Canada in 1776. He married Miriam Kent, a cousin of Chancellor Kent. He removed to Hebron, N. Y., and kept a tavern on the turnpike several years. He died in 1830, aged 82.

HOPKINS, ERVIN, only son of James Hopkins, on his father's removal succeeded to the homestead. He was educated at Middlebury, but on account of a personal disagreement with one of the professors, did not graduate. He had the reputation of being the best scholar in his class, and in 1818 received the honorary degree of A. M. He raised a large family, of whom James is an attorney; Ervin was member of the New York assembly in 1863, and Frank was secretary of Wisconsin and is now member of congress; all of whom, with their father, are in Wisconsin.

HOSFORD, HENRY R., married Melvina Smith and succeeded to the homestead of his step-father, Ephraim Robinson, Jr.

FAMILY SKETCHES. 205

HOUGHTON, Dr. CHARLES, from Marlboro, 1835, m. Eliza Woodman, of West Brattleboro, and settled in the practice of medicine at the village. He was an active, wide-awake member of society. He removed hence to Bennington in 1847, and thence to Philadelphia, Pa.

HOUGHTON, Dr. A. SIDNEY, from Ellisburg, N. Y., 1844, m. Fanny M. Woodman, of West Brattleboro, and settled at the village in the practice of his profession. He was in the legislature in 1861 and '62, and during the war a member of the State Medical Board.

HULETT, DANIEL, from Killingly, Conn., 1780, settled on the Willard tract. He was at the battle of Saratoga and severely wounded, but refused to leave the field while he could "load and fire." He was noted for great energy, industry and perseverance, and amassed a large property. He raised a family of three sons: Paul, Daniel and Joshua, and seven daughters. These children, all in turn, raised large families, many of whom reside in this and neighboring towns. He and his wife both died in 1838, the former 90, the latter 83.

HULETT, PAUL, m. Olive Wooden, and first settled in Danby, but moved on the John Cobb place, near the village, in 1820. He became a large owner of land, having several farms in this town, Wells and Danby. He was one of the earliest anti-slavery men in town and maintained a decided stand. He raised a family of nine children: Orestes B., Orlin, Josiah, Jared, Orson G., John S., Philetus N., Alzina and Paulina. John S. Hulett was in the legislature from Wells in 1846 and 1847. Mr. Hulett died in 1845, aged 69; his widow in 1854, aged 74.

HULETT, DANIEL, Jr., settled near his father. He married Hannah Buxton; next Betsey Phillips,

18

who died in 1813, aged 24; next Betsey Woodworth, who died in 1864, aged 79. He raised a family of ten children, of whom Tobias succeeded to the homestead; Marshal m. Margaret, da. of William Clark, and moved to Wisconsin; Martha m. Apollos Hastings and is dead; Sally m. Robert Cobb. Mr. Hulett died in 1836, aged 59; his widow in 1864, aged 79.

HULETT, DYER, son of Daniel Hulett, Jr., married Anna Forbes of Wallingford and settled on the Seth Sheldon farm. They have raised a family of eight children, four of whom were deaf mutes. These have had the benefit of an education at the deaf and dumb asylum at Hartford, Conn. Two of these latter only survive.

HULETT, JOSHUA, m. Harmony Woodworth and settled in the east part of the town, near Danby. He raised a family of ten children. He was a hard working man, and, like his brothers, accumulated a handsome property. He built a beautiful family cemetery near his residence, inclosed with an iron fence. He died in 1858, aged 78; his wife in 1861, aged 76.

HULETT, JOSHUA, Jr., m. Lydia Kelly and lives on the Nathaniel Smith farm. They raised three children: Eunice, Juna and Adelia. Eunice married William White, Juna married Galen L. Hulett.

HUTCHINS, BULKLEY, from Putney, 1795; m. Elizabeth Johnson, and raised eleven children. Of these, only two survive: Irene, who followed the business of teaching 37 years, mostly in Troy, N. Y., and m. deacon Samuel Gilbert, of Shushan, in 1860, and Lois, who taught school 16 years. Mr. Hutchins died in 1850, aged 85; his wife in 1846, aged 77.

HYDE, Rev. AZARIAH, from Randolph, succeeded Samuel M. Wood in the pastorate of the

Congregational church, 1859. He had been teacher in the Castleton Academy, and was a graduate of Middlebury. Dignified, yet conciliatory, of pure diction and classic tastes, faithful and untiring in his pastoral duties, he commanded the respect and confidence of his people. He was a prompt worker in the national cause, during the rebellion. His reports, as town superintendent of schools, which office he held during most of his residence in town, were searching and sometimes caustic, but were listened to with great deference, and were productive of beneficial results. He removed in 1865, to Polo, Ill.

HURLBUT, ASHBEL, from Wethersfield, Conn., 1810; m. Lucy Blin, who died in 1811, aged 29. Next, m. Betsey, da. of Peter Stevens, and settled at West Pawlet. They raised a family of three children, Lucy B., Lucius B. and Walter S. Lucy B. was a graduate of Troy Female Seminary, and one of the first principals of the Troy Conference Academy at Poultney. She m. Gen. Isaac McDaniels, of Rutland, and was drowned at the burning of the Henry Clay steamer, near Yonkers, N. Y., in 1852, aged 38. Lucius B. followed the profession of teaching at Fredonia, N. Y. Walter became an attorney, settled in Buffalo, but died in Granville, N. Y., in 1849, aged 30. Mr. Hurlbut was an ambitious, stirring man, devoted to education, and an ingenious mechanic. He died in 1828, aged 46.

JENNINGS, JOSEPH, son of Jonathan Jennings, who was an early settler in Rupert, married Sally Tooley, and settled on the mountain. He raised a family of three children, James, Linus and Laura.

JOHNSON, Capt. JAMES, from Granville, N. Y., m. Ruth, da. of James Williams, and settled at West Pawlet, of which he is one of the oldest inhabitants. He raised a family of two sons, Leonard and Florace. Leonard m. Harriet, da. of Henry Viets, and has been station agent at West Pawlet depot, since 1853. Florace m. Mehala, da. of James Whedon, and is deputy post master.

JONES, EPHRAIM, from Plainfield, Conn., 1790; settled on our present homestead. He was popularly known as deacon Jones. He retained a strong attachment for his native state, to which for many years, he made an annual pilgrimage. Though outwardly rough and rather forbidding, he was a man of great hospitality and friendliness. He m. Rachel, da. of Capt. John Stark, one of a "nest of twelve sisters, with a brother in it." They raised a family of eleven children: Joel, Harry, Asa S., Ahira, Ephraim, John, Harrison, Jared, Rosanna, Mariette and Rachel. These children are mostly living, but none of them in town. Rosanna m. David Kelly, Illinois; Rachel m. Isaac T. Parris, of Fairfax; Ephraim m. Sophia Page, and was almost instantly killed by the falling timbers of a barn, in which he had taken refuge during a tornado, in 1858. Joel and Asa S. carried on the woolen manufacture several years, in the mill now owned by Enoch Colvin. Dr. Frank H. Jones was a son of Ephraim, Jr., and died in Dorset, in 1865. Deacon Jones died in 1839, aged 69; his widow survived him but a few years.

JONES, JOSEPH, from Greenwich, Mass., 1781; settled on the present farm of John A. Orr. He died in 1816, aged 84; his wife in 1810, aged 80.

JONES, SILAS, son of Joseph, settled on the present homestead of his grandson, Merritt C. He raised a family of five children: Joseph, Eli, Fanny, Silas and Hiram. Joseph m. Deborah Viets; Eli, Chloe Goodspeed; Fanny, Walliston Hawley, who died in 1863, aged 76; Silas, Sarah Weeks, and

Hiram, Catharine Baldrige. These children are all dead.

JUDSON, Dr. NATHAN, from Arlington about 1825; settled and built the house now occupied by Sherman Weed. Though a medical graduate, he never entered on the profession. He removed west about 1845.

KIERNAN, Rev. JOHN, a native of Ireland, was assigned to the Methodist church at the village, in 1866. Scholarly in his tastes and attainments, high toned in moral and religious purpose, he seems well calculated to exert a beneficial influence over the people of his charge.

KNIGHTS, GEORGE W., from Rupert, 1863; settled on the Samuel Taylor, Jr., place in 1866. He m. Louisa M., da. of Samuel Coburn. Her father was killed while in the army in Tennessee, July 5, 1864. Her mother, who resides in town, was with her husband in the army, as nurse and laundress, 21 months, and drew soldier's pay and rations.

LAMPSON, TRUMAN, from Rupert, settled near the Town farm. He was a gunsmith, and as a marksman, was unrivaled. Dignified and gentlemanly in his deportment, he won the admiration and esteem of numerous friends. He was an ingenious mechanic and inventor. He now resides in Bennington.

LAY, AMOS, from New Hampshire; was one of the earliest map publishers of the country. He was for several years a resident of this town. He published a township map of this state, on a large scale, from surveys by Gen. James Whitelaw. He was a brother of the first wife of Rev. John Griswold.

LEACH, JAMES, from Canterbury, Conn., about 1780; settled on the present homestead of his son, Lovell. He was a substantial, independent citizen, and exerted a great influence in shaping and controlling the political fortunes of the town. He was in the legislature three years. He died in 1835, aged 76; his widow in 1842, aged 87. He left three children, Lovell, James and Ebenezer.

LEACH, LOVELL, m. Amy Barsley, succeeded to the homestead, and raised nine children: Lucretia, Louisa, Ellen, Lucy, Elizabeth, William, Lorenzo, Wesley and Martin V. Elizabeth died in 1850, aged 19. William died in 1849, aged 31. Ellen m. Elkanah Danforth, of Rupert. Lucy m. James N. Robinson. Mr. Leach was one of the first members of the Pawlet band and its leader. By industry and economy, he acquired a handsome property, and now lives retired from business, at the age of 81, respected by all his acquaintances.

LEACH, JAMES, Jr., m. Olive Carver, who died in 18 . Next, he m. Harriet Peck. He occupies the Doctor Sargent homestead. He was in the legislature of 1859–60. His children are Gideon C. m. Lois B., daughter of Philo Harwood; Lophelia m. William U. Phelps, and Casper N., who married Frances, da. of Adams L. Bromley, and died 1866, aged 26.

LEACH, EBENEZER, has accumulated one of the largest properties in town, and is still active in acquiring more. His wife died in 1864, aged 78. His son, Henry W., is a medical graduate; has kept a drug store at the village several years, but removed to Norwich, Conn., in 1860.

LINCOLN, LEWIS, from Cheshire, Mass., 1837; settled at North Pawlet, in the carriage making business. He was agent of the union store during its existence, from 1851 to 1861. His family consisted of two daughters, Lettie T. and Fidelia. Lettie T. was a graduate of Troy Conference Academy, and married Alonzo Raynor, of Evansville,

Ind. Fidelia died of diptheria, in 1864, aged 21. He removed to Indiana in 1865.

LINCOLN, LUTHER P., from Cheshire, Mass., 1837; m. Deborah, da. of Henry Wooster, Jr., and succeeded to his homestead. He removed to Fort Ann, N. Y., some twenty years ago, and was instantly killed by being thrown from a wagon, about 1862.

LOOMIS, OLIVER, from East Windsor, Conn., 1785; m. Jude, da. of Gideon Adams, who died in 1814, aged 50, leaving three children, Jerusha, Gideon A. and Mary. He was a man of staunch political principles of the Jeffersonian school. He died in 1837, aged 73. Jerusha is the wife of J. Ward, of Norwich, Conn.

LOOMIS, GIDEON A., m. Amanda, da. of Elijah Brown, and settled on the present homestead of his only surviving son, Orla. His wife died in 1835, aged 42, leaving six children, Orla, Lucia, Laura, Candace, Owen and Lester. Lucia married Benoni Blossom, of Poultney; Laura m. Loammi Lee, of Granville, N. Y.; Candace m. George D. Martin; Owen was in the army from Minnesota; was with Sherman in his march through the south, and died in South Carolina; Lester died in 1854, aged 20.

LOOMIS, ORLA, m. Julia C., da. of David Robinson, and succeeded to the homestead. Their only son, George B., m. Hattie Snell.

LOOMIS, NATHANIEL, from East Windsor, Conn., 1810; settled on the John Stark homestead. He died in 1829, aged 49, leaving four children, Maria, Miranda, Benjamin N. and Henry W. Maria m. Josiah Goodspeed, and removed to Illinois; Miranda m. Orlin Hulett, who died near thirty years since; Benjamin N. is an attorney at Binghamton, N. Y., and has been law partner of the Hon. Daniel S. Dickinson; Henry W. is in Saratoga.

LOOMIS, ELIJAH M., is a son of Abner Loomis, who came from Connecticut in 1801. His mother dying in his infancy, he was brought up by his uncle, Roswell Loomis, whose widow, Mercy, still lives, at the age of 86, and is the oldest person in town. He m. Jane, da. of James Bassford, who died in 1834, aged 27, leaving two children, Edmund and Mary. Edmund m. Maria, da. of Hiram Smith, of Rupert; Mary m. George Clark. Next, Mr. Loomis m. Nancy, da. of Thaddeus Smith, of Rupert, who died in 1861, aged 54, leaving five children.

LOUNSBERRY, NATHAN M., from Connecticut, 1781; settled near Capt. Benoni Smith's. He was seven years in the war of the revolution, serving under Gen. Knox, and the most of the time was attached to the immediate command of Gen. Washington. He was a man of great physical strength and endurance, and attained the age of one hundred years. At that age, he held plow for a short time, at a county fair at Rutland. He died in Clarendon.

LUMBARD, Capt. ABNER, from Brimfield, Mass., 1784; m. Sarah, da. of Asa Andrus, and settled at the village in the cloth dressing business. Modest and unobtrusive in his deportment, honorable in his dealings, he won the respect of all. He died in 1861, aged 88; his wife in 1858, aged 80. They raised a family of seven children: Chester, Sophia, Fanny, Pamela, Julia, Hiram and Franklin. Hiram m. Fanny, da. of Samuel Potter, and died 1851, aged 41.

LUMBARD, CHESTER, m. Sina, da. of Daniel Clark, and settled at the village in the manufacturing business. He was a man of few words, quiet and retiring in his manners, and was held in high esteem. He died in 1856, aged 54.

LYON, JACOB, from Danby, 1843; owns the William Boyce farm, but lives at the village. He m. Anna Boomer. They raised a large family, of whom Lydia m. Alonzo Smith; Harriet, Albert A. Boynton; Emily, Wesley Rowe, of Wells; and Anna, Harvey Rowe, of Poultney, and died recently.

MAHER, JAMES, from Ireland, about 1783, settled on the present homestead of Samuel Culver. He died in 1824, aged 78; his wife in 1814, aged 68. We know of but three children: William, Catharine and Margaret. William was an ingenious mechanic, and was among the first in the country to manufacture cut nails. Margaret married John Ottarson, who died in 1829, aged 44. Their son, B. Fitch Ottarson, was post master at Granville, N. Y., from 1861 to 1867.

MARKS, CORNWELL, from Glastenbury, Conn., 1785; m. Sarah Goodrich, and settled on the road near James M. Shaw's; was a kind hearted and exemplary man, and died in 1857, aged 88. His wife was a skillful nurse, and devoted much of her time to attendance on the sick; she died in 1857, aged 87. They raised a family of five children: William, Elisha, Ira, Prudence and Electa. William m. Rosanna, da. of Ephraim Robinson, and settled at Nunda, N. Y.; becoming attached to the Mormons, he followed them in their wanderings to Nauvoo, Ill. He was acting mayor of the city, when the Mormon prophet, Joseph Smith, was arrested by the civil authorities of Illinois, and issued a writ of habeas corpus, through which he was released from custody. The infuriated mob took after Smith, followed him to Carthage, and killed him. Elisha married Ann, da. of

Reuben Smith, and removed to Burke, N. Y.; Ira m. Sarah Ann Goodrich, and settled at West Pawlet, where he kept a store, run a starch factory, and also a stocking factory at the village. Prudence m. John C. Prescott, between whom a separation took place, leaving with her one son, Gustavus A. She then married William Miles, and became attached to the Mormons and followed them to Utah, where she recently died. Electa married John Smith, Burke, N. Y.

MARSH, WILLIAM, from Woodstock, 1816, settled first in this town, whence he soon removed to Granville, N. Y., thence, about thirty years since, retnrned to the village. He died in 1864, aged 91, leaving no children; his wife died in 1846, aged 68. He was a pioneer in the anti-slavery cause, meeting its opponents "in season and out of season," with firmness and great ability. He wrote numerous articles in its advocacy and showed his sincerity by donating during his lifetime a large property, over twenty-five thousand dollars, to the furtherance of the cause. He lived to see his principles triumph in the councils of the nation. He was also noted for his liberality in private charity. He was an uncle of Hon. George P. Marsh, who has been in congress from this state, minister to Turkey and is now minister to Italy.

MARTIN, GEORGE D., married Candace, daughter of Gideon A. Loomis, and settled on the John Toby place.

MASON, JAMES N., married Alta, a daughter of Joel Simonds, Jr., who died in 1864, aged 43, leaving eight children. Next he married Almira Bannister. He was from Pownall, 1839, and settled on Hascall farm.

MCFADDEN, STEPHEN, from Waterford, N. Y., settled on the Samuel Baldwin farm. While in Waterford he kept store several years. He married a daughter of Jacob Braymer, of Hebron. His family of four sons, Michael, Henry, Jacob and Edward, are all settled in the vicinity, and are intelligent, thrifty farmers.

McNAUGHTON, FINDLAY, from Washington county, N. Y., was one of the earliest settlers near the present homestead of John Stearns. He married a sister of Palmer Cleveland and died in early life, leaving a large family. His widow married David Stearns and raised another family, making in the whole fourteen, most of whom lived to adult age.

McWAIN, ELHANAN, from Manchester, settled at the blacksmith business. He married Lucy Tooley, who died in 1851, leaving four children: Eliza, who married Palmer Clapp, who died in prison at the south; Leroy D., Nathaniel and Sylvanus; all of whom were in the service. Next he married Mahala Shaw.

MEACHAM, Capt. ASA, settled in this town in 1781, and removed to Richland, N. Y., in 1804. His son, Col. Thomas Meacham, made the large cheese (1,800 pounds) presented to President Jackson in 1830.

MEACHAM, Capt. ABRAHAM, settled here in 1787, raised a large family and removed to the west.

MEIGS, Rev. BENJAMIN C., step-son of Rev. John Griswold, received his theological education with him and was one of the first missionaries of the American Board to Ceylon, about 1820. After laboring there forty years he returned to this country and died in New York city a few years since.

MEIGS, CHARLES, brother of Benjamin C., came when a lad to this town, and was bred to the profession of law. He removed to the north part of the state, thence to Michigan.

MENONA, PAUL, the Indian preacher, spoken of in

Goodhue's *History of Shoreham*, sojourned a few years in this town, near the lower covered bridge, on Pawlet river. His wife was the daughter of the renowned Indian preacher, Sampson Occum, who bequeathed to him his extensive and valuable library. This library was carelessly packed in boxes and when it reached its destination was nearly spoiled. He is represented as having been, in his prime, an interesting and effective speaker; we remember him only in his old age. He removed hence to Lake George.

MOFFITT, JUDAH, married Nancy Hancock, niece of Governor John Hancock, and settled in a secluded nook on the mountain near Rupert. He was from Brimfield, Mass. He was with the detachment of soldiers under Ethan Allen, who surprised Ticonderoga in 1775. He was in the battle of Saratoga in 1777, and at the siege of Yorktown in 1781. He was long a respected citizen in his secluded home. He died in 1852, aged 92; his wife died in 1848, aged 83. Of his children we know only Hiram and Nancy, who have lately removed to Wells.

MONROE, Capt. JOSIAH, from Canterbury, Conn., 1784, married Susan, a daughter of Asa Andrus, and settled on the present homestead of his son, Asa A. Monroe. He was held in great respect and esteem. He died in 1846, aged 84; his wife died the same year, aged 79. He raised a family of four sons: Jesse, who removed to Michigan; William, Asa A. and Chauncey, who married Emeline Brown, and died in 1828, aged 28.

MONROE, WILLIAM, m. Alta, da. of Joseph Clark, who died in 1837, aged 35, and succeeded to his homestead. Next he married the widow of David Curtis. His only son, Joseph C., settled near his father.

FAMILY SKETCHES. 217

MONROE, ASA A., m. Axa, da. of Elkanah Phillips, and succeeded to his father's homestead. He was in the legislature in 1856 and '57.

MONROE, JESSE, from Canterbury, Conn., a brother of Josiah, settled on the present homestead of Edward S. Soullard. He removed to Poultney several years since where he died in 1858, aged 87. His family, whom we know, are Calif Monroe, who married a daughter of John C. Hopson, of Wells. He was in the legislature from Wells two years, and now lives in Poultney. Giles Monroe is a Methodist preacher; Nathan Monroe lives in Poultney; Lucinda married Welcome Wood, who died in Poultney in 1864, aged about 60.

MONROE, Dr. RENSSELAER G., from Granville, N. Y., 1853, m. Lucy, da. of James Whedon, and settled in his profession at West Pawlet. He removed to Rutland in 1866.

MONTAGUE, ADONIJAH, from Massachusetts at an early day, married a sister of Joel Simonds, Sen. He was a man of singular piety and discreetness. Suffering for many years from chronic ailments and slender means, he was aided by the Congregational church, of which he was a prominent member. He removed to Oswego county, N. Y.

MOORE, HENRY J., from England, settled several years ago at the village in the blacksmithing business. He removed to East Rupert in 1867.

NORTON, THERON, from Granville, N. Y., about 1820, settled in the mercantile business at West Pawlet. He accumulated a large property. He employed as clerks, successively, Col. William Woodward, Henry Bulkley and Arch Bishop. The latter has been widely known as secretary of the Washington County (N. Y.) Insurance Company, an institution which did an immense business. Mr.

19

Norton removed to Chicago, Ill., about 1834, where he soon after died, aged about 40.

NYE, TIMOTHY, from Falmouth, Mass., about 1783, married a daughter of Josiah Goodspeed, of Wells, and settled on the place now in possession of James Alexander. He was of quiet and domestic habits and mingled but little with the busy world. He died in 1847, aged 85; his widow in 1857, aged 84. Their two children, Nathaniel and Louisa, widow of David Goodall, own the homestead.

OLDS, Rev. ABEL W., from Bradford, Pa., 1866, called to the pastorate of the Church of the Disciples at West Pawlet has, during the past year called together the scattered elements of his charge and obtained a large increase in the membership of his church. He was in the 76th regiment Pennsylvania volunteers for three years.

ORCUTT, HUGH, from Cambridge, N. Y., married Philinda, widow of Martin Blakeley, and settled on the east road, near Wells. His wife died in 1860, aged 40. Next he married Mrs. Herrick.

ORR, Maj. GEORGE S., m. Henrietta da. of Ervin Pratt. He was one of the first to respond to the first call of the president of the U. S. for volunteers in 1861. He entered as private in the first Vermont regiment and was at the battle of Great Bethel, Va., where the gallant Winthrop was slain. Soon after his discharge he again enlisted as private in the 77th N. Y. regiment, and rose step by step to the position of major. This regiment was in the 3d brigade, 2nd division, of the 6th army corps of the army of the Potomac. It was in the disastrous campaign of Gen. McClellan and was first engaged with the enemy at Yorktown from April 6th to May 4, 1862, and then in succession at Williamsburg, May 5; at Chickahominy from

May 20 to 26; at Hanover C. H. May 27; Fair Oaks, June 1; Golden's Farm, June 20; Savage Station, June 27; White Oak Swamp, June 28; Charles City cross roads, June 30; Malvern Hill, July 1. After the discomfiture and retreat of McClellan, the brigade was under the command of Gen. Pope, and were engaged with the enemy at the second Bull Run. Next the command devolved on Gen. Burnside and the regiment was at Fredericksburg, Dec. 13. Gen. Hooker taking the command it was again at Fredericksburg, May 3, 1863, and at Franklin's Crossing, June 5. It was again under fire, under Gen. Mead at Gettysburg, Pa., July 2 and 3; at Fairfield, July 5; Rappahanock Station, Nov. 7; and at Mine Run, Nov. 24. At the opening of the campaign in 1864, under Gen. Grant, it was in the terrible battles of the Wilderness, May 5 and 6; at Spottsylvania, May 8 and 10 and 12; at Anderson's House, May 20; at Cold Harbor, June 1 to 13; at Petersburg, June 16 to July 10; at Fort Stevens, July 12; at Winchester, Sept. 15; at Fisher's Hill, Sept. 22; and at Cedar Creek, Oct. 19. Here Major Orr being on the staff of General Bidwell had his left arm shattered by the explosion of a shell which instantly killed Gen. Bidwell. This was the first wound he had received in all the battles we have here enumerated. This ended his campaigns. The brigade continued in the field and was in most of the hard fought battles around Richmond until it was taken April 3, 1865. We have been more particular in giving in brief detail the military career of Maj. Orr, inasmuch as he was in the same division with the "Old Vermont brigade" composed of the 2d, 3d, 4th, 5th, 6th, and part of the time the 11th regiments of Vermont volunteers. Hence *his* record is *their* record! This brigade in which there were forty-three representatives from this town, though the army with which it was connected met with many and terrible reverses, never dodged the post of danger, and never flinched in the face of the enemy, only retreating when ordered by the commanding general. Their banners never trailed in the dust, nor were captured by the enemy. They were the balance-wheel of the army of the Potomac, and nobly they fulfilled their mission.

ORR, Capt. MOSES E., enlisted with his brother George S. in the 1st Vermont, and next in the 96th N. Y. He served longer in the war than any other man from this town, and though engaged in but comparatively few battles was ever prompt to fill the position assigned him. He was never wounded in the service. At the conclusion of his term he was touched in a tender spot, which was soon healed by his marrying Lena Smith of N. J.

ORVIS, ELIHU, from Granville, m. Sina, a daughter of Joseph P. Upham, succeeded Theron Norton of West Pawlet, thence removed to Troy, N. Y., where he died. His oldest son, Joseph U. Orvis, has become noted in mercantile and financial circles in New York city, and is now president of the Ninth National Bank.

PARRIS, HARVEY, from Danby, married a daughter of Edward Herrick, who died, leaving two children, Levi and Orla.

PEARL, Col. STEPHEN, was an early settler in the south part of the town, where he kept a store and tavern. He was a prominent man among the early settlers. He was in command to suppress the "Rebellion" at Rutland in 1786. The court there had been overawed by the mob and prevented from sitting for several days. It made a requisition on the several towns in the county to send an armed force the following day at nine o'clock in the morning.

## Family Sketches. 221

To this requisition Pawlet, though farthest off, was the first to respond, her quota of troops being first at the rendezvous. In 1794 Col. Pearl removed to Burlington and was among the foremost in building up that city. Pearl street is named for him. He died in 1816, aged 69.

PENFIELD, JOHN, born in Fairfield, Conn., married Patience Penfield, of Vergennes, and came to this town in 1803, from Pittsford, and settled on the present homestead of Joel H. Sheldon. They raised twelve children, all of whom lived to adult age: Horace, Eunice, Alma, Sarah, Daniel, Amoretta, Mary Ann, Laura, Maria, Harriet D., Fanny A. and Betsey S. Horace m. Caroline Chandler, and died in Whitehall in 1864 aged 61; Amoretta m. John T. Barden, who died in Chautauque Co., N. Y.; Mary Ann m. ——McLaughlin, of Rutland; Betsey S. died in 1862. He was deacon of the Congregational church several years until 1840, when he removed to Whitehall, N. Y., where he died in 1848, aged 74; his wife died in 1846, aged 64.

PEPPER, SIMEON, from New Braintree, Mass., 1783, m. Esther, da. of Joseph Jones, and settled on the present premises of H. W. King. He served through most of the war and was at the battle of White Plains. He raised a family of six children: Simeon, Asahel, John, Chauncy P., Philene and Narcissa. He died in 1822, aged 68; his wife in 1821, aged 64.

PEPPER, SIMEON, Jr., m. Lucy Leonard, who died in 1812, aged 22, next he m. Helotia Brooks, and raised nine children: Danforth, Seth B., Simeon, Ashbel H., Willard, Louisa, Lovina, Mary and Philena. These children, with their wives and husbands, were all present at the funeral of their mother in 1865. He died in 1851, aged 64.

PEPPER, JOHN, m. Anna Roach, and settled near

his father's. They raised three children: James, who married Caroline Preston and removed to Ohio; Esther m. Harry Goodspeed and died in 1862, aged 43; Anna m. Clark Bent, of Poultney. Mr. Pepper died in 1830. His widow m. Elijah Billings, who died in 1853, aged 63.

PEPPER, CHAUNCY P., m. Seba Derby and settled at West Pawlet at brick-making. They raised seven children: Hamilton, Warren D., Hiram, Melissa, Flotilla, Julia A. and Lefa. Hamilton m. Amelia Andrus; Warren D. m. Katie Warner; Hiram m. Orcelia Williams and died 1864, aged 34; Melissa m. Allen Mills, of Pittsford; Flotilla m. Albert A. Ransom, of Castleton, and Julia A. m. Benjamin Reed, of Hebron, N. Y. Mrs. Pepper died in 1858, aged 62.

PERKINS, JACOB, from Canterbury, Conn., 1779; was the first settler on the west road, on premises now owned by George Barker. He married Mary Fitch and raised a large family, all of whom, with most of their descendants, have left town. He died in 1801, aged 56, and was the first person interred in the West Pawlet cemetery; his widow in 1835, aged 89.

PERKINS, RUFUS, son of Jacob, m. Olive Wilcox, who died in 1819, aged 35, leaving four children, Lydia, Mary, Walter and Electa. These children all died of consumption; Lydia in 1821, aged 21; Mary in 1826, aged 23; Walter in 1827, aged 19, and Electa, who married James Cox, of Wells, in 1845, aged 29. Mr. Perkins was a devoted member of the Baptist church, to which he bequeathed two hundred dollars; he also gave three hundred dollars to the Hamilton Theological Seminary, "the interest to be applied for the education of some colored brother." He died in 1857, aged 80; his wife, Salinda Smith, in 1857, aged 67.

## Family Sketches.

PERKINS, WILLIAM F., from Canterbury, Conn., 1779; settled near West Pawlet. He was an expert mechanic and performed most of the nice work on the old Congregational church. He raised a family of ten children, all of whom are supposed to be living, most of them at Otto, N. Y., where he and his wife died some twenty years since.

PHELPS, MERRITT C., from Rupert, 1865; married Ann, da. of Henry Braymer, of Hebron, N.Y., and settled in 1865, on the Stephen Dillingham place.

PHILLIPS, ELKANAH, from Massachusetts, 1820; settled on the Samuel Porter place, in the southeast corner of the town. He died in 1861, aged 77; his widow survives at the age of 85. His son, Samuel, succeeded to the homestead, and married Mary, daughter of Josiah Monroe.

PITKIN, Capt. SYLVESTER, from Marshfield, 1815; m. Hannah Randall, who died in 1844, aged 49. Next, he m. Mary Ann Clark. He was among the pioneers of the temperance reform, and almost the last survivor of the early members of the Methodist church. He died in 1865, aged 75.

PLUMB, Rev. ELIJAH W., D.D., from Halifax; married Sarah Woodman, of West Brattleboro, and succeeded Rev. John Griswold and Rev. Fayette Shepherd in the pastorate of the Congregational church, May 18, 1831. He continued pastor until 1843. During his pastorate, and greatly by his exertions, the present beautiful church edifice was erected, which, at the time, was scarcely equalled in the state. He graduated at Middlebury in 1824. His intellectual resources were immense and profound, and, for deep and comprehensive thought, he had few superiors. His wife dying in 1846, aged 43, he married Alta Griswold, widow of Harry Griswold. He removed to Potsdam, N.Y., in 1843, where, besides services in the ministry, he had charge of an academy.

POMROY, JOHN, settled first on the present homestead of Samuel Cole. He was noted as among the first to give attention to improvement of sheep. Several of his descendants remain in the town and county. He died in 1804, aged 64.

PORTER, Dea. MOSES (by Hon. John K. Porter). He was a native of Connecticut, son of Experience Porter, and a descendant of Thomas Porter, of Farmington, Conn. He came to Vermont in 1780, where many of his near relatives resided, among whom were Col. Seth Warner, of Bennington, and Nathaniel Chipman, afterwards chief justice of the state. In 1765 he married Sarah, the daughter of Phineas and Thankful Killam, and widow of Rev. Paul Park, of Preston, Conn. She was a lineal descendant of Capt. Miles Standish and was a woman of much culture and intelligence. She retained to an unusually advanced period the remains of her early attractions, and lived to the extreme age of one hundred and one years, with her mind still clear and her eyes scarcely dimmed. At the time of her death, in 1843, she had more than one hundred living descendants. Dea. Porter entered the revolutionary service as one of Putnam's (Conn.) volunteers and took an honorable part in several of the leading engagements of the war. He exhibited conspicuous gallantry at the battle of Bemis's Heights, Oct. 7, 1777, where he won his commission as major by his active and efficient part in the charge led by Gen. Arnold, which drove the British forces to their intrenchments. He was compelled by failing health to retire from the service, and he afterwards laid aside his military title as inappropriate to a civilian who had religious scruples as to the lawfulness of any but defensive war. He was a man of resolute purpose, of sterling worth and strong practical sense. He died in 1803, aged 64. His oldest son, Dr. Elijah Porter, was a learned and eminent physician of Saratoga county, residing at Waterford. He died in 1841.

His surviving son, John K. Porter, is now one of the judges of the court of appeals, residing at Albany. Dr. Moses R. Porter, of Ohio, and Hervey Porter, of Oswego, two of the sons of Deacon Porter, died many years since, each leaving a large number of descendants. One of his daughters was the wife of Timothy Hatch and the mother of Moses Porter Hatch, who was formerly a member of the N. Y. state senate. Another daughter, Sally, was the wife of Ephraim Fitch.

PORTER, Dea. JOSEPH, youngest son of Moses Porter, m. Sarah, da. of Dea. Benajah Bushnell, and succeeded to his father's estate, and to the office of deacon of the Congregational church, made vacant by his death. He was a man of uncommon excellence of character and his influence always beneficially exerted. He died in 1840, aged 65. He raised a family of six children: Dorothy, Sophia, Caroline, Sarah, Benjamin and Moses. Dorothy m. Hon. Dorastus Wooster, of Middlebury; Sophia m. —— Sampson, of Cornwall, and died in 1832; Sarah m. Jacob Chapin, of Manchester; Moses is a physician at the west and m. Helen, da. of Phineas Strong, who died recently. His widow removed west and died some years ago.

POTTER, Capt. WILLIAM, from New London, Ct., settled on the late homestead of his son Joshua Potter at a very early day. He raised a large family of children. Two of his sons Samuel and Joshua, settled in this town, the others mostly in Wells. He had been a captain of a vessel trading to the West Indies. His mother's house in New London,

Conn., was burnt by the infamous Arnold during his raid on that city.

POTTER, Dr. SAMUEL, practiced medicine in this town and Wells several years. His intuitive perception, judgment and skill were remarkable. He died in 18 . He raised a family of eight children, Samuel, Fayette, Collins, Charles W., George, Edwin, Phebe and Helen L. Samuel is a physician at Buffalo; Fayette, an attorney; Collins, a noted millwright; Charles W. has been a druggist and postmaster at the village, and is now about to take charge of the Lake House in Wells. George is a physician near Buffalo; Edwin an attorney in Michigan. Phebe married Rev. Mr. Sprague and is dead. Helen L. married Abbot Robinson.

POTTER, JOSHUA, succeeded the homestead of his father, and raised six children: George, James, Joshua, Jane, Amanda and Betsey. George m. Sylvia Oatman and lives in Wells. Joshua occupies the homestead. Mr. Potter was a man of uncommon shrewdness and intelligence and retained his faculties remarkably to the time of his death in 1863, aged 81. His widow died the same year. He was in the legislature in 1837 and held many responsible town offices.

PRATT, Capt. JAMES, a native of Ware, Mass., from Halifax to this town in 1792, settled on the mountain, on the premises now owned by his son Ervin Pratt. His wife's name was Lucy Giles. He was an officer in the revolution and a fine specimen of the hardy, thrifty and intelligent farmers who laid the foundations of society in this town. His home was ever the seat of hospitality and good cheer. His conversational and story-telling powers were unrivaled. He died in 1854, aged 92, the last survivor of the revolution in town. His wife died in 1834, aged 68. He raised nine children, Elisha,

FAMILY SKETCHES.  227

Miner, James, Alva, Ervin, Dorcas, Sally, Lucy and Esther. Elisha removed to Michigan and died some years since. Rev. Minor Pratt is a graduate of Middlebury and Congregational minister. He is now agent of the American Colonization Society at Andover, Mass. Alva m. Sarah, da. of Ithamar Crouch, and removed to Michigan where she recently died. James m. Philene Sheldon, removed to Westfield, N. Y., where his wife died some years ago. Dorcas m. Braman Fitch; Esther m. Ephraim Giles; Sally m. Stephen Loomis.

PRATT, ERVIN, m. Caroline Elwell and succeeded to his father's estate. He was in the legislature in 1863 and '64. He will be long remembered by our volunteer soldiers for the liberal supplies he sent them in the field. He has a family of seven children, James, Byron A., Quincy, Sarah, Henrietta, Francelia and Minor. James m. Phebe Woodard, and removed to Hebron. Byron A. m. Alta da. of Ira Gibbs, who died in 1865, aged 28. Next he m. Marrietta Roberts, and now occupies his father's homestead.

PRATT, Capt. ELISHA, father of James Pratt, from Ware, Mass., came with his son in 1792. He was an active, thorough man and expert in the use of the rifle (see Game). He died in 1807, aged 78; his widow in 1827, aged 90.

PRATT, Capt. SAMUEL, was a captain in the revolution and commanded a company in which James Pratt was a sergeant. Though living to a great age he was for many years bowed together with rheumatic disease. He was a recipient of public charity for several years in this town and died at Daniel Clark's, aged about 80.

PRATT, MARTIN V. B., from White Creek, N. Y., 1854, married Mary Rising, of Rupert, and settled in the mercantile business at West Pawlet. He has been post master and is now the oldest merchant in town.

PRESCOTT, GUSTAVUS A., m. Nancy, da. of Alpheus Wade, and settled at Sandy Hill, N. Y. He is the inventor and patentee of several useful inventions connected with the business of machinist and edge tool manufacture. He is a noted vegetarian and horticulturist. We believe in his horticulture, but we are afraid by the time he gets thoroughly schooled in his vegetarian habits there will be nothing left of him.

PURPLE, GEORGE H., m. Sophia, da. of Rev. John Griswold, and kept store at the village in connection with Reed Edgerton, closing in 1830. He was post master three years. He removed to Ohio in 1831, where his wife died in 1861, aged 57.

RANDALL, JONATHAN, a native of Concord, N. H., came to this town in 1817, when 15 years of age, and married Anna, daughter of Jonathan Blakeley. He has held the office of justice twenty-seven years.

REED, SIMEON, from Dutchess county, N. Y., 1776, m. Abial Rice and settled in the northeast part of the town. He was serving as minute man at Ticonderoga in 1777, at the time of the invasion of Burgoyne. Upon the dispersion of the militia at Hubbardton, he hurried home and started with his family for his old home on the Hudson. Afterwards he served several turns in the army and when the war closed in the north returned with his family to his farm. He raised twelve children: Simeon, James, Colby, Enoch, Eliakim, Stephen, Silas, Ezra, Ruth, Abigail, Esther and Abial. Ruth m. Jasper Armstrong; Abigail m. Chauncy Baker; Esther m. Heman Sheldon, and Abial m. Mr. Hull. Mr. Reed was greatly beloved and confided in by his fellow citizens and his memory is fondly cherished. He died in 1840, aged 84.

## Family Sketches. 229

REED, ENOCH, m. Abial, da. of Joshua Cobb, and moved to Wisconsin, where he died in 1860, aged 78. Two sons remain in town, Simeon, who married Alta, da. of Jacob Edgerton, and Curtis, who married Almira, da. of Dan Blakeley, and is settled on the Daniel Branch farm.

REED, ELIAKIM, m. Laura Coleman, of Tinmouth, and settled in Moriah, N. Y., where he now lives, at the age of 84.

REED, STEPHEN, m. Phebe Hill, of Danby, and settled near his father. He was a worthy and liberal citizen. By his will, he bequeathed an annuity of fifty dollars to the Congregational society, to be continued while preaching shall be sustained. His wife died in 1854, aged 55, when he married Sophia Smith; he died in 1862, aged 75.

REED, SILAS, m. Mary, da. of deacon Joel Sheldon, of Rupert, settled near his father, and raised a family of eleven children: Allen H., Ira S., Elliott, Charles A., Louise, Harriet, Fanny, Julia Ann, Mary Ann, Sarah and Delia L. Ira S. and Allen H. are merchants in Troy, N. Y,; Elliott m. Betsey, da. of Silas Gregory (second wife), and is a merchant in Chicago; Charles A. is in Illinois; Julia Ann m. —— Horr, teacher in Boston, Mass.; Sarah m. Rollin J. Harwood; Delia L. m. Augustus Edgerton.

REED, EZRA, m. Sophia, da. of Joel Swallow and, died in 1826, aged 30. His widow m. Capt. John Harwood, and lives at the village.

REED, JEDEDIAH, from New Lebanon, Conn., 1770; settled on a farm now owned by Daniel H. Bromley which still bears his name. He was a prominent actor in the stirring scenes of the revolution, and was frequently intrusted with important business by the Council of Safety. He removed to Orwell, in 1820; he raised four children: Jedediah, Lyman, Elijah and a daughter who married Elias Kingsley. Elijah was a physician and removed to Williston.

REED, PHILIP, from New Lebanon, Conn., 1770; married a daughter of Col. William Fitch, and settled on the place now owned by Austin S. Whitcomb. He removed to Richmond, N. Y., 1798, and died in 1828, aged about 80.

REED, ISAAC, settled in the southeast corner of the town, near Dorset mountain. He was a soldier of the revolution. He died about 1850, aged 83. His son, Solomon, succeeded to his place, and has become famous for his encounters with bears, which appear to have lingered longer in that vicinity than elsewhere.

REYNOLDS, Rev. WORDEN P., from Manchester, 1831; settled at the West Pawlet parsonage. He was a fluent and impressive speaker, and was instrumental in organizing and building up a large church of the Disciples. He now lives in Worcester, Mass.

RICE, JAMES, from Granville, N. Y., 1840, married Catharine Cushman, who died in 1844; next he married Lois, daughter of Bulkley Hutchins. He served as deputy sheriff eighteen years and was county commissioner two years. Since 1861 he has been post master and kept store at the village. His children's names are: Daniel, Caroline, Catharine, Ann and Warren, who married Marcia Smith.

ROBINSON, Capt. NATHANIEL, from Attleboro, Mass., 1812; was an officer of the revolution and held commissions, which are now in possession of his granddaughter, Mrs. Amos W. Bromley, of lieutenant and captain, which were signed respectively by John Hancock and Samuel Adams. The chief interest that attaches to these papers is, the autographs of these distinguished champions of

American independence. Without much effort of the imagination, we can reach back through the intervening ages, and grasp these venerable statesmen by the hand. Capt. Robinson was a man of great humor and wit, and was highly esteemed. He, in connection with his sons, was the first to establish the spinning of cotton by machinery in the county. Four sons and several daughters came with him: Jonathan, Nathaniel, William, David, Mary and Hannah. He died in 1841, aged 89; his widow in 1845, aged 90; Hannah in 1863, aged 76; Mary in 1841, aged 63; William in 1863, aged 76.

ROBINSON, JONATHAN, m. Laura Sykes, and settled near the village. He was a great reader and of uncommon intelligence, and stood high in the masonic fraternity. He died in 1862, aged 85; his widow survives at the age of 82. His family are Laura, who married Amos W. Bromley and Frank.

ROBINSON, NATHANIEL, Jr., was a man of great mechanical skill, and was machinist for the cotton factory, over 30 years, constructing nearly all its complicated machinery with his own hands. He married Betsey Brown, who died in 1816, aged 28, leaving two children, William B. and Ezra H., of Janesville, Wis. Next, he married Lydia Belden, who left three children: Betsey, Sally and Louisa. Next, he married Rachel Haskins; her children are, James N., Fayette S., George and Francis. Mr. Robinson died in 1864, aged 81.

ROBINSON, WILLIAM B., m. Sally Woodward, and raised a family of children. Clarissa m. Thomas C. Mosher, who died in 1862, aged 30; Charles, and Chauncey H.

ROBINSON, JAMES N., m. Marietta, da. of Robert

Clark, who died in 1860, aged 31. Next m. Lucy, da. of Lovell Leach.

ROBINSON, DAVID, m. Mary French, and settled at the village. They raised a family of eleven children: George B. died in 1840, aged 36; David W. m. Maria Clapp; Denzill F. m. Rhoda Bigelow, Chrystal Lake, Ill.; Thomas C. m. Sophronia Barnard; Mary Ann; Nathaniel H., Chrystal Lake; Benjamin m. Desdia Howe, Chrystal Lake; Julia C. m. Orla Loomis; Abbot m. Helen L., da. of Dr. Samuel Potter; Eliza Jane m. Marshal Brown, and Henry M. m. Luthera Davis. Mr. Robinson died in 1828, aged 47; his wife in 1828, aged 43.

ROBINSON, Capt. EPHRAIM, from Windham, Conn., 1785, settled on the present homestead of Henry R. Hosford. He was among our most valuable and enterprising citizens. His wife died in 1820, aged 62, leaving five children: Ephraim, Samuel, George, Rosanna and Sophia. Ephraim, Jr., married Anna Fitch, who died in 1825, aged 22; next Mrs. Hosford, who died in 1852, aged 50. Capt. Robinson next married Jemima, widow of Seely Brown and daughter of Capt. Benoni Smith. He died in 1843, aged 83; his wife in 1834, aged 66. Ephraim, Jr., succeeded to the homestead and died in 1847, aged 47. He was in turn succeeded by his step-son, Henry R. Hosford, who married Melvina Smith.

ROBINSON, Richard, brother of Ephraim, settled on the height of land west of his brother's and raised a large family. We remember as his sons: Ezra, Willis, Erastus and Otis, who was an antimasonic politician in 1830. Mr. Robinson died in 1838, aged 75; his wife in 1832.

ROBINSON, ABEL, another brother, settled in the same neighborhood. One of his daughters, Rhoda, married Maj. Salmon Weeks, and another married

Arunah Hanks, Jr., and is the only one of the family remaining in town.

ROLLIN, EBENEZER, settled opposite Dea. Samuel Cole's about 1800, in the tanning business, where he raised a large family. He was a leading member of Elder Beale's church and chorister in the time of fugue tunes. He removed to Johnsburg, N. Y., about 1820, and when last heard from was near one hundred years old.

ROSE, Major ROGER, settled before 1770, on the present homestead of Daniel Hulett 2d. He was one of the delegates from this town to the convention that sat in Dorset in 1776, which adjourned to Westminster in January, 1777, and declared the present territory of Vermont a free and independent state, under the name of New Connecticut, alias Vermont. He died about 1800, aged 75.

RUSH, GEORGE, from Schoharie, N. Y., 1775, settled in the east part of the town near Danby. He died in 1820, aged one hundred and ten years, having attained a greater age than any other person who ever lived in town. He had two sons: Jacob and Aboltus. Jacob settled in Rush Hollow, but soon left town. Aboltus left one daughter, who married Obadiah Kelly, of Wallingford. Their oldest daughter married Samuel Thompson, who owns the Joseph Armstrong farm. Their son, Holden Kelly, owns the Joshua Hulett farm. There are in town six of the fifth generation from George Rush.

SAFFORD, Dr. JONATHAN, from Bennington, 1793, succeeded Dr. Eliel Todd, on the place now in possession of Joseph B. Safford. He was a successful and popular practitioner until his death in 1821, aged 56; Dr. Safford raised a large family: Horace, Jonathan W., Edwin B., Annis, Eliza, Delia and Caroline. Horace m. Rebecca, da. of Dr. Ithamar Tilden and died recently in Ohio; Jonathan W. m. Jane, da. of Joshua Potter, and died in 1864, aged 60; Edwin B. is a merchant in West Rupert, married a daughter of Edward Baldridge, who died in 1862; Annis m. Hon. Elisha Allen; Eliza m. Zerah Wright, now of Wisconsin; Delia m. Col. Lee T. Rowley.

SARGENT, Dr. JOHN, from Mansfield, Conn., 1761, was the descendant in the sixth generation from an English family who emigrated to this country in 1638. He first moved to Norwich with his father's family, where he married Delight Bell, of Welsh origin. He entered the revolutionary service at the age of 18, was severely wounded and taken prisoner to Quebec. In the spring he was paroled, when he returned to Norwich and studied medicine under Dr. Lewis. In 1780 he removed to Dorset where he commenced a successful practice, often going his rounds on foot. He was distinguished in the practice of both medicine and surgery and his reputation extended to a wide circuit. He removed to this town in 1798, as the successor of Dr. Lemuel Chipman, and was the first president of the Rutland County Medical Society. He built the elegant mansion, now the homestead of James Leach, where evidences of his taste still exist. He was the first captain of the light artillery, organized in 1802, and was promoted to the rank of colonel. He was in the legislature in 1803 and of the Washingtonian school of politics. He died in 1843, aged 82; his wife in 183 , aged 74. He raised a family of ten children: Ralph, John, Leonard, Daniel, Royal, Epenetus A., Warren B., Martha, Nancy and Delight.

SARGENT, Dr. JOHN, Jr., m. Miranda Morrison. He graduated at Middlebury in 1811. He practiced medicine in this and adjoining towns several years, but was more at home in the school-room.

He removed to Fort Ann, and was county superintendent of schools. He died at Rochester, N. Y.

SARGENT, Hon. LEONARD, commenced the practice of law in this town, but removed to Manchester soon after. He has held the office of lieut. governor two years, judge of probate seven years, states' attorney three years, state senator two years, council of censors one year, constitutional convention two years, and town representative four years. He still lives in a green old age, having attained the age of 75.

SARGENT, Dr. WARREN B., m. Betsey, da. of Capt. Joshua D. Cobb, settled at the village where he has been in the practice of medicine forty years.

SARGENT, DELIGHT, went as a missionary teacher to the Cherokees in 1826. After several years' service she married Rev. Elias Boudinot, an educated native Cherokee. When the Cherokees were partly coaxed and partly driven out of Georgia, Mr. Boudinot, who was one of their chiefs, favored their emigration. For this offense he was led into an ambush and foully murdered by men of his own tribe who were opposed to emigration. Mrs. Boudinot returned to this state after the death of her husband, where she has since resided.

SARGENT, SILAS, came into town in 1810. In 1814 his wife died leaving two sons: Silas and Lemuel. Silas removed to California. Next he married the widow Cushman and raised two daughters: Mercy and Chloe. Mercy married Zadoc Frisbee and died in 1834, aged 24. Mr. Frisbee then m. her sister Chloe and died in 1845, aged 38; his widow died in 1848, aged 36. Mr. Sargent was an industrious and useful citizen. He died in 1833, aged 51.

SHELDON, Capt. SETH, from Suffield, Conn., 1782, married Mary Henchitt and settled on the present homestead of Dyer Hulett. He was a prominent citizen and raised a large family, none of whom remain in town. He died in 1810, aged 72; his widow in 1820, aged 73.

SHELDON, Capt. SETH, Jr., m. Philene, da. of Simeon Edgerton, and succeeded to the homestead. He was an active business man. He removed to Chautauque county, N. Y., about 1831, and died recently. He raised a family of nine children: Tichenor, who married Lucinda Brown; Nancy, Philene, Alta, who married Levi Ingalsbee; Franklin, David, Julia, Esther and Sarah. His wife died in 1852, aged 72.

SHELDON, JOEL, Jr., m. Sally, da. of Capt. Simeon Edgerton. He settled in the south part of the town, but removed to Chautauque, Co., N. Y., some thirty years since. He raised a family of twelve children: Sally, Harvey, Hiram, Ira, Cornelia, Newton, David, Ezra R., Henry, Chauncy, Daniel and Mary. Dr. Hiram Sheldon removed to Ohio and is dead. Mr. Sheldon died in 1853, aged 81; his wife in 1851, aged 74.

SHELDON, JOEL H., son of David F. Sheldon, of Rupert, married Marcia, a daughter of Samuel Farrar, and settled on the John Penfield place.

SHEPHERD, MOSES, from Connecticut, 1790; settled on a road now discontinued, in the west part of the town. He was an industrious and peaceable citizen. Several of his sons were among the first colonists to the republic of Liberia.

SHIPHERD, Rev. FAYETTE, son of Hon. Zebulon R. Shipherd, of Granville, N. Y. He became assistant pastor of the Congregational church about 1825, and continued until 1831. During his ministry, this church received a large accession to its membership. He was active and untiring in the discharge of his pastoral duties. His style of public speaking was graceful and impressive, and seldom failed to fix the attention of his audience. During his pastorate, he was greatly beloved by his people; but when he afterwards became identified with the anti-slavery movement, he was denied the use of the church, in which to deliver his lectures. He removed hence to Troy, N. Y., and thence to Oberlin, Ohio.

SHERMAN, JOSIAH R., from Salem, N. Y., married Lydia S. Walker, and succeeded Fitch Clark on the Joshua Cobb place. He has recently built on the site of the old house, a beautiful and commodious dwelling.

SIMONDS, JOEL, from Massachusetts, about 1780; m. Patience Hall, and settled on the present premises of Ossian H. Simonds. They raised twelve children, two sons and two daughters in alternation until the quota was filled: Joseph, John, Bethiah, Lucy, Joel, Justin F., Mary, Sarah, Jonah, Ira, Patience and Hannah. Bethia m. Benjamin Coy; Lucy, Jacob Meacham; Mary, Eli Oatman; Sarah, Samuel Miles; Patience, Warren A. Cowdrey, and Hannah, Joseph Douglas. Mr. Simonds died in 1821, aged 77; his widow in 1832, aged 86.

SIMONDS, JOEL, Jr., m. Mary, da. of Bethel Hurd, and succeeded to the homestead. He was a prominent member of the Methodist church, and gave his children unusual educational advantages. He raised a family of nine children: Ossian H., Joel, Justin F., 2d, Annis, Louise, Patience, Mary, Alta and Helen. Joel removed to Illinois; Dr. Justin F. removed to Iowa, and was a surgeon in the late war; Annis m. Artemus Wilcox; Louise, Nathan Swift; Patience, Lucien B. Meacham, and died in 1833, aged 23; Mary, James L. Lee, of Poultney; Alta, James N. Mason, and Helen, Joseph Parker, of Cazenovia, N. Y. Mr. Simonds died in 1850, aged 78; his wife in 1849, aged 65.

SIMONDS, OSSIAN H., m. Marion Semple, who died in 1839, aged 32. Next m. Fanny Conant, who died in 1849, aged 34, leaving two children, George O. and Fanny, who married Samuel Bailey. Next he married Melissa Strong, of Sandy Hill. Mr. Simonds has been justice of peace 26 years.

SIMONDS, JUSTIN F., settled on the present homestead of Artemus Wilcox. He was a quiet domestic man and when entrusted with public business always did it well. He was thrown from his wagon and hurt so that he soon died in 1839, aged 69. His widow died the same year, aged 70.

SIMONDS, Col. BENJAMIN, a brother of Joel Simonds, Sen., was in command of the military post in this town in 1777, which was the head-quarters of Col. Herrick's regiment of rangers and was used as a recruiting station and a depot for stores for our troops and for plunder taken from the enemy. On the 15th of August, 1777 the day before the battle of Bennington an order was issued by Col. Simonds to Jedediah Reed, directed to his wife in Lanesboro, Mass., and endorsed by the council of safety for six or seven pounds of lead " as it is expected every minute that an action will commence between our troops and the enemies within four or five miles of Bennington and the lead will positively be wanted." Col. Simonds was grandfather of Hon. John B. Skinner, of Genesee Co., N. Y.

SMITH, Capt. NATHANIEL, from Conn., at an early day came to this town with several brothers among whom was Judge Pliny Smith, of Orwell. All the brothers but himself left town in a few years. He was in the legislature in 1795–96. We have often heard the old inhabitants speak of him in the highest terms of respect. He died 1807, aged 57. His widow in 1820, aged 69.

SMITH, Capt. BENONI, from Glastenbury, Conn.,

1781 settled on the present premises of his son Robert H. Smith. He brought with him and encouraged to come from time to time large numbers of settlers who looked upon him almost as a father. He was a man of life and energy, and contributed greatly to promote the settlement of the neighborhood. He built a grist and saw mill on his premises soon after he came to town. His wife died in 1788, aged 47, leaving seven children: Josiah, Arthur, Reuben, Hoel, Ira, Jemima and Anna, who m. Benjamin Tyler of Claremont, N. H. Next he m. Elizabeth Smith, who died in 1832, aged 77, leaving two children, Robert H. and Eliza, who m. David Hitchcock, of Granville, N. Y. Robert H. Smith has been in the legislature two years. Capt. Smith died in 1799, aged 59.

SMITH, JOSIAH, m. Ruth Goodrich and settled on the present premises of Horatio Hollister. He was a leading Episcopalian and senior warden of Trinity church, Granville, from its organization to his death in 1823, aged 56. His widow died in 1846 aged 77. His death was caused by a kick from a horse. In his domestic and church relations he was greatly beloved and esteemed. He raised ten children: Ephraim, Noah, Hoel, Josiah, Betsey, Penelope, Julia, Ruth, Mima and Laura. The three first named removed to Illinois; Josiah removed to Londonderry; Betsey m. Allen Blossom; Mima m. Hoel Clark, of Wells.

SMITH, REUBEN, m. Sarah da., of Col. Samuel Willard, and settled near his father. He was a kind-hearted and pleasant man, and highly esteemed. He kept tavern some twenty years before 1832, when he removed to Burke, N. Y. He raised six children: Benjamin, John, Arthur, Ann, Abigail and Emily. These all removed to Burke, N. Y., and vicinity. Mr. Smith died in 1862, aged 96.

SMITH, ARTHUR, settled south of his father's. He was a scholarly intelligent man. He removed to Scipio, N. Y., with all his family, about 1810. Some of his family have become distinguished in the professions. He was deacon of the Congregational church in Scipio, and died recently at a very advanced age.

SMITH, HOEL, m. Ruth, da. of John C. Bishop the head of the well known Bishop family in Granville, N. Y. He entered upon the mercantile business in that place and died in 1806, aged 35, leaving no children. He commenced life with the most flattering prospects and his untimely death was greatly deplored. His widow did not cease to mourn her loss through a long life.

SMITH, IRA, m. Maria, da. of Col. Samuel Willard, and removed in early life to Franklin county, N. Y. We know little of him, but we understand he maintained a creditable position in society. He died in 1856, aged 76.

SMITH, Rev. ZEPHANIAH H., from Glastenbury, Conn., came here as a missionary before there was any settled minister in town. He returned to Conn., and was pastor of a church in Newtown, His religious views being changed, he adopted the profession of law, in which he became very distinguished. He was uncle of the Rev. George Smith, of Hebron, N. Y., who was the first preacher of the Methodist church at the village in 1825, and founder of the Methodist Protestant church in 1832, in the south part of the town.

SMITH, Dr. JUSTIN, m. Irene, da. of Col. Ozias Clark, and removed to Lima, N. Y. He was a physician of the highest order of talent, but became insane, which destroyed his usefulness. His son James, well known in town, recently lost his life by the caving in of a well in Iowa.

## Family Sketches.

SMITH, Gov. ISRAEL. We have been often told by the old residents that Gov. Smith was for some years a resident of this town. History seemed to contradict this, as he was the representative of Rupert at the same time he was claimed to be a resident here. Our solution of the question is that he lived on disputed land between Rupert and Pawlet, which on a final settlement was adjudged to this town. He was from Suffield, Conn., 1783, a graduate of Yale, an attorney, in the legislature four years, and member of congress from 1791 to 1797. In 1797 he was chief justice of this state. In 1800 he was again in congress and served one term when he was elected U. S. Senator, which office he held until 1807, when he was chosen governor. He died in Rutland, in 1810, aged 51.

SMITH, Hon. NOAH, a brother of Gov. Smith, and who graduated at Yale with him, came here during the early years of the revolution; he too was an attorney. At that day it was confidently expected that this town would become the county seat of the present counties of Bennington and Rutland; hence the influx of distinguished men to this place. Being disappointed, Noah Smith returned to Bennington and delivered the first anniversary oration in commemoration of the battle of Bennington in 1778. he was states' attorney from 1781 several years, and judge of the supreme court of the state; in the whole five years. He removed to Chittenden county about 1800, and soon after died.

SMITH, ALONZO, from Wells, 1860, settled on the homestead of George Willard. He m. Lydia, da. of Jacob Lyon. His oldest son Frederic m. Harriet, da. of Curtis Weeks.

SMITH, JOHN, settled in Fairfax county, Va, whence he was driven in 1861, by the confederates. He has been lessee of the town farm since 1864.

SMITH, SIMON, from Minerva, N. Y. He m. Abigail, da. of James Williams, and settled in North Pawlet. They raised a family of six daughters and one son: Deborah, Harriet, Vesta Ann, Alta, Lydia, Amanda, and Judson O. Harriet m. Daniel Cobb, and died 18 . Vesta Ann m. Edward Wall, of Granville; Amanda m. William Dean, of Fort Ann, N. Y.; Alta m. William Bigelow, of St. Lawrence Co., N. Y.

SNELL, JOHN, from Gilmamton, N. H., m. Lois Whiting, who died, leaving one son, John. Next he m. Rhoda Sheldon, of Rupert, and died in 1856, aged 56, leaving five children, Lois, Samuel, Julia, Hattie and James; Lois m. Dr. Jacob J. Denham, of Benton, N. Y.; Julia m. Martin V. Leach.

SOULLARD, EDWARD S., from Saratoga, N. Y., 1828, m. Fanny, da. of John Crapo, who died in 1852, aged 49. Next he married Julianna, da. of Shubel Barden, of Rupert, and settled on the Jesse Monroe farm. He was several years a preacher of the Methodist church, which connection he left in 1831. He afterwards became a Baptist minister, and was pastor of the church in Middletown. He retired from the clerical profession some twenty years since.

SPENCER, Hon. CHESTER, is the son of Stephen Spencer, one of the early and respected citizens of this town. He was brought up to the trade of clothier under Capt. Abner Lumbard. He has long been a resident of Castleton, where he has filled many responsible offices.

SQUIER, TRUMAN, a native of Woodbury, Conn., settled as an attorney on the present premises of Daniel F. Cushman. He was here at an early day, and removed about 1800 to Manchester, where he held the office of states' attorney two years, judge of probate three years, and was secretary to the go-

## FAMILY SKETCHES. 243

vernor and council several years. He died in 1845, aged 81.

STAPLES, JONATHAN, from Danby, succeeded Daniel Fitch on the present homestead of Lucius M. Carpenter. He was a man of great activity and energy. He removed to Granville, N. Y., in 1852, where he now lives at the age of 70 years.

STARK, Capt. JOHN, we believe from New Hampshire, prior to 1770. He was a leading citizen and large landholder. He settled on the farm, and built the house now owned by Mr. Hammond, which is one the oldest houses in town. He was a cousin of General John Stark, and commanded a company at Bennington battle. He raised a family of twelve daughters and one son, Samuel, who removed to Oswego Co., N. Y. He was one of the first judges appointed in the state (in 1788). The records of the town show him to have been a man of standing and influence. He removed to Grand Isle about 1800, and was soon after instantly killed by the kick of a horse. His son Samuel raised a family before he left town, of ten daughters and four sons.

STEARNS, JOHN, son of David Stearns, married Nancy Hopkins, and succeeded to his father's estate. His wife died, leaving four children: John, who married Mary Hitt, and settled in Kansas; Mary, James and Janett, who married Harry B. Jones.

STEARNS, SETH, from N. H., settled near Smith Hitt's and was engaged in the manufacture of starch, several years, until burnt out in 1851. He then removed to North Granville, N. Y.

STEVENS, PETER, from Glastenbury, Conn., 1783, married Mercy House, and settled on the present homestead of James M. Shaw. He was of a kind and genial disposition and of very industrious habits. His father's name was Joseph, who was the son of

Rev. Timothy Stevens, who for thirty years was the Congregational minister of Glastenbury, and died in 1726. Peter Stevens was one of a family of fourteen children: Joseph, Thomas, Mary, Elisha, David, Jerusha, Samuel, Elijah, David, Jonathan, Jerusha, James, Peter and Ashbel. He raised a family of six children: Jared, Jonathan, Sector, Hoel, Joel and Betsey. Jared died in 1850, aged 66; Sector in 1859, aged 73. Hoel, who was a shrewd business man, died in 1844, aged 44. Mr. Stevens died in 1838, aged 80; his wife in 1833, aged 70.

STEVENS, JONATHAN, m. Margaret, da. of Robert Riley. He may be considered the father of the woolen manufacturing business in this town. In 1812, in connection with John Strong, he erected the first woolen mill in town at West Pawlet. In 1832 he built a large mill on Pawlet river, which was burnt about 1850. He then removed to Granville, N. Y., where he run a mill several years, and was succeeded by his son, Robert R. He died in 1865, aged 76; his wife in 1860, aged 72. He raised a family of six children: Annis, Malona, long a teacher of the higher and ornamental branches; Lora, who died in 1853, aged 38; Mary, who married Hon. Oscar F. Thompson, of Granville, N. Y.; Joel and Robert R., who married a daughter of Luther Cathcart.

STEVENS, JOEL, twin brother of Hoel, married Rachel S. Phelps, and succeeded to his father's estate on which he built, in 1845, the beautiful and convenient mansion now occupied by James M. Shaw. He removed to Granville, N. Y., about 1852, where he erected a paper mill at a cost of $7,000, which was burnt, uninsured, soon after he commenced business. This was a staggering blow, but Joel is one who never gives up. He was the inventor of the cheese pan and stove combined, which was a great improvement in the manufacture of cheese.

STEVENS, ELIJAH, from Glastenbury, Conn., settled on the Burton farm and raised a large family, who have all removed to the west. His children's names were: William, who married Sally Hurlbut; Asa, who married Alvira Bowker; Ashbel, who married Laura Hollister, and Esther, who married ―― Goodrich, and subsequently Elijah Brown. Mr. Stevens died in 1816, aged 72; his wife in 1807, aged 66.

STEWART, PHILO P., nephew of Deacon John Penfield, served an apprenticeship to the harness business under him. About 1825 he went as lay missionary to the western Indians, where he continued a few years. He next turns up in Troy, N. Y., where he has achieved a wide reputation as the inventor of the Stewart stove.

STODDARD, Capt. NATHAN A., from Connecticut about 1810; m. Ruth Judson, and settled last at the village. He was an active and zealous member of the Congregational church, and prominent in the temperance reform. He removed west some thirty years since. His youngest son, Rev. Judson B. Stoddard, is a Congregational minister in Connecticut.

STODDARD, WILLIAM, m. Abigail, da. of Capt. Joshua Cobb, and settled last on the mountain above Henry R. Hosford's. He raised a numerous family, of whom only one, the widow of Luther B. Wood, remains in town. He died in 1854, aged 75; his wife in 1854, aged 73.

STONE, Rev. LEVI H., from Northfield, succeeded Rev. Azariah Hyde in the pastorate of the Congregational church in 1866. Chaste and elegant in diction and elocution, he fixes impressions on his hearers with uncommon force and brilliancy. He commands in advance the respect and confidence of all classes of community. He was chaplain to the first Vt. regiment in 1861.

STRATTON, SAMUEL, from Greenwich, Mass., 1783; m. Bulah, da. of Joseph Jones, and succeeded to his homestead. His wife died in 1803, aged 35, leaving a large family. Next, he m. Tabitha Simonds, who spent a long life mostly in attendance on the sick. He died in 1823, aged 60; his wife in 1857, aged 88. Two daughters only of a numerous family remain in town: Roxana, the widow of Hiram Weeks, and Tryphena, who m. Avery Wooster.

STREETER, Dr. M. H., from Hebron, N. Y., settled at West Pawlet in the practice of medicine in 1866 as successor to Dr. R. G. Monroe.

STRONG, RETURN, from Suffield, Conn., 1784; built the house now owned by Lucius M. Carpenter. His wife was a sister of Deacon Ezekiel Harmon, and after his decease, in 1807, aged 59, became the wife of Daniel Welch. We have knowledge of only four sons, Zopher, Phineas, Return and Walter.

STRONG, PHINEAS, m. Anna, da. of Asa Field, and settled at the village in the mercantile business. He was a worthy and highly esteemed citizen; was in the legislature two years. He died in 1839, aged 51; his widow in 1861, aged 67. They raised ten children: Justin, Rollin F., Martin D., Gustavus, John, Phineas, Return, Guy C., Ann F. and Helen. Justin was burnt to death at Fort Plain, when about 25 years old; Rollin F. was a graduate of Middlebury, 1827, settled as attorney at Middleburg, N. Y.; Martin D. m. Betsey, da. of Dorastus Fitch, who died in 1839, aged 24; next he married a daughter of Capt. Joseph Short, of Granville, N. Y.; he succeeded to his father's business; was post master four years, and town clerk six years; he removed to Michigan in 1854, and is now judge of probate. Gustavus was a printer; John a teacher; Phineas m. Eliza Ann, da. of Ezra Andrus, and is a physician at Buffalo, N. Y.; Return was a volunteer in the Mexican war, and died in New Orleans; Rev. Guy C. Strong is a graduate of Middlebury, and a Congregational minister in Michigan; Ann F. m. William F. Bascomb, late principal of the Burr and Burton Seminary, and now clerk in a department of government at Washington; Helen m. Dr. Moses Porter, 2d, and recently died.

STRONG, RETURN, Jr., m. Laura, da. of Gen. Thomas Davis, of Montpelier. He settled at the village in the mercantile business. He was in the legislature three years, and deputy sheriff several years. He was universally esteemed and beloved. He died in 1833, aged 42, leaving two children, Thomas D. and Laura D. The former is a physician at Westfield, N. Y.; the latter follows the profession of teaching and was late female principal of Burr and Burton Seminary.

STRONG, Capt. WALTER, m. Nancy, da. of Seth Sheldon, Jr., who died in 1864, aged 64. He removed to Chautauque county in 1827, and raised a family of six daughters who, all but one, live in that county. Capt. Strong is a man of standing and influence; he removed lately to Cleveland, O.

STRONG, Capt. TIMOTHY, from Connecticut about 1810; settled on the Jonathan Willard place. He was an enterprising citizen and noted for his exertions to improve the breed of sheep. He was a friend, we understand a relative, of Col. Humphreys, of Connecticut, who brought to this country the first Spanish merino sheep. Some of these sheep were brought here, and distributed about the country. He removed to Washington county, Vt., in 1816, where he died in 1842.

STRONG, JOHN, m. Nancy a daughter of Findlay McNaughton, and settled at West Pawlet in the woolen manufacture. He was from Glastenbury, Conn. He removed some years since to Sandy Hill, N. Y. where he died in 1857, aged 68. They raised a family of eight children: Marcellus, Sabra, Melissa, Helen, Thomas J., Gustavus A., Laura and Ann Eliza. Marcellus is a printer and editor at Madison, Wis.; Melissa m. Ossian H. Simonds; Thomas J. lost a foot at "Dutch Gap" canal, and is a Brig. General; Gustavus A. was in the service; Helen m. Mr. Holbrook, and Ann Eliza m. Edna Vaughn.

SWIFT, NATHAN, from Fort Ann, N. Y., 1866, m. Louisa, da. of Joel Simonds, Jr., and settled on the James Bigart place. His family consists of three daughters: Mary m. Philander White of Fort Ann, Alta and Ann.

SYKES, JACOB, from Connecticut, 1782, settled on the present homestead of Wilson Clark. Several brothers came with him who settled in Dorset, where their descendants are numerous. He was a substantial thrifty farmer. His wife died in 1816, aged 59, when he married the widow of William Stevens. Of his family we know but little. One daughter m. Jared Francis, of Wells; his son Jacob married Minerva Goodspeed, and died in 1836, aged 36, leaving a large family. She is now the wife of Samuel Wood. Mr. Sykes died in 1843, aged 83.

TAYLOR, SAMUEL, from Springfield, Mass., 1780, m. Olive Pomroy, settled at the village where he wrought at blacksmithing fifty years. He had five sons brought up at the same business: Samuel, Elias P., John P., Zadoc and Daniel P. There were several

## Family Sketches.

daughters, one of whom m. Seth Viets, another Jared Hulett, and another Lamson Allen. He died in 1844, aged 76. His wife in 1813, aged 42.

TAYLOR, SAMUEL, Jr., m. a da. of Aaron Bennett and settled on the mountain on the Asa Denison place. He raised nine children: Sylvester, Neville, William, Elias, Ahira, Charles P., George W. Cyrus P., and Eliza. He died in 1852, aged 60. His widow in 1862, aged 65.

THOMPSON, SAMUEL, from Wallingford, m. Judith Kelly, and settled on the Joseph Branch farm. His wife is a great, great granddaughter of George Rush. They raised two daughters: Harriet who m. Fayette Andrus and Prudence who m. Daniel Brown.

TOBY, JOSIAH, from Falmouth, Mass., 1783, m. Lydia Baker, and settled on the present homestead of Luther Cathcart. He succeeded Joseph Hascall as deacon of the Baptist church in 1815. He raised seven children: John, Josiah, Zeno, Mercy, Betsey, Hannah and Lydia. John m. Chloe, da. of Dr. Ithamar Tilden and removed to Ohio, about 1844; Zeno died in 1836, aged 32. Mary m. David Downs, of West Haven, and died in 1839, aged 60. Deacon Toby died in 1843, aged 81; his wife in 1825, aged 62.

TOBY, Col. JOSIAH, Jr., m. Lorette, da. of Joseph P. Upham and succeeded to his homestead. He was held in high estimation as a citizen, and magistrate, having held the office of justice 28 years. He died in 1863, aged 63. He raised a family of three sons, Azro, Chipman J. and George. Azro died in 1857, aged 26. Chipman J. has gone west. George m. Laura, da. of John C. Bishop and succeeded to the homestead.

TOBY, REUBEN, from Falmouth, Mass., 1783, m. Rebecca Weeks, and settled near Timothy Allen's.

He was noted for industry and economy, and acquired a handsome property. He was one of the first deacons of the Second Baptist church. He removed to Pittsford, N. Y., 1850, and died in 1852, aged 83. His wife a few days after aged 82. They raised six children: Arthur, Zenas, Reuben, Sally, Rebecca, and Emily. Arthur m. Abigail, da. of Seth Blossom and removed to Pittsford, N. Y. Zenas m. Ruth, da. of Jacob Putnam, and moved to Mendon, N. Y. Reuben m. Betsey, da. of Jacob Putnam, who died in 1843, aged 33, leaving 2 children. Next he m. Salina Rogers of Pittsford, N. Y. Sally m. Dea. Seth P. Stiles, of Auburn, N. Y., and died in 1863, aged about 63. Emily m. John Simonds, and died in 1852, aged 43.

TODD, Dr. ELIEL, settled on the present homestead of Joseph B. Safford, and was the first physician in the north part of the town. He was a skillful and talented physician and tradition invests him with rare endowments. He was a lieutenant in the revolution. He died in 1793, from poison accidentally taken. His son, Jonathan, first settled near George W. Burt's. He removed to Granville, where he was known as an intelligent and influential politician. About 1850, he kept the brick tavern at North Granville, whence he went west, but did not long survive.

TRYON, JESSE, from Glastenbury, Conn., 1783, settled near Timothy Allen's. He was a blacksmith and farmer, and acquired a handsome property. Some years before his death he removed to Granville, N. Y., where he died in 1839, aged 75. He raised a family of eight children: Jonathan, David, Jesse, Dennis, Mary, Sally, Penelope and Nancy. David removed to Texas; Jesse raised a large family and removed to Oregon. He married a daughter of Dr. Socrates Hotchkiss, of Wells. His son, Socrates H., became a physician; Sally married Samuel Smith, and removed to Burke, N. Y. Dennis is the only survivor of the family in this vicinity, and has been noted for his efforts to mine the precious metals on Haystack mountain.

UPHAM, JOSEPH P., from Sturbridge, Conn., 1810, settled on the present homestead of George Toby. He was a prominent and influential citizen. He married Huldah, daughter of Rosabella Tuttle, who died in 1828, aged 60, leaving eight children : Sina, Huldah, Ann, Clarissa, Maria, Lorette, John and Joseph. Sina m. Elihu Orvis; Clarisa m. Arch. Hay: Huldah m. Rev. Nehemiah Nelson, who died in 1852, aged 62; his wife died in 1838, aged 44; Ann m. Arch Bishop, long a merchant at Granville. They removed some years since to Wisconsin, where their daughter, Maria, married Hon. Charles A. Eldridge, member of congress. Maria m. Chipman R. Johnson, who died in 1834, aged 31; next she married Jonathan Dayton, of Michigan; Lorette m. Col. Josiah Toby; John m. Paulina, da. of David C. Blossom, and lives in Winooski; Joseph has been a merchant in Brooklyn, N. Y. Mr. Upham died in 1857, aged 93; Mrs. Rosabella Tuttle in 18  , aged 93.

UTLEY, Capt. LEONARD, m. Fidelia, da. of Arunah Hanks, and succeeded to his homestead. His wife dying, he married a widow Eastman, and removed to Otto, N. Y., where he died in 1864, aged 70. He was considered the best military officer the town ever produced. He raised a family of seven sons and one daughter: Jane, who married Jonathan Goodrich and is the mother of eighteen children, all living.

VIETS, SETH, from Granby, Conn., 1780, settled on a farm near Charles Phillips. He was a cousin of the Rt. Rev. Alexander Viets Griswold, bishop of the Eastern diocese, which, until 1823, included Vermont. He died in 1823, aged 85; his wife in 1817, aged 68.

VIETS, SETH, Jr., succeeded to the homestead and raised a large family, among whom are Seth, who married a daughter of Samuel Taylor; Harvey, who married Emeline, daughter of Seely Brown; Henry, Eunice and Mary, the widow of Franklin Jones. Mr. Viets died in 1847, aged 75; his wife in 1859, aged 80.

VIETS, Capt. HENRY, married Harriet Shaw and is one of the oldest residents of West Pawlet. They have raised four children : Harriet; Fayette, who married Lura Davis; Helen, who married Amyll B. Searl, and Martin.

WADE, ALPHEUS, from Rhode Island, 1785, settled near the centre of the town. He m. Mary, da. of Henry Wooster. He raised a large family who enjoyed good educational advantages of which he himself was deprived. Their names so far as remembered, follow : Alpheus, John, Hiram, Nelson, Rachel, Nancy, and Anne. Alpheus is a Methodist preacher, Amsterdam, N. Y. John was a physician in Ohio, died in 1866 ; Hiram is at Sandy Hill, N. Y.; Nelson at Warrensburg, N. Y. ; Rachel died at Granville ; Nancy m. G. A. Prescott, Sandy Hill; Anne m. —— Brock, Newark, N. J. Mr. Wade died in 1841, aged 70.

WALLACE, WILLIAM, married a sister of Deacon Penfield, and settled near the base of the hill north of the village. We have often heard him highly spoken of. He died in 1816, aged 46; his wife in 1835, aged 59. His family have all left town.

WALKER, Rev. JASON F., from having been principal of the Troy Conference Academy at Poultney, assumed charge of the Methodist church at the village in 1853. About his first service was the preaching of the dedication sermon. He soon became of the "Progressive" school and under his auspices an independent religious society was soon after organized. Whatever the defects or excellences of his views and theories, he exerted a magnetic and fascinating influence over the adherents to his peculiar views. He removed to Wisconsin.

WARNER, MARK, from Northampton, Mass., 1799, was an industrious and worthy citizen. He raised four sons: Elisha, Spencer, William and Mark. Spencer m. Lucy, da. of Heman Hastings, and is a liberal and wealthy capitalist of Chicago. William resides in Franklin county, where he has been a merchant. Mr. Warner died in 1839, aged 78; his wife in 1857, aged 70.

WARNER, ELISHA, m. Mary, da. of Oliver Loomis, who died in 1861, aged 68, leaving two sons, Oliver L. and Walter S. Oliver L. married Mary A., da. of John Moore of Dorset. Walter S. m. Marcia, da. of Sylvanus B. Lathe, who died in 1862, aged 29. Next, he m. Olive J., da. of Galusha Hanks. Mr. Warner is now in Norwich, Ct.

WARNER, MARK, Jr., m. Angelia, da. of Lyman Finney, and has a family of five daughters, of whom the oldest, Julia, m. Francis S. Hollister.

WARRINER, GAD, from Conn., 1788; settled on the farm now owned by Horace Clark. His son, Chester, m. Drue, da. of Joshua Cobb; Willis m. Nancy, da. of Joseph Armstrong, and moved to Hopkinton, N. Y., in 1811. The rest of the family moved to Gainsville, N. Y.

WEED, JAMES, from Rupert, m. Caroline, da. of James Rice, and settled on the Moses Porter place. He has just opened a store at the village.

DAVID WEEKS, from Hardwick, Mass., 1801; settled south of the village and conducted the tanning business over 50 years; the latter part of the time in connection with his sons, Rich and Seth B. He was a man of quiet and genial manners, and was much respected. He married Abigail, da. of Seth Bond, and raised eight children: Elijah, Salmon, Rich, Seth B., Matilda, Abigail, Eliza and Nancy. Elijah m. Alma Morrison, and died in 1859, aged 67; Salmon m. Rhoda Robinson and settled at the village in the tanning business; he removed to Long Island, where he died. Rich m. Catharine, da. of Asahel Clark, and lives near the homestead; Seth B. m. Fanny Keeler of Brandon, who died in 1846, aged 29; he died in 1850, aged 48. Matilda m. Hiram Wickham; Abigail m. Fowler W. Hoyt, of Manchester; Eliza has followed teaching near forty years, and m. in 1865 ——— Daniels, of Troy, N. Y.

WEEKS, SAMUEL, from Hardwick, Mass., 1801; settled on the present homestead of Arthur Goodspeed, and raised nine children: Wheeler, John, Curtis, Hiram, Safford, Harvey R., William P., Cyrus and Sarah. Wheeler removed to Penn., and died recently; John m. Clara Willard, and died in Whitesboro, N. Y.; Safford died at the same place. Hiram m. Roxana, da. of Samuel Stratton, and died in 1866, aged 62; Harvey R. m. Roxana Perry, and died in 1866, aged 58; William P. m. Laura, da. of John Williams; Sarah m. Silas Jones, Jr., who died in 18  . Next, she m. John Williams, of Granville, and died in 18  .

WEEKS, CURTIS, m. Almira, da. of Chauncy King and raised five children: Chauncy K., Edward P., William C., Clarinda and Harriet. Chauncy K. m. Catharine Hanks and died in 1849 aged 23, leaving one son Henry; Edward P. m. Charlotte Perham who died in 1857.* William C. m. Annette

## FAMILY SKETCHES. 255

Reed; Clarinda m. Simeon Pepper, now of Rupert; Harriet m. Frederic Smith.

WELCH, DANIEL, from Norwich, Conn., 1768, was one of the earliest settlers in town. He settled on the present Town Farm. He was a wide-awake thorough-going man, and was familiarly called "Governor" Welch. He was m. four times: first to Polly Bryant; next to Catharine Risden, in 1788; next to Return Strong's widow in 1813; next to Widow Kent, of Dorset. His numerous family of children are all dead or have left town, and he has few descendants left here. In 1822 he removed to Mendon, N. Y., where he died in 1827, aged 81.

WHEDON, EDMUND, from Conn., 1787, settled on the present homestead of Allen Whedon. He was one of the first members of the Baptist Church which was organized at his house in 1791. He was a substantial enterprising man, and contributed largely to build up West Pawlet, where he erected some of the first mills in town. He removed to Cayuga Co., N. Y., 1815, and lived to an advanced age.

WHEDON, ANSEL, from Conn., 1787, settled a few rods south of his brother Edmund. He was a spirited wide-awake man and accumulated a large estate all in one body, sufficient to give each one of his seven children an excellent farm. He died in 1826, aged 62; his widow Rachel in 1837, aged 71. His children were David, Ansel, John Samuel, Rachel, Lorene and Agnes. Ansel m. Jane, da. of Nehemiah Allen and died in 1831, aged 36. His widow m. William Clark, of Whitehall, N. Y., and died in 1850, aged 50. John m. Lovice, a da. of Joshua Harndon and died in 1820, aged 32. His widow m. General Covill, of Hartford, N. Y. Samuel m. another da. of Joshua Harndon and removed to Illinois in 1844. Rachel m. Washington

Z. Wait, of Hebron, N. Y., who removed to Belleville, Wis., where his wife died in 1858, aged 65. Lorene m. Rev. Archibald Wait, who removed to Chicago where she died in 1865, aged 60. Mr. Whedon lived on the present homestead of Nath. G. Folger after 1810.

WHEDON, DAVID, m. Lucy, da. of Nehemiah Allen, and settled on Edmund Whedon's homestead. He was an exemplary citizen and was highly esteemed. He died in 1858, aged 70. His widow survives at the age of 71. They raised seven children : James, David, Ansel, Allen, Oscar, John M. and Lucinda. Ansel m. Mary Hatch and settled in Fairfax Co., Va., whence he was driven off by the confederates in 1861. Their oldest daughter Charlotte, m. Jacob McFadden. Allen m. Ruth, da. of Jonathan Staples. Oscar m. Julia, da. of Joel Winchester and removed to Albion, N. Y. John M. m. Mary, da. of Col. Parker, of Rupert. Lucinda m. John A. Orr, postmaster at West Pawlet.

WHEDON, JAMES, married Roxana Howe, and raised four children : Mehala, Lucy, Anne and Charles. He has been music teacher and chorister over thirty years. He removed to Poultney, in 1867.

WHEDON, DAVID, Jr., married Maria, da. of Isaac Wickham, and kept store at the village from 1843 to 1854, the latter part of the time in connection with Hiram Wickham. He was a director of the Bank of Manchester several years. He removed to Albion, N. Y., in 1854.

WILCOX, JARED, settled on the present homestead of John W. Nelson, where he raised a family of ten children : Jared, Walter, James, Edmund, Cyrus, Olive, Lydia, Betsey, Mary and Electa. A melancholy interest attaches to the history of this family. All of them, except the father, Edmund and Electa, fell victims to consumption, most of them in early life. Electa married Jonathan T. Evarts, a brother of Jeremiah Evarts, late secretary of the American Board of Foreign Missions. Mr. Wilcox removed to Georgia, Vt., and died at an advanced age.

WILCOX, JOHN, from Halifax, 1780, settled on the north line of the town, near Wells. He raised a large family, several of whom, with their descendants, reside in the vicinity. He died in 1827, aged 72; his wife in 1819, aged 57.

WILCOX, ARTEMUS, son of John Wilcox, married Annis, daughter of Joel Simonds, Jr., and settled on the homestead of Justin F. Simonds. They have raised ten children: Harvey, Joel S., Amos, John H., Eugene, Jerome, Catharine, Laura, Merrien, who died in 1858, aged 18, and Annis. Harvey m. Marcia, da. of Rufus P. Conant, and moved to Canada West; Joel S. m. Emma, da. of James L. Lee; Catharine m. Charles N. Carver; Laura m. Phipps Dean; Annis m. Thomas Folger, of Granville, and Amos m. Louise, da. of Samuel Culver.

WILCOX, HORACE, from Berlin, Conn., 1819, m. Sophia, da. of Abner Lumbard, and died in 1852, aged 59, leaving three children. He was in the legislature in 1840 and '41. His sons, Francis H. and Edward, are merchants in Potsdam, N. Y. Francis H. m. Maria, da. of Laurel Armstrong, of Dorset; Edward m. Mary Putnam, and Helen m. George W. Bonney, now of Potsdam, N. Y.

WICKHAM, ISAAC, from Glastenbury, Conn., 1799, settled on the present homestead of George W. Burt. He was a man of great shrewdness and circumspection, and exerted a commanding influence in society. He was deacon of the second Baptist church from 1825 to his death in 1835, aged 64. His widow, whose name was Ruth Bidwell, died in 1857, aged 82. They raised five children: Robert,

Hiram, William, Willis and Maria. Robert m. Louisa, da. of John Edgerton, who died in 1867, aged 62; Hiram m. Matilda, da. of David Weeks, who died in 1859, aged 56, leaving two sons: Merritt and Rollin C. Merritt m. Mary E. Sherwood; Rollin C. m. Mary E., da. of Abel H. Denio, of Rupert. Hiram Wickham has been town clerk since 1858 and one of the directors of the Battenkill Bank several years. William m. Eunice, da. of Benjamin Fitch, who died in 1862, aged 53. He is a Methodist preacher and resides in Chester, N. Y. Willis died in 1830, aged 20.

WHEELER, RUSSELL C., m. Julia, da. of Abner Lumbard, who died in 1848, aged 37. He kept store and the post office several years at the village from 1831. He resides in Middle Granville, N. Y.

WHEELER, MARGARET. We find it recorded on the tomb-stone in the village cemetery, that Margaret Wheeler was the first person interred in that yard. She died in 1776, aged 88. From the best information we can obtain we believe she was the mother of the wife of Col. Elisha Clark.

WHITCOMB, AUSTIN S., from Rupert, married Alzina, daughter of Paul Hulett, and settled on the John M. Clark place.

WHITING, EDMUND C., married Charlotte Decker, and settled at West Pawlet. Thence he removed to Granville, and thence, in 1863, on the Samuel Wright farm. He built the Baptist church at West Pawlet.

WILLARD, Capt. JONATHAN (by Henry Willard). Capt. Willard, the principal grantee and settler of this town, was born in Roxbury, Mass., about 1720. He m. Sarah Childs, who died, leaving three children: Samuel, Mary and Joseph. Next, he married in succession —— Hough and a widow Stark, neither of whom had issue by him; he died in

Rutland 1804, aged 84. In early life, he was for many years an inhabitant of Colchester, Conn. His principal business appears to have been that of a trader. He owned and commanded a vessel trading from ports in New England to New York. A short time subsequent to 1750, he removed to Albany, N. Y., where he kept a public house, the only English tavern then in the city. About this time, by contract with government, he furnished stores for the army then at lake George, in which business he employed forty yoke of oxen. Tradition tells us that he made a large amount of money, and it is related that at one time, when his fears were excited by an expected invasion, he filled a strong cask with silver, rolled it beside the chimney and sealed it up, making it appear as though there was no space there. After residing in Albany eight years, he removed to old Saratoga and engaged in the lumber business. In 1760, he paid a visit to the Hampshire Grants, in company with two others. They selected three townships of land, each of six miles square, and then drew lots for choice. Pawlet fell to our grantee, and at the same time he had large rights in the other two which were Danby and Mt. Tabor. He then entered the names of his old neighbors in Connecticut, and obtained a charter Aug., 1861. Immediately after the location of the township, he repaired to Colchester and informed his friends of what he had done. For a mug of flip or a new hat he purchased many of their rights until he became possessed of just two-thirds of the town. The other third, he was extremely anxious to have immediately settled. Accordingly this same year Simon Burton and Wm. Fairfield came into town. Mr. Burton settled and made the first clearing on the farm now owned by Daniel Cushman, and here the first fifty acres of land were given to the wife of Mr. Burton for being the first woman settled in town. On this ground the first celebration of the fourth of July was held in 1777, when an ox was roasted whole. The next year, 1762, Capt. Willard came into town with nine hired men and several horses. He pitched his tent near Henry Allen's and by fall had cleared several acres and sowed it with wheat. He then returned to his home on the Hudson, where he remained two or three years. Meeting with heavy losses in the lumber business about this time, in 1764 or 1765 he returned with his family to his clearing in this town. At this time he had lost half his capital, which was the sole cause of his settling in the township which he bought for the purpose of speculation. As a man, Capt. Willard was strong, elastic, wiry and enduring; mentally he was a quick discerner of the intentions of men, shrewd and sound in judgment. He sprung from a noble stock being descended in the fourth generation from the ninth son of Major Simon Willard, who came from the county of Kent, England, to Boston, 1634. He was a thorough business man, and in testimony of his uprightness, it is said that he was universally respected by those with whom he did business. His name is held in great veneration by his numerous descendants. His last wife died in 1804, aged 74.

WILLARD, Col., SAMUEL (By Henry Willard), m. Sarah Stark, da. of his father's third wife and raised seven children; Jonathan, Samuel, Benjamin, Archibald, Robert, Sarah and Maria. Jonathan m. Abigail, da. of Major Roger Rose; Samuel m. a da. of John Burnham, and Robert m. —— Gardner, both of Middletown; Sarah m. Reuben Smith and Maria, Ira Smith. This family of Willards all left town many years since, and settled mostly in northern

## FAMILY SKETCHES. 261

New York, where in some places the name is quite common. From one of these sprung Daniel Willard Fisk, of the Astor Library, N. Y., who is a distinguished linguist. Col. Willard was a leading man during his short life. Our tradition is that he was a colonel of militia in the latter end of the French war. He was also at the battle of Saratoga. He built the old red grist mill; he died in 1788, aged 43. Mary, only da. of Capt. Jonathan Willard m. Elkanah Cobb, and raised seven children: Elkanah, Willard, John, Joshua, James B., Mary and Sophia (see "Elkanah Cobb)," James B. was educated at Burlington, and afterwards a graduate of West Point. He recruited a company for the war of 1812, but not being allowed by government to command it he broke his sword and resigned his commission of lieutenant. He was a man of uncommonly prepossessing appearance and decided abilities; soon after this he went south, and settled in the state of Georgia. From him sprung the Hon. Howell Cobb. Sophia, youngest da. of Elkanah Cobb, m. Zadoc Remington, of Castleton, and was the mother of Rev. Frank Remington, D.D., of the Episcopal church, now of Brooklyn, N. Y., and of Henry Remington, of Castleton.

WILLARD, JOSEPH (by Henry Willard), youngest son of Capt. Jonathan Willard, was born in Colchester, Conn., 1750. He m. Sarah Hare, and raised five children; Margaret, Betsey, John, Andrew and George. The singularity of the marriage of Joseph may be considered worthy of record. Her father was an English officer in command at Fort Stanwix, and fell in a hand to hand conflict with the American officer, in which both were killed. Capt. Hare's widow with three or four children and a black servant, sought refuge in Canada, and by a roundabout way to avoid our forces, journeyed through this town, and put up at Capt. Willard's tavern, expecting to proceed in the morning. During the night a sudden thaw ensued and they were compelled to remain. Soon an attachment sprung up between Joseph and Sarah, and her parent was induced to stay to see how it would end: which was by marriage in her 17th year. It may be of interest to some to state that her father was a captain in Butler's Rangers under Col. Butler the noted tory. When Butler held Fort Stanwix (Rome N. Y.), he sent Capt. Hare with his company, and three hundred Indians out upon a scouting expedition. A man named Davis who had married Capt. Hare's sister, was a captain in the American service. Accidentally they met upon this occasion. Each demanded of the other a surrender, which each denied. Each fired upon the other, when both fell at the same instant, mortally wounded at each other's feet. (Col. Hare's family history, Canada West). This was indeed a melancholy fate for the two brothers-in-law, especially when it is remembered that they had always been warm friends aside from political animosities. She was left behind while the family proceeded on their way. She was a woman of great judgment, memory and physical endurance. To her the writer of this sketch is indebted for many facts in relation to the family. Joseph Willard passed his days at the present residence of Daniel McGrath, and died in 1829, aged 80. His widow in 1846, aged 80.

WILLARD, ANDREW, m. Mary, da. of David Blakeley, who died in 1866, aged 70. He owns and occupies land which has been in the family from the first settlement of the town. He has been confined mostly to his house and bed for the last twelve years with a spinal complaint, which he has

FAMILY SKETCHES. 263

borne with cheerful fortitude. His only son Henry lives with his father.

WILLARD, GEORGE, m. Lucretia, da. Fitch Clark, and succeeded to the homestead, subsequently he moved on the present farm of Alonzo Smith. He now resides in Castleton.

WILLARD, SILAS, m. a da. of Ebenezer Baker, and settled at the village. He struggled through life against the adverse influences of poor health and slender means, and maintained a highly respectable character. He died in Grandville, N. Y., in 1859, aged 66, leaving four children; Cyrenius M., Eunice, Mary and Ersa, who all reside in Castleton. Hon Cyrenius M. Willard is an attorney, and judge of probate. He was cashier of the Castleton Bank, from 1853 to 1865.

WILLARD, Dr. JAMES H., a brother of Silas Willard, M. Nancy, a da. of Ephraim Fitch, and practiced his profession here a few years. He removed to Brownhelm, Ohio, in 1830, and died in 1858; his wife in 1863.

WILLEY, ASA, from Colchester, Conn., 1778, settled in the northeast part of the town. He died in 1825, aged 80; his widow in 1827, aged 79. They left eleven children: Asa, Zechariah, Israel, Betsey, Abigail, Rachel, Patience, Lydia, Lucy, Polly and Sally. Asa lives in Unadilla, N. Y., at the age of 88. Zechariah died in 1866, aged 85; Israel in 1847, aged 53. Betsey married Gideon Gifford, who died in 1810, aged 50. Next she married Nathan Brown, and died in Castile, N. Y., in 1855, aged 91. Rachel married Hon. John H. Andrus, and died in 1821, aged 50. Sally is the widow of Capt. Bushnell, and with her sister, Lucy, 81 years of age, lives on the homestead. Polly is the widow of Thomas T. Newton, Fon du lac, Wisconsin.

WILLIAMS, NATHAN, settled on the late homestead

of his son, Edward. He raised a large family, none of whom remain in town. Daniel, John and James settled in Castleton. Edward m. Laura A., da. of Col. Asa Thompson, and died in 1865.

WILLIAMS, OLIVER, from Granville, N. Y.; m. Minerva Roach, and settled on the Jonathan Arnold place. They have two sons, John and David.

WILLIS, ALLEN, from Shelburn, Mass., married Nancy, a daughter of Lemuel Barden, and settled on the David Cleveland farm. He died in 1858, aged 80. His widow survives at the age of 78.

WILLIS, GUILD, from Cheshire, Mass., 1815, settled near the village. He died of cancer in 1856, aged 74, leaving six children: Eliza, Sally Ann, Adeline, Alvarado, Fanny and Emily. Eliza m. Capt. Isaac Crosby, and died of cancer in 1865, aged 46, Sally Ann m. David Andrews; Adeline m. Henry Belden.

WINCHESTER, ANDREW, from New Lebanon, Conn., 1786; settled on the present homestead of his grandson, Norman. His wife, whose name was Lydia Carver, was a direct descendant of Gov. John Carver, the first governor of Plymouth colony in 1620. He died in 1827, aged 66.

WINCHESTER, JOEL, m. Sophia Armstrong, of Castleton, and succeeded to the homestead of his father, Andrew. He was a worthy and exemplary citizen. He died in 1846, aged 56; his widow in 1862, aged 70. They raised eight children: Horace, Charles, Norman, Lydia, Mary Ann, Harriet, Ellen and Julia. Horace m. Ardelia, da. of Elkanah Phillips, who died in 1852, aged 35. Next, Lucina, da. of Moses Whitcomb, who died in 1858, aged 39. Next, to Harriet Simonds, of Whitehall. Charles graduated at Wesleyan University, became an attorney, and is county judge at Springfield, Mass. Norman m. Harriet Lyon, and succeeded

## FAMILY SKETCHES.

to the homestead; Lydia m. N. W. Bourn; Harriet m. Joseph Peck, of Middletown; Ellen m. John Allen, and Julia m. Oscar Whedon.

WISEMAN, JOHN, born in England, 1765; came to this country during the revolution, a soldier in the British service. He deserted while the army lay on the Hudson, and being hotly pursued, swam the river. When his pursuers came up, they fired upon him, but to no purpose. He waved his hat in triumph and exclaimed, "Boys, you are too late." He joined our army and continued in it to the end of the war. He settled in the southwest part of the town, the only guide to his place then being marked trees. He died in 1815, aged 60. He raised a family of ten children, all of whom lived to marry and settle. John Wiseman, Jr., married a daughter of Nehemiah Bourn, and succeeded to the homestead, but afterwards built a house across the line in Rupert. He raised a large family of children: John, Milton B., Josephine, and others. Milton m. Ann, da. of James Whedon; Josephine m. Dewitt C. Wait.

WOOD, DAVID, from Plymouth, Mass., 1792, settled on the late homestead of his son, Luther B. Wood. He had several children of whom we knew: Timothy, Luther B. and Calvin, who died in 1867. Timothy raised a large family, and died some years since. Mr. Wood died in 1836, aged 87. His wife in 1825, aged 77.

WOOD, LUTHER B., succeeded to the mountain home of his father. He was m. four times, and raised a very numerous family. His two last wives were daughters of William Stoddard. His son, Martin P. was killed at Spottsylvania, Va., May 12, 1864. Another son, Henry C. was among the first to enter the service for three years. Mr. Wood died in 1865, aged 80.

WOOD, Rev. SAMUEL, M. succeeded Rev. Mr. Bonney in the pastorate of the Congregational church in 1854, and continued until 1859, when he removed to Brunswick, N. Y. The church is represented as having been at a low ebb at the time he assumed the pastorate. Diffident and unassuming in his deportment, he was faithful and diligent in the discharge of his ministerial duties.

WOODARD, JOHN J., married Margaret Hopkins, and settled at West Pawlet, in 1851. He was in the mercantile and produce business. He died in 1864, aged 45.

WOODWARD, ANDERSON D., from Townsend, 1846; m. Sarah Norcross, and settled at the village. He has run the mail stage from Manchester to Pawlet and Granville, several years. His da. Ellen S., married Louis Piaget, of Paterson, N. J.; his da. Emily A., m. George Tingue, of Union village, N. Y.

WOOSTER, HENRY, from Connecticut, about 1780; settled on the present premises of Daniel Folger. In 1793, the Episcopal convention of Vermont met at his house, and elected the first Bishop of Vermont, Dr. Edward Bass, who, however, did not enter on its duties. He died about 1820, aged 80. He left two sons, Henry and Amos.

WOOSTER, HENRY, Jr., married Dorothy Baldwin, who died in 1817, leaving two children: Asa and Amanda. The latter married Rev. Mr. Stannard, and was a missionary to the Indians. Next he m. Deborah Loomis, and died in 1839, aged 63, leaving one daughter, Deborah, who m. Luther P. Lincoln.

WOOSTER, Amos, m. Zeriah Hall, and succeeded to the homestead of his father. He raised a family of twelve children: Amos, Avery, Andrew, Alpheus, Aaron, Albert, Asa, Mary, Mercy, Martha, Manda and Maria. Avery is the only one living in

FAMILY SKETCHES. 267

town. He married Tryphena, a daughter of Samuel Stratton. Amos is a Methodist preacher. Mr. Wooster died in 1836, aged 56; his widow in 1849, aged 57. Mrs. Wooster's sister, Miss Polly Hall, long a resident of this town, died in 1866, in Pittsford, aged 88.

WRIGHT, SAMUEL, settled on the present homestead of Edmund C. Whiting. He was noted as a hunter and trapper, and spent a portion of each year, until over seventy years of age, in the northern forests in pursuit of his favorite game. He raised three sons: Samuel, Zerah and Resha. Zerah m. Eliza, da. of Dr. Jonathan Safford, and moved to Ohio. Resha m. Minerva, da. of William Stevens, and died in early life. Mr. Wright died in 1828, aged 81.

WRIGHT, SAMUEL, Jr., m. Rebecca, da. of Tracy Cleveland, and settled near his father's. He was an intelligent and influential citizen. He built a linseed oil mill in 1814. He had two sons: Hoel and Lucien B. Hoel m. Aurelia, da. of Calvin Cleveland, and removed to Green Bay, Mich. He was one of the first settlers in that region, and is a prominent and wealthy citizen. Rev. Lucien B. Wright became an Episcopal minister and settled in Alabama, where he died at an early age. Mr. Wright removed to Green Bay about 1830, and recently died.

## TOWN CENSUS, JANUARY 1, 1867.

Whole number of inhabitants, 1,363 : Males, 674; Females, 689. Aggregate age, 40,233 years. Average age 29.562. Of these, 362 are voters. Of men over 21, there are farmers, 283; carpenters, 11;

manufacturers, 7; blacksmiths, 6; shoemakers, 6;
masons, 6; wagon makers, 3; painters, 3; weavers, 2;
millwrights, 2; harness makers, 2; tinners, 3; tailors,
2; gunsmith, 1; photographer, 1; merchants, 8;
produce dealers, 5; grocer, 1; hotel keepers, 2;
station agent, 1: railroad employees, 5; mail carriers, 2; clergymen, 3; physicians, 3; attorneys, 2.

*Table showing the number of each age and sex from under one year of age to eighty-nine years:*

| Years. | Male. | Female. | Years. | Male. | Female. | Years. | Male. | Female. | Years. | Male. | Female. |
|---|---|---|---|---|---|---|---|---|---|---|---|
| 1 und. | 13 | 11 | 23... | 15 | 11 | 46... | 13 | 7 | 69... | 3 | 3 |
| 1.... | 12 | 10 | 24... | 9 | 12 | 47... | 7 | 8 | 70... | 4 | 4 |
| 2... | 17 | 14 | 25... | 9 | 14 | 48... | 9 | 7 | 71... | 3 | 1 |
| 3.... | 13 | 15 | 26... | 13 | 17 | 49... | 7 | 9 | 72... | 2 | 2 |
| 4.... | 16 | 16 | 27... | 5 | 9 | 50... | 9 | 6 | 73... | 3 | 2 |
| 5.... | 16 | 15 | 28... | 6 | 13 | 51... | 11 | 4 | 74... | 4 | 3 |
| 6.... | 13 | 8 | 29... | 7 | 7 | 52... | 9 | 5 | 75... | 2 | 1 |
| 7.... | 16 | 9 | 30... | 15 | 8 | 53... | 7 | 10 | 76... | 2 | |
| 8.... | 15 | 16 | 31... | 9 | 6 | 54... | 2 | 6 | 77... | 2 | 3 |
| 9.... | 14 | 8 | 32... | 6 | 10 | 55... | 7 | 6 | 78... | 2 | 2 |
| 10.... | 14 | 18 | 33... | 10 | 9 | 56... | 10 | 7 | 79... | | 2 |
| 11.... | 15 | 13 | 34... | 6 | 8 | 57... | 4 | 7 | 80... | | |
| 12.... | 18 | 20 | 35... | 7 | 5 | 58... | 3 | 4 | 81... | 3 | 1 |
| 13.... | 12 | 16 | 36... | 6 | 11 | 59... | 7 | 3 | 82... | | 1 |
| 14.... | 9 | 17 | 37... | 6 | 9 | 60... | 5 | 10 | 83... | 2 | |
| 15.... | 12 | 10 | 38... | 5 | 11 | 61... | 7 | 3 | 84... | 1 | |
| 16.... | 16 | 11 | 39... | 6 | 9 | 62... | 3 | 5 | 85... | | |
| 17.... | 13 | 18 | 40... | 9 | 9 | 63... | 4 | 7 | 86... | | |
| 18.... | 12 | 19 | 41... | 5 | 8 | 64... | 5 | 5 | 87... | | |
| 19.... | 8 | 15 | 42... | 6 | 5 | 65... | 4 | 3 | 88... | | |
| 20.... | 16 | 14 | 43... | 11 | 5 | 66... | 2 | 1 | 89... | | 1 |
| 21.... | 13 | 11 | 44... | 4 | 10 | 67... | 4 | 2 | 90... | | |
| 22.... | 15 | 15 | 45... | 8 | 12 | 68... | 4 | 5 | 91... | | |

# APPENDIX.

*Obituary of Deceased Soldiers.*

NYE, EDWARD, son of Nathaniel Nye, enlisted for three years in Co. B, 9th Vt. regiment. He died in hospital, March 30, 1864, aged 23.

WARREN, JOHN, enlisted in Co. F, 169th N. Y. regiment for three years. He was killed instantly at the capture of Fort Fisher, 1864. He was the youngest of four sons of a widowed mother, all of whom were in the service. His patriotic mother needs and deserves, but does not receive a pension.

*Cheese Factories.*

The first cheese factory in the state was established on the premises of C. S. Bardwell, in West Pawlet, in March 1864. It is run by a joint stock company incorporated by the legislature in 1865, and has a capital of about five thousand dollars invested in buildings and necessary fixtures. The milk of about 475 cows, on an average, has been delivered here for the last three years. The whole amount of milk for three seasons is 4,849,759lbs. making 486,267lbs. of cheese, market weight, being a fraction more than one pound of cheese to ten pounds of milk. Net proceeds of the cheese, all expenses paid, $90,000, being a fraction over $18\frac{1}{2}$ cents per pound. The cost of manufacturing cheese at this establishment, including every expense until delivered at the depot has been two cents per pound. The whole management is under the supervision of a board of three directors, and so well are its patrons satisfied with this method of cheese making that the association will the present year very much enlarge its manufacturing capacity.

Another factory was established at the village in 1865, by Rollin C. Wickham, on a rather larger scale, which has been equally successful. We have no returns from it. Still another factory just over the line in Wells was established in 1865 by James Norton. More than half its milk comes from this town. We are assured that the cheese from all these establishments brings the highest price in market.

# Fullname Index

----, Willis 164
ABBOT, John 40
ABBOTT, Samuel 143
ACKERMANN, K 13
ACKLEY, Joseph 98 111 162
ADAMS, 45 82 Abiah 184
  Benoni 71 95 156 Frederic
  W 100 George Jones 162
  Gideon 20 39-41 118 156 211
  Jesse 156 Jhn 139 John 23
  Joseph 20 35 184 Jude 156
  211 Margaret 156 Mary 156
  Samuel 230 Squire 94
AGAN, Michael 23 Thomas 23
AGARD, Caleb 143 Lydia 143
AGRICULTURE, 5554
AIKIN, Dr 168 Mary 168
ALEXANDER, Benjamin 156
  Elizabeth 156-157 Ellen 157
  Harriet 157 Henrietta 157
  Henry 157 Issac H 23 James
  218 John 156 Mary 156
  Mary Ann 156 Susan 156
  Sylvia 157
ALLEN, Alanson 157 Anna 158
  Annis 159 234 Barna 157
  Caleb 41 115 157 179
  Charles 42 158 Daty 100
  157-158 Daty 2nd 150
  Deacon 157 Ebenezer 12-13
  83 Elisha 39 41-42 145-146
  158-159 171 179 234 Eliza
  158 Ellen 158 265 Ethan 10
  17-18 118 157 188 204 216
  Hannah 180 Henry 111 138
  158 260 Horace 67 102 159
  Ira 14-15 Ira A 66 Isaac 102
  158 Jane 158 255

ALLEN (cont.)
  John 20 40 98 158 265 Julia
  158 Kate 159 Lamson 249
  Lucy 159 256 Mary 68
  Merritt 102 159 Mervin 66
  Nathan 36 39-40 146 158
  Nehemiah 20 158 255-256
  Parmalee 12 39 157 Sarah
  68 158-159 Timothy 12 157
  249-250 Timothy Jr 20 157
AMES, Joseph 147
ANDERSON, David 39
ANDRE, Maj 203
ANDREWS, David 264 Reuben
  161 Sally Ann 264
ANDRUS, Allen 100 160
  Almeda C 160 Amelia 222
  Ann 160 Asa 139 212 216
  Asa Jr 160 Asa Sr 160
  Benjamin 160 Betsey 160
  Chapin 111 160 Cordelia
  159 David 60-61 142 160 180
  186 197 Eliza Ann 159 247
  Elizabeth 176 Emily 160
  Esther 159 Eunice 161 Ezra
  159 170 247 Fayette 160 249
  Harriet 160 249 James Mcd
  159 John H 159 263 Judge
  159 Julia 159 Lemon 71 142-
  143 160 Merritt 159 Mr 160
  Mrs Zebadiah 104 Nancy
  159 Paulina 160 Rachel 263
  Sarah 212 Sarah Ann 159
  Susan 216 Sylvania 186
  Sylvester 160 William 160
  Zeb'd 139 Zebadiah 176
  Zebadiah Jr 160-161
  Zebadiah Sr 159-160

ANDURS, James Mcd 27
ANTI-SLAVERY, 83
APPENDIX, 269 Cheese
  Factories 269 Obituary Of
  Deceased Soldiers 269
ARCHITECTURE, 108
ARMSTRONG, Candace 188
  Clarissa 161 Eunice 161
  Harriet 161 Jasper 161 228
  Jesse 161 Joseph 112 161
  233 253 Judge 188 Laurel
  257 Maria 257 Nancy 161
  253 Phineas 21 161 Polly
  161 Ruth 228 Sally 161
  Sophia 264
ARNOLD, 226 Gen 224
  Jeremiah 112 143 148 161
  Jonathan 161 Luther 21 148
  Mary 161
ATTORNEYS, 102
AVERILL, Elisa 35 Elisha 20 37
  39 161 185 Mary 185
BABBITT, Amos W 23 John H
  23
BAILEY, Fanny 238 Samuel
  238
BAKER, 98 100 Abigail 228
  Chauncy 228 Ebenezer 163
  263 Elijah 162 Harvey 97
  163 Ichabod 163 Laura 175
  Lydia 249 Mariettea 163 Mr
  200 Philene 200 Remember
  59 162 Rufus 163
BALDRIDGE, Daniel 144
  Daniel Jr 163 Edward 234
BALDRIGE, Catharine 209
  Daniel 163 Daniel Jr 163
  Edward 163 Edwin S 163
  Fanny 163 James 41 163
  James Jr 163 Mary 163
BALDWIN, Alpheus 189
  Dorothy 266 Frederick 182
  Jane 189 Jeremy 144 163

BALDWIN (cont.)
  Joel 149 Nellie 182 Samuel
  61 163 214
BANKS, Gen 130
BANNISTER, Almira 214
BARBER, Daniel 145 Mr 66
BARDEN, Amoretta 221
  Amorette 164 Clara 164 198
  John T 36 111 153 163 198
  221 Julianna 242 Lemuel 20
  111 152 163 181 190 264
  Nancy 264 Polly 181 Sarah
  190 Shubel 242
BARDWELL, Amy 183 C S 60
  116 188 269 Consider S 61
  107 115 164 177 Lawson 183
  Maggie 73 Maggie E 164
  Mahala 164 Merritt W 164
  177 Minerva 164 Mr 107
  Sally 164
BARKER, George 173 222
BARNARD, Sophronia 232
BARNES, Martha 190
BARRETT, Charles 22-23 28
  131 133 165 Elijah 28 165
  Elisha 165 Emily 165 Levi
  165 Merritt C 23 28 165
  Sally 165
BARSLEY, Amy 210
BARTON, Lucy Ann 167 Seth
  167
BARWELL, Merritt W 164
BASCOMB, Ann F 247 William
  F 247
BASE, Ball 121
BASS, Edward 144 266
BASSFORD, 201 Dorcas 173
  James 173 212 Jane 212
  Mary 191
BATES, James T 148 165
BEALE, Elder 233
BEALL, Elder 47 143 182 Isaac
  47 143 164 Mrs Isaac 104

FULLNAME INDEX.      273

BECKWITH, Harry 176 Julia 176
BEEBE, Anna 174 Ezekiel 35 Harvey C 23 Lewis 138 165 195 Mr 138 140
BEECHER, Althea 166 Charles 166 David 148 166 Elder 148 Lyman 85
BELDEN, Adeline 264 Ann 160 Henry 160 264 Lydia 231
BELDING, Wm H 23
BELL, Delight 234
BEMAN, Charles 100 Jacob 147
BENNETT, Aaron 20 144 149 165-166 249 Ahira 165 Banks 166 Benjamin Jr 166 James 142 Leonard 149 165 Mary 143 Roswell 20 Samuel 20 166 Uriah 21 Wesley 166
BENNING, Gov 8
BENT, Anna 222 Clark 222
BETTS, Anna 192 Franklin 167 John 166 192 Laura 167 Lydia 166 Marshal 166 Melissa E 166 Mrs Selah 104 Orson F 39 43 166 Royal C 102 166 Selah 20 166 192 Selah Jr 166 Sibel 166-167 192 Sidney 167 Willis W 23 166
BIDWELL, Anson 167 Betsy 167 Caroline 167 Emily 167 Gen 219 Harriet 167 Jonathan 167 172 Laura 167 172 Lucy Ann 167 Mr 167 Ruth 257
BIGART, Francis 27 James 27 112 124 167 248 Lola 167 Mr 125
BIGELOW, Alta 242 Rhoda 232 William 242
BILLINGS, Christopher 20 168

BILLINGS (cont.)
Elijah 222 Margaret 168
BISHOP, Ann 251 Arch 217 251 Isaac 124 Isaac W 184 John C 240 249 Laura 249 Maria 251 Ruth 240
BLACK, John H 23 Robert 23
BLACKSTONE, 18
BLAKELEY, Almira 229 Anna 228 David 42 262 Jonathan 228 Martin 218 Mary 179 262 Philinda 218 Robert 179
BLAKELY, A J 67 A Judson 23 67 102 168 Abby H 168 Abigail 168 Almira 168 Angenette 168 Ann 167 Anna 168 Billings 168 Collins 67 98 168 Cythera 167 Dan 110 167-168 229 David 20 41 101 142 167 David Jr 36 167 Esther 167 Fayette 39 42 168 Franklin 168 Hannah 168 Hewit 41 Hewitt 167-168 Hiland H 168 Jacob E 67 142 167 Jonathan 168 Margaret 168-169 Maria 167 Marshal 167-168 Martin 167-168 Mary 168 Mrs David 104 Mrs Jonathan 104 Phebe 167 Philinda 168 Quincy 67 142 167-168 Robert 59 168 179 Robert S 102 Sheldon 67 102 168 Walton 167-168 William 59 147 168
BLAKLEY, Jacob E 168
BLIN, Lucy 207
BLOOD, Elder 143
BLOSSOM, Abigail 169 250 Allen 239 Anna 169 Benjamin 169 Benoni 169 211 Bethiah 169 Betsey 239 David C 169 251 David G 41

BLOSSOM (cont.)
　122 157-158 169 Elizabeth
　169 Henry 169 Hiram 23
　Hiram S 169 Jane 169
　Joseph 100 169 Laura 169
　Lucia 169 211 Lucy 169
　Mary I 169 Paulina 169 251
　Pauline 169 Phebe 169
　Rebecca 169 Sarah 169 Seth
　35 59 147 169 250 William
　169 William Jr 111
BLOSSON, Fidelia 169
BLOWERS, Andrew J 23
BOND, Abigail 254 Seth 21 254
BONNEY, Elijah 170 Elijah H
　141 George W 257 Helen
　257 Jane 170 Rev Mr 266
BOOMER, Anna 213
BORDER, War 116
BOSTWICK, Henry 28 111 171
　Noble C 23 28 Royal E 23
BOUDINOT, Delight 142 235
　Elias 142 235 Mr 235 Mrs
　235
BOURN, 187 Celinda 196
　Charles W 100 Fanny 163
　Lydia 265 N W 156 265
　Nehemiah 163 196 265
　Royal E 23
BOWKER, Alvira 245
BOYCE, William 150 213
BOYNTON, Albert A 159 171
　201 213 Hannah 171
　Harriet 213 Ziba 149
BRACE, Joantahn 170
　Jonathan 41 67 102-103 137
BRADFORD, Joseph 139
　William 59 188
BRANCH, Daniel 11 20 170 229
　Joseph 170 249 Miner 170
　Philinda 168
BRAYMER, Ann 223 Henry 223
　Jacob 215

BRAYTON, Daniel 146
BREWSTER, Joanna 177
　Timothy 40 143 159 170
BRIGHT, Julia 191
BROCK, Anne 252
BROMLEY, Adams L 37 98 115
　171 175 210 Alta 171 Amos
　W 171 231 Angenette 171
　Daniel H 42 98 171 229
　Daniel W 98 103 Fayette
　171 189 Frances 210 George
　W 35 100 171 Harriet 171
　175 Helen M 68 Henry 171
　Jane 68 Jerome B 39 102-
　103 171 175 Laura 231
　Laura B 171 175 Lovine 35
　171 Lucy 171 Mary 171 Mrs
　Adams L 189 Mrs Amos W
　230 N M 175 Nancy 171
BRONSON, Abraham 145
BROOKS, Helotia 221 Zilpha
　202
BROUGHTON, Ebenezer 20
BROWN, Amanda 172 211
　Betsey 172 186 231 263
　Calista 176 Castera 172
　Celestia 172 Col 12 16
　Daniel 249 David 172
　Densia 172 Elder 142-143
　Elijah 20 150 171 211 245
　Eliza Jane 232 Elizabeth
　157 Emeline 216 252 Esther
　172 245 Eunice 171 Gerry
　39 167 171-172 James S 98
　111 Jane 172 Jemima 172
　232 John 6 21 72 84 183
　Laura 167 172 Lucinda 236
　Lydia 172 Maria 172
　Marshal 172 232 Marshall
　39 156-157 Mary Ann 156
　Milton 37 40 42 98 142 153
　171 186 Mr 153 Nathan 263
　Phebe 171 Polly 172

BROWN (cont.)
  Prudence 249 Russell 172
  Seely 60 98 115 144 172 232
  252 Seely 2nd 172 Seety 143
  Selden S 172 Seth 172
  Solomon 142-143
BRYANT, Polly 255
BUCKLEY, Fayette 98
BUFFUM, David M 23
BULKLEY, Henry 217
BULL, John 76
BURCH, Porter 172
BURGOYNE, 10 12 118 188 228
  Gen 19
BURKE, Edmund 155
BURNHAM, B S 147 Jacob 124
  John 18 260 Samuel A 67
BURNS, John 23 Sylvester 23
BURNSIDE, Gen 129 131 219
BURROUGHS, Thomas 23
BURT, Cordelia 173 George W
  173 250 257
BURTON, 245 Mr 259-260
  Simon 9 39 100 173 259
BUSBEE, Dorcas 173 Jeremiah
  173
BUSHBEE, Jeremiah 40
BUSHEE, Jeremiah 35 101
  Orlando 23 Peroy M 23
BUSHNELL, Benajah 139 173
  225 Capt 263 Sally 263
  Sarah 225
BUTLER, Col 262
BUTT, Samuel 137
BUTTS, Ruth 192 Samuel 139
BUXTON, Hannah 205 Henry H
  67
CAMPBELL, Alexander 149
CAPEN, Abram 23
CARPENTER, Lucius M 37 41-
  42 100 115 173 189 246
  Phebe 173
CARTER, David 139

CARVER, Ahiva 173 Anna 174
  Betsey 173-174 200
  Catharine 174 257 Charles
  N 39 174 257 Chester L 173-
  174 David 36 41 101 148
  173-174 Edgert H 68 Egbert
  174 Emeline 174 Helen 174
  James A 174 Jane 174 John
  21 173-174 264 Joseph H
  174 Lucy 173 195 Lucy M
  174 Lydia 173-174 184 195
  264 Maria 174 Martha 174
  Mary 174 Mr 174 Mrs
  Nathaniel 104 Nancy M 174
  Nath 200 Nathaniel 20 173
  184 195 Olive 210 Ransom
  H 174
CASTLE, Charles D 27 David
  40 Peter 23 Tracy 27
CATHCART, Luther 244
CAVANAUGH, James 23
CEMETERIES, 115
CENSUS, Of 1867 267
CHANDLER, Caroline 221 John
  L 100
CHAPIN, Emily 160 Jacob 225
  Sarah 225
CHARLES, Ii King Of ? 116
CHASE, Lemuel 150 Mrs
  Lemuel 104
CHESTER, Rev Mr 141
CHILDS, Sarah 258
CHIPMAN, 82 Anna 175 Cyrus
  100 175 Fitch 67 Lem 139
  Lemuel 40-42 99-100 174-
  175 234 Nathaniel 224 Sina
  174
CHITTENDEN, 188 Bethuel
  144 Thomas 15-17 58
CHURCH, Daniel 102-103
  History 136 History 1st
  Baptist Church 142 History
  1st Congregational Church

CHURCH (cont.)
    137 History 2nd Baptist
    Church 147 History Church
    Of The Disciples 148
    History Methodist Episcopal
    Church 145 History
    Mormonism 150 History
    Protestant Episcopal
    Church 144 History
    Protestant Methodist
    Church 149
CHURCHILL, Gilbert 100
    Oliver 20
CLAPP, Eliza 215 Maria 232
    Palmer 215
CLARK, 55 Aaron 103 176
    Addie 176 Alta 175 195 216
    Amelia 73 176 Angenette
    171 Annis 175 Asahel 175-
    176 182 187 254 Betsey 73
    175-176 Calista 176
    Caroline 176 182 Catharine
    176 254 Col 111 Corilla 176
    186 Cornelia 176 Cyrus 176
    Daniel 36 139 175-176 180
    186-187 212 227 Darius 176
    David 176 Deacon 84 E
    Fitch 111 Elisha 15 20-21 37
    175-176 258 Elisha Jr 40
    Elizabeth 176 Enos 185
    Ephraim F 176 Fanny 176
    Fitch 36 146 171 175 263
    Flora 175 George 212
    George Jr 151 Harriet 171
    175 Harry G 175 Henry W
    23 Hoel 239 Horace 97 177-
    178 253 Horace A 176 Irene
    175 240 Jane 158 174 176
    255 Jeremiah 98 148 John
    146 176 178 John M 36 153-
    154 175-176 258 Jonas 177
    Jonathan B 175 Joseph 35
    175-176 216 Josephine 178

CLARK (cont.)
    Julia 176 Kittie 176 Laban
    146 Laura 175 Laura B 171
    175 Lemira 176 Lemuel 39-
    40 Lucretia 175 263 Lucy
    176 203 Margaret 206
    Marietta 231-232 Mariette
    175-176 Mariettea 163
    Martha 73 178 197 Mary
    212 Mary Ann 223 Merritt
    178 Merritt W 197 Mima
    239 Mrs Asahel 104 Mrs
    Elon 174 Mrs Ozias 104 N
    M 175 Nancy 175 178 Ozias
    35 37 39-40 83-84 86 111
    139 142 152 163 175 178 195
    240 Philip 171 176 Polly B
    176 Rachel 175 Rebecca 192
    Robert 111 146 175-176 231-
    232 Roswell 192 Russell C
    42 Sally 187 Sarah 175
    Sarah J 178 Sheldon 175
    Sibel 176 Sina 176 212
    Wheeler 176 William 36 158
    176 203 206 255 Wilson 178
    248
CLAYTON, Alex 60 196 Elder
    149
CLEVELAND, Asa 177
    Augustus 21 177 Aurelia
    267 Calvin 177 267 David 35
    40 177 264 David A 178
    Joanna 177 John 36 100
    John Jr 100 Luther 177
    Lydia 177 Moses 177 Mrs
    Luther 104 Mrs Moses 104
    Olive 177 Palmer 40 60-61
    164 177 215 Rebecca 267
    Tracy 267 Zuba 177
COBB, 55 Abial 229 Abigail 245
    Betsey 235 Daniel 147 242
    Drue 253 Ebenezer 144
    Elkanah 40 98 179 183 261

COBB (cont.)
  Gideon 40 178 Hannah 178
  184 Harriet 242 Howell 179
  261 James 179 James B 261
  Jane 176 John 36 39-40 115
  139 178 205 261 Joshua 35
  160 178 184 229 237 245 253
  261 Joshua D 35-36 142 176
  178 185 235 Josiah 175
  Mary 179 261 Nancy 178
  Rachel 185 Robert 206 Sally
  206 Sophia 261 Willard 21
  35 39 112 179 261 William
  59
COBURN, Louisa M 209
  Samuel 209
COLE, David D 179 Electa 179
  Samuel 148 179 224 Smauel
  233 Whitman 179
COLEMAN, Laura 229
  Seymour 146
COLVER, Erastus D 170
  Nathaniel 170
COLVIN, Enoch 58 169 179 208
  Mary 169 179
COMBE, Elder 148
COMSTOCK, Willard 23
CONANT, Charlotte 180 Daniel
  180 Fanny 180 238 John 21
  35 180 John C 144 John G
  180 Marcia 257 Maria 68
  180 Martha 180 Nancy 180
  Orlando 180 Rufus 148
  Rufus P 148 180 257
CONGDON, Althea 166
CONLIN, John 23
CONSTITUTIONAL, Officers
  41
COOK, Allen 180 Charlotte 180
  186 Chloe 179 190 Cornelia
  180 Elisha B 41 Ephraim
  180 Ephraim F 180
  Erasmus D 29 180 186

COOK (cont.)
  James 61 179 John 67 100
  180 Mahlon 35 180 Mr 180
  Samuel 179 Simeon E 23 29
  Titus A 40 109 152 179 182
  190
COOLEY, William 151
CORNELL, Elder 143
COUNTY, Officers 42
COVILL, Gen 255 Lovice 255
COWDREY, Oliver 181
  Patience 180 237 Warren A
  180 237
COWDRY, Warren A 100
COX, Electa 222 James 222
  Robert 20 36
COY, Benjamin 237 Bethiah
  237
CRAPO, Alden B 181 199 Fanny
  242 John 146 181 242 Mrs
  John 104 Polly 181
CRAWFORD, Elias 146 John 23
CROCKER, Benjamin 181 Ezra
  181 James 103 181 John 181
  Josiah 181 187 Mr 181 Mrs
  Josiah 104 Thomas 35 181
  Timothy 181
CROFOOT, Horace 172 Lydia
  172
CROKER, John 149
CROSBY, Eleazar 181 Eleazur
  177 Eliza 181 264 Isaac 35
  181 264 Lydia 177 Margaret
  181
CROUCH, David 182 Elizabeth
  143 Ithamar 181-182 227
  John 143 Phineas 182 Sarah
  227
CROWLEY, Dr 201 Michael 23
  Sarah 201
CULVER, Albert 27 Amanda
  179 182 Betsey 182 Erastus
  27 182 Jennie 73 Jenny 182

CULVER (cont.)
   Louise 68 182 257 Nellie 182
   Samuel 182 213 257 Seth E
   27
CURTIS, Aaron 182 Amos 139
   David 216 Eldad 182
CUSHMAN, Caroline 176 182
   Catharine 230 Daniel 259
   Daniel F 176 182 242
   Huldah 183 Rowland 182
   Widow 235
DAMON, George B 133
DANA, Daniel 75
DANFORTH, Elkanah 110 210
   Ellen 210 Mary 201
DANIELS, Eliza 254
DAVIS, 262 Laura 247 Lura 252
   Luthera 232 Mary 190
   Thomas 190 247
DAY, Charles 183
DAYTON, Jonathan 251 Maria
   251
DEAN, Amanda 242 Catalina
   183 Danforth 183 Jane 183
   Laura 257 Narcissa 183
   Phipps 183 257 Seth 183
   Simeon 183 William 242
DECKER, Charlotte 258
DELONG, Miles H 23
DENHAM, Jacob J 242 Lois 242
DENIO, Abel H 258 Mary E 258
DENISON, Asa 21 183 249
DERBY, Benjamin 183
   Benjamin Jr 183 Hiram 183
   James C 183 Seba 183 222
   Warren 183
DICKINSON, Daniel S 212
DILLINGHAM, Amy 183 Dilla
   183 Judith 183 Mary 183
   Reuben 27 183 Stephen 183
   223
DODGE, Elder 143
DONATIN, Festivals 120

DONNELLY, Edward 23
DOOLITTLE, Eliakim 71 James
   R 71
DOUBLEDAY, Gen 135
DOUGLAS, Hannah 237 Joseph
   237
DOWNS, David 249 Mary 249
DRAKE, Eldridge G 149
DUNCAN, William 24
DUNTON, Andrew 157 Harriet
   157
DURLING, Edward 23
DUTTON, Calvin 184 Polly 184
DYER, Palmer 145 184
EARLL, William 147
EASTMAN, Widow 251
EDGERTON, Abiah 184
   Abraham 42 185 Alta 185
   229 Amanda 185 Augustus
   186 229 Betsey 184-186 195
   Capt 184 Charles 186
   Charles F 36 42 60 185-186
   Charles M 27 Charlotte 180
   186 Chester 103 186 Corilla
   186 Cornelia M 73 187
   David 184-186 Delia 186
   Delia L 229 Elisabeth 186
   Elizabeth 186 Esther 167
   184-185 Fanny 186 Frances
   185 George 27 98 185
   Hannah 168 178 184-185
   Harriet 186 Helen 187
   Henrietta 186 Henry 186
   Hiram 185 Horace 187
   Jacob 21 27 39 42 167-168
   184-185 229 Jacob Jr 153
   159 Jedediah 21 36 139 184
   John 39 60 184-185 258
   John G 186 John L 67 107
   185 Joseph 184 Joseph K
   103 Joseph R 185 Joshua
   100 185 Kate 159 Louisa
   185 258 Lucy 186 Lydia 173

FULLNAME INDEX. 279

EDGERTON (cont.)
184 Marson 27 98 Mary 51
53 73 185 187 Mason 186
Matilda 187 Mrs Simeon
104 Mrs Simeon Jr 104
Narcissa 185 Philena 184
Philene 236 Polly 184
Porter 186 Rachel 185 Reed
97 185-186 228 Rollin A 27
Sally 184 236 Sheldon 41-42
153 185-186 Simeon 21 40-
41 142 173 184 236 Simeon
Jr 36 40 180 186 195 Simeon
Sr 160 178 Simon Jr 173
Sophia 185-186 Sylvania
186 William G 27 William U
67 100 185
EDUCATION, 65
EIGHTS, Professor 106
ELDRED, Abigail 168
ELDRIDGE, Charles A 251
Maria 251
ELLSWORTH, Col 191 Mary
161
ELWELL, Caroline 227
EMIGRATION, 63
EVANS, Abiathar 21 109 187
201 Abiathar Jr 187-188
Elijah 187 Henry 187 Mary
187-188 Mrs Abiatha 104
Osborn 187 Sally 187
Truesdell 187
EVARTS, Electa 257 Jeremiah
257 Jonathan T 257
EVEREST, Zadoc 16 40-41 118
187
EVERETT, Betsey 73 176
Harrison 176
FAIRFIELD, William 9 187 Wm
259
FAMILY, Sketches
(alphabetical) 155
FARR, A A 147

FARRAR, David 181 187 Esther
M 187 Marcia 236 Samuel
236
FAY, Jonas 100 187 Jos 14-17
Joseph 15-16
FELCH, Elizabeth 186 Willis
186
FIELD, 147 Anna 246 Asa 40
139 246
FIFTY, Years Ago 75
FINNEY, Abiathar E 188
Angelia 188 253 Harriet 188
Helen 188 Lucetta 188
Lyman 188 253 Mary 188
FIRST, Constables From 1776
39 Settlement 8
FISH, John 23
FISHER, Ogden 27 Timothy 21
FISK, Daniel Willard 261
FITCH, 82 Abial 188 199 Alice
199 Ann 191 Anna 175 188
191 232 Appleton 190
Asahel 60 189-190 Ashbel 39
Benjamin 35 40-42 188-190
258 Betsey 191 246 Braman
190 227 Camilla 189
Candace 188 Capt 190
Chloe 190 Cynthia 189
Cyrus 189 Daniel 40 139
152 188 243 Daniel H 189
Daniel Jr 173 188 Daniel Sr
188 Delia 191 Dorastus 42
60 97 142 171 189 191 246
Dorcas 190 227 Elisha 40
137 Ephraim 47-48 97 111
151 163 189 225 263 Eunice
258 Fayette S 103 191
Ferris 67 142 190-191
Hannah 189 Helen 191
Hiram 189 Isaac 188 Jane
189 Jared 188 John 35 86
177 188 190 Joseph 39-40
139 171 189 Julia 191

FITCH (cont.)
    Lucy 188 191 Margaret 188
    Martha 190 Mary 171 189-
    191 222 Moses P 42-43 190
    Mr 189 Mrs Benjamin 104
    Nancy 190 263 Philene 188
    Prosper 188 Rachel 175 188
    Return 188 Rhoda 189
    Rufus 139 Salina 188 Sally
    189 191 225 Sarah 190-191
    Sibel 176 188 Silas 97 189-
    190 Sina 174 188 Sophia 190
    Stephen 189 William 14 21
    35 37 40-41 97 118 174-176
    188 198-199 230
FLOWER, Anson 191 James T
    191 Mary 191 Vesta 191
FLOWERS, Byron 100
FOGARTY, John 24
FOLGER, Annis 257 Daniel 191
    266 Eunice 193 Frederick
    24 Nath G 256 Nathaniel G
    61 Susan 191 Thomas 257
FORBES, Anna 206
FORD, 147
FOSTER, Gilmore 27 Ira 27
FRADENBURGH, Mr 67
FRANCIS, Jared 248 Nathan
    122
FRANK, Augustus 75
FREEMASONRY, 151
FRENCH, And Indian War 11
    Mary 232
FRISBEE, Chloe 235 John M 24
    Mercy 235 Mr 235 Zadoc
    235
FULLER, John 139
GALLUP, Robert 24
GALUSHA, Amos 21 40
GAME, 87
GARDNER, 260
GARRETT, Camilla 189
GARRISON, William Lloyd 83

GENERAL, Census Of The
    Town 129 History Of The
    War 129 History Of The
    War 10th Regiment 133
    History Of The War 11th
    Regiment 133 History Of
    The War 14th Regiment 134
    History Of The War 1st
    Regiment 131 History Of
    The War 1st Regiment
    Cavalry 133 History Of The
    War 1st Regiment U S
    Sharp Shooters 134 History
    Of The War 2nd Battery
    Light Artillery 135 History
    Of The War 2nd Regiment
    131 History Of The War 5th
    Regiment 132 History Of
    The War 7th Regiment 132
    History Of The War 9th
    Regiment 132 History Of
    The War Volunteers In Ny
    Regt 135
GEOLOGY, 106
GEORGE, 202 Emeline 174 Ii
    King Of? 116
GIBBS, Alta 227 Beysey 191
    Clemons 191 Ira 111 191
    227 James R 24 Mr 191
    Spencer 191 Zebulon 191
GIBSON, James 24
GIDDINGS, 83
GIFFORD, Betsey 192 263
    Gideon 21 191 263 Martha
    174 Mrs Gideon 104 Noah 4
    21 192 Ruth 192 Sgt 192
    Warren 24
GILBERT, C C 147 Harriet 167
    Irene 206 Joseph 167
    Samuel 206
GILES, B F 112 Braman F 193
    Ebenezer 21 193 Ephraim
    193 227 Esther 227

GILES (cont.)
    Eunice 193 Lucy 193 226
    Mary 193
GILLINER, Col 13
GONE, William 149
GOODALL, David 218 Louisa 218
GOODHUE, 216
GOODNOUGH, Capt 14
GOODRICH, Anna 169 Bethiah 169 Daniel 169 Esther 245 Fidelia 169 Ira 98 Jane 251 Jonathan 251 Lucy 169 Nancy 180 Orson 169 Ruth 239 Sarah 202 Sarah Ann 214
GOODSPEED, Aaron 67 100 Alvin 167 Anna 192 Arthur 192 254 Chloe 192 208 Esther 192 222 Hannah 192 Harry 192 222 Heman 192 Jemima 192 Josiah 192 211 218 Lola 167 Lucius 192 Maria 211 Mercy 192 Minerva 248 Mr 193 Peter 61 192 Phebe 192-193 Polly 192 Rebecca 192 Samuel 192 Susan 192 Sylvia 192 Zenas 21 192
GOULD, 21 Daniel B 30 Maria 30
GRANT, Gen 130-131 219 Lewis A 132 Peter 24
GRAVES, Allen 75 Amos 193 Azariah R 67 142 193 Mary 75 Mr 193
GRAVIN, Joseph 24
GRAY, James W 183 Jesse C 27 183 Josephine 178 Judith 183 Mary 183 William 147
GREEN, Beriah 83-84 193-194 Beriah Jr 67 142 193 Elder 143 George 24

GREEN (cont.)
    Jonathan S 68 142 193-194
GREGORY, Alfred 100 194 Betsey 186 195 229 Clarissa 194 Elmira 194-195 Lucy 186 195 Lydia 195 Maj 195 Minerva 104 194 Mrs Sylvanus 104 Narcissa 185 Polly 194-195 Silas 36 61 186 194-195 229 Simeon 194 Sophia 190 194 Sylvanus 37 39-40 61 109 139 190 194
GRISWOLD, Alexander Viets 251 Alta 195 223 Betsey 160 195 Elisabeth 186 Fanny 186 195 Father 95 Harriet 186 195 Harry 36 39 111 142 195 223 John 47 68 138-139 151 160 178 186 191 195 209 215 223 228 Mr 48 138-140 Mrs John 104 Rev Mr 141 Sally 191 195 Sarah 195 Sophia 195
GROSWOLD, John 71
GUILD, Abigail 196 Celinda 196 Chauncy 146 196 Eunice 171 196 James W 24 John 40 98 152 171 196 Lucy 196 Milton 196 Napthali 152 Plina 196
GUILDER, Alonzo V 24 Wallace V 24
GUILFORD, Fayette 175 Maria 172 Samuel G 172 Sarah 175
HAGER, Albert D 107
HALL, Daniel H 29 196 Daniel H Jr 24 Hiland 167 James L 24 Patience 237 Polly 104 267 Selden A 24 29 Seldon A 196 Thomas 142 Zeriah 266
HAMBLIN, Lorin 21

HAMBLIN (cont.)
  Nathaniel 102-103
HAMMOND, Cordelia 173
  David F 173 Francis D 24
  Mr 243
HANCOCK, Amasa 21 Elder
  148 John 216 230 Nancy 216
HANKS, Arunah 196-197 251
  Arunah Jr 197 233 Camillus
  197 Catharine 254
  Deidamia 197 Ermina 197
  Festus 67 197 Fidelia 251
  Galusha 29 183 197 253
  George G 24 29 Hannah 143
  Isaac 27 197 Jane 197 Jarvis
  21 197 Joseph 196-197 Levi
  27 Lovina 197 Lucinda 197
  Lucy 197 Marcia 197
  Martha 178 197 Milton H 27
  Mr 197 Mrs Arunah 104
  Olive J 197 253 Oliver 40 42
  71 196 Rebecca 197 Romeo
  197 Safford 197 Walter S 24
  133 William 59 196-197
HANNAH, Abel 100
HARD, Times And Seasons 79
HARE, Capt 261-262 Sarah 261-262
HARLOW, Caroline C 203 Isaac
  157 Judson R 98 Lucy M
  174 Ransom 174 Sylvia 157
HARMAN, Nathaniel 198
HARMON, 82 Abial 199 Alice
  198 200 Berintha Hulett 199
  Clara 164 198-200 Deacon
  198 Diantha 201 Ezekial
  139 Ezekiel 21 39-40 68 142
  197-198 246 Ezekiel Jr 100
  George W 41 102-103 198
  Ira 103 198 Joel 21 40-41 97
  137 139 142 199 Joel Jr 35
  40 47 49 71 199-200 Lydia
  197 Mary Ann 198

HARMON (cont.)
  Merit 67 Nathaniel 41 102
  143 164 198 200 Oliver L
  100 198 Proserpine 198
  Reuben 9
HARNDON, Joshua 255 Lovice
  255
HARRINGTON, Judge 83
HART, 97
HARWOOD, John 168 199 229
  Justus W 24 Lois B 210
  Mary 168 Otis W 24 Philo
  210 Rollin J 199 229 Sarah
  199 229 Sophia 199 229
HASCALL, 82 214 Alice 198-200
  Asa 103 200 Betsey 200
  Clara 199-200 Daniel 67 143
  200 David A 100 200 Deacon
  200 Joseph 40-41 142-143
  198-199 249 Lebbeus 21 103
  200 Mrs Joseph 104 Nancy
  200 Philene 200 Ralph 103
  200 Safford 21 39 59 200
HASKINS, Rachel 231
HASTINGS, Apollos 206 Heman
  39 201 253 Lucy 201 253
  Martha 206
HATCH, Mary 256 Moses
  Porter 225 Timothy 225
HAWKINS, Cornelia 68 200
  Don 200 Hattie 200 John 86
  Maria 200 Riley 200
HAWLEY, Fanny 208 Walliston
  208
HAY, Arch 251 Clarisa 251
HAYES, Helen 187 James 187
HAYNES, Lemuel 146 Rev Mr
  137
HAYWARD, Ebenezer 61 Uriel
  R 24
HENCHITT, Mary 235
HENRY, Andr 139 Andrew 40
  98 201 Jeffrey J 201

HENSHAW, Elizabeth 169
HERRICK, Alta 171 Col 12 83
    97 157 238 Edward 171 220
    Mrs 218 Samuel 15
HERRING, Susan 191
HICKS, Edmund 24
HIGGINS, Zadock 151
HIGHWAYS, And Bridges 112
HILL, Abial 228 Charles K 201
    Diantha 201 Dorothy 202
    George 166 Nathaniel 21
    191 201 Nathaniel Jr 201
    Phebe 229 Vesta 191
HITCHCOCK, Adolphus F 189
    Cynthia 189 David 239
    Eliza 239
HITT, Anson 201 Caleb S 201
    Caroline 201 Galen R 103
    201 John E 100 201 Maria
    201 Mary 201 243 Samuel
    169 Sarah 201 Smith 201
    243 Sophia 201 William H
    201
HITTS, Smith 59
HOLBROOK, Helen 248 Mr 248
    William C 132
HOLLISTER, A Sidney 202
    Albert E 24 203 Amos 202-
    203 Anna 202 Ashbel 21 40
    59-60 202 Ashbel W 202
    Augusta C 203 Calvin 100
    203-204 Caroline 202
    Caroline C 203 Catharine
    203 David 148 202 Dorothy
    202 Elijah 21 204 Emory
    203 Estelle 203 Francis S 24
    203 253 Franklin 27
    Frederic M 203 Frederick M
    27 98 Hartley 203 Harvey
    202 Hiel 41-42 98 202-203
    Horace 202 Horatio 203 239
    Innett 21 150 203 Innis 27
    39 111 203-204 Iunett 40 42

HOLLISTER (cont.)
    Jane 203 Joan 202 John 202
    John Jr 202 Josiah 202 Julia
    202-203 253 Laura 203-204
    245 Lois 204 Lucy 203
    Martha 202 204 Marvin 103
    204 Mary 202-204 Mrs
    Ashbel 104 Orange 202
    Orange S 203 Penelope 202
    Sarah 202 Sarah M 203
    Thomas 202 Willis H 24 203
    Zilpha 202
HOLMES, Melissa E 166
HOMESTEAD, 81
HOOKER, 181 Gen 129 131 219
HOPKINS, Ervin 40 68 204
    Frank 204 James 21 40 103
    183 204 Margaret 266
    Miriam 143 204 Nancy 243
HOPSON, John C 217
HORR, Angenette 168 Ann 167
    John 167 Julia Ann 229
HOSFORD, Henry R 41 204 232
    245 Melvina 204 232 Mrs
    232
HOTCHKISS, Socrates 250
HOTELS, 111
HOUGH, 258 John 141
HOUGHTALING, J B 146
HOUGHTON, A Sidney 42 71
    100 205 Charles 100-101
    205 Eliza 205 Fanny M 205
    James 98
HOUSE, Mercy 243
HOWARD, Sewell F 24
HOWE, Desdia 232 Ellen 157
    Roxana 256 Samuel 146
HOY, James 24 Michael 27
    Michael Jr 27
HOYT, Abigail 254 Fowler W
    254
HSOFORD, Henry R 232
HUBBARD, 147 Anna 191

HUGGINS, Mary 204 William R 204
HULBERT, 147
HULETT, Adelia 206 Alzina 205 258 Anna 206 Betsey 205-206 Charles 195 Chester B 24 Daniel 21 104 111 171 205 Daniel 2nd 233 Daniel Jr 205-206 Dewitt 111 Dyer 206 235 Eunice 206 Galen L 206 Hannah 205 Harmony 206 Jared 205 249 John S 122 205 Joshua 116 205-206 Joshua Jr 36 206 Josiah 205 Juna 206 Lydia 206 Margaret 206 Marshal 206 Martha 206 Miranda 211 Mr 205-206 Nancy 171 Olive 205 Orestes B 205 Orlin 169 205 211 Orson G 205 Paul 40 83-84 145-146 169 205 258 Paulina 169 205 Philetus N 205 Sally 206 Tobias 206 Warren E 24
HULL, Mr 228
HUMPHREY, John O 24
HUMPHREYS, Col 126 247
HUNT, Nathaniel 102-103
HURD, Bethel 112 237 Mary 237
HURLBURT, Lucy B 68
HURLBUT, Ashbel 207 Betsey 207 Catharine 203 Lucius B 207 Lucy 207 Lucy B 207 Mr 207 Sally 245 Walter 103 Walter S 207
HUTCHINS, Benjamin 21 Bulkley 21 206 230 Elizabeth 206 Irene 206 Lois 206 230 Mr 206 Nathan 21
HYDE, Azariah 67 141 206 245 Betsey 184 Charles B 24

HYDE (cont.)
Elijah 184 Lt 16
INCORPORATED, Manufacturing Companies 152
INGALSBEE, Alta 236 Levi 236
INTRODUCTION, 3
JACKSON, Gen 46 76 80 President 215
JENNINGS, James 207 Jonathan 207 Joseph 207 Laura 207 Linus 207 Sally 207 Walter 58
JEWETT, Stephen 145
JOHNSON, Austin 149 Campbell 100 Chipman R 251 Delia 186 Elizabeth 206 Florace 61 208 George 24 29 Harriet 208 J G 135 James 36 111 207 John G 24 29 Leonard 27 41 43 61 208 Mahala 208 Maria 251 Ruth 207
JONES, Ahira 208 Asa S 37 58 170 208 Bulah 246 Catharine 163 209 Charles 89 Chloe 208 Deacon 208 Deborah 208 Eli 208 Ephraim 27 60 150 208 Ephraim Jr 208 Esther 221 Fanny 208 Frank 27 100 Frank H 208 Franklin 252 Harrison 208 Harry 208 Harry B 243 Hiram 208-209 Jane 170 Janett 243 Jared 208 Joel 58 208 John 208 Joseph 208 221 246 Julia 159 Lewis F 159 Mariette 208 Mary 252 Merritt C 208 Mrs Joseph 104 Parker 159 Rachel 208 Rosanna 208 Sarah 159 208 254 Silas 20 208 Silas Jr 254 Sophia 208

## FULLNAME INDEX. 285

JUDSON, 97-98 Nathan 67 100
  163 209 Ruth 245
KEELER, Fanny 254
KEIGWIN, Joseph 156
  Margaret 156
KELLEY, Mrs 192
KELLY, David 208 Holden 233
  Judith 249 Lydia 206
  Obadiah 233 Rosanna 208
  Roswell 146
KELVIA, William 25
KENDALL, Mary 203 Zuba 177
KENNEDY, Ronald A 132
KENT, Chancellor 204 Miriam
  204 Rev Mr 137 Sylvester
  100 Widow 255
KIERNAN, John 147 209
KILLAM, Phineas 224 Sarah
  224 Thankful 224
KING, Almira 254 Chanucy 254
  H W 221
KINGSLEY, Charles M 24 Elias
  230
KINNEY, Lyman 164 Minerva
  164
KIRBY, John 156 Mary 156
KITCHEL, Alson L 24
KNAPP, Harriet 188 Merrick
  188
KNIGHST, Louisa M 209
KNIGHTS, George W 209
KNOX, Gen 212
KOSCIUSKO, 202
LACKEY, James 24
LAING, Thomas 148-149
LAMB, Caroline 167 Charles
  169 Mary I 169 Nicholas 24
  William 167
LAMPSON, Truman 209
LASELL, Abby H 168 Amanda
  185
LASSOR, Baptiste 24 Vital 24
LATHE, Fanny 180

LATHE (cont.)
  Henry S 24 156 Marcia 253
  Sylvanus 253
LAY, Amos 209 Betsey 195
LEACH, Amy 210 Casper N 39
  210 Ebenezer 210 Elizabeth
  210 Ellen 210 Frances 210
  Gideon C 210 Harriet 210
  Henry W 98 100 210 James
  20 40-42 170 174 209-210
  234 James Jr 40 210 James
  Sr 156 Jude 156 Julia 242
  Lois B 210 Lophelia 210
  Lorenzo 210 Lorenzo D 24
  Louisa 210 Lovell 36 209-
  210 232 Lucretia 210 Lucy
  210 232 Martin V 210 242
  Mr 210 Mrs James 104
  Olive 210 Wesley 210
  William 210
LEE, Emma 257 Gen 134 James
  L 237 257 Laura 211
  Loammi 211 Mary 75 237
LEFFINGWELL, Jeremiah 158
  Julia 158
LEONARD, Jacob 147 Lucy 221
LEWIS, David 169 Dr 234
  Phebe 169
LIBRARIES, And Periodicals 68
LICENSE, Caroline 201
LINCOLN, Deborah 211 266
  Fidelia 210-211 Lettie T 68
  210 Lewis 98 210 Luther P
  211 266 President 13
LITTLE, Eugene 24
LOCAL, Government 38
  Literature 47 Militia 34
  Politics 43
LOOMER, Joseph 100
LOOMIS, Abner 212 Amanda
  172 211 Annis 175 B
  Newbury 103 Benjamin N
  211 Candace 211 214

LOOMIS (cont.)
  Deborah 266 Edmund 212
  Elijah M 212 George B 211
  Gideon A 27 35 39 169 172
  211 214 Hattie 211 Henry W
  211-212 Jane 212 Jerusha
  211 Johnson 175 Jude 211
  Julia C 211 232 Laura 211
  Lester 211 Lucia 169 211
  Maria 211-212 Mary 211-
  212 253 Mercy 212 Miranda
  211 Mr 212 Mrs Roswell 104
  Nancy 212 Nathaniel 211
  Oliver 211 253 Orla 112 211
  232 Owen 27 211 Roswell
  212 Sally 227 Stephen 227
  William F 24
LOUNSBERRY, Nathan M 212
LOUNSBURY, Nathan M 20
LOVEJOY, 83
LOVELAND, Hosea 166 Laura
  172 Lydia 166
LOWELL, Elder 148
LUMBARD, Abner 35 59 212
  242 257-258 Chester 59 212
  Fanny 212 Franklin 212
  Hiram 212 Julia 212 258
  Mrs Abner 104 Pamela 212
  Sarah 212 Sina 212 Sophia
  212 257
LUTHER, Martin 69
LYMAN, Eleazer 111 202 Mary
  202
LYON, 150 186 Anna 213 Emily
  213 Hannah 171 Harriet
  213 264 Jacob 171 173 213
  241 Lydia 213 241 Mr 151
MACOMBER, Wyman L 25
MAGITT, S O A 25
MAHER, Catharine 213 James
  213 Margaret 213 William
  60 213
MANNING, George 25

MANUFACTURES, 557
MARKETS, 98
MARKS, Ann 213 Cornwell 213
  Electa 213-214 Elisha 98
  111 213 Goodrich 213 Ira 36
  39 42 60-61 98 213-214 Mrs
  Cornwall 104 Mrs Cornwell
  150 Prudence 213-214
  Reuben 98 Rosanna 213
  Sarah 213 Sarah Ann 214
  William 213
MARSH, George P 214 William
  40 83 214
MARSHALL, Helen 188 J W
  100 John W 188
MARTIN, Candace 211 214
  George D 211 214 Job H 67
MASON, 24 Almira 214 Alta
  214 237 James N 199 214
  237 Joel A 25 133
MATTIS, Dinah 13 Nancey 13
MCARTHUR, Franklin S 25 29
MCBRINN, James 29 Michael
  25 29
MCCLELLAN, 219 Gen 129 131
  218
MCDANIELS, Isaac 207 James
  159 Lucy B 207 Nancy 159
MCFADDEN, Charlotte 256
  Edward 215 Henry 215
  Jacob 27 215 256 Michael
  215 Stephen 61 144 163 214
MCGRATH, Daniel 30 262
  James 25 30 John 25
  Patrick 25
MCKENNA, Edward 25
  Thomas 25
MCLAUGHLIN, Mary Ann 221
MCNAUGHTON, Findlay 215
  248 Findley 40 180 Martha
  180 Nancy 248
MCWAIN, Elhanan 27 215 Eliza
  215 Emily 165

## FULLNAME INDEX. 287

MCWAIN (cont.)
  Leroy D 27 215 Lucy 215
  Mahala 215 Nathaniel 27
  215 Sylvanus 25 215
MCWHORTER, Caroline 202
  Samuel 202
MEACHAM, Abraham 139 Asa
  215 Isaac 139 Jacob 237
  Lucien B 237 Lucy 237
  Patience 237 Proserpine 198
  Silas 100 Thomas 215
  Willard 198
MEACHAN, Abraham 215
MEAD, Elder 147 Gen 129 131
  219 Timothy 14
MECHANICS, 62
MEEKER, Cyrus 147 Mr 66
MEIGS, Benjamin C 215
  Charles 103 215 Dr 195
  Sarah 195
MENONA, Paul 215
MERCHANTS, 96
MERRILL, 100
MEXICAN, War 22
MICHAEL, Mary 191
MILES, Prudence 214 Samuel
  237 Sarah 237 William 214
MILLER, 183 Lucy 203 Martha
  202 William 151
MILLS, Allen 222 Melissa 222
MINER, Lamson 66 Sherman
  147
MOFFATT, Joel 139
MOFFITT, Alvin 27 Hiram 27
  216 Judah 20 216 Luther 27
  Mrs Judah 104 Nancy 216
MONROE, Alta 216 Asa A 42
  160 216-217 Asa L 25 30
  Atherton 25 30 Axa 217
  Calif 217 Chauncey 216
  Emeline 216 Giles 217 Isaac
  67 100 Jesse 149 216-217
  242 Jonathan 61

MONROE (cont.)
  Joseph C 216 Josiah 20 35
  40 160 216-217 223 Lucinda
  217 Lucy 217 Mary 223
  Nathan 217 Nelson 67 R G
  67-68 246 Renselaer G 100
  Rensselaer G 217 Susan 216
  William 176 198 216
MONTAGUE, Adonijah 217
MONTGOMERY, Hugh 21
MOON, Lois 204
MOORE, Grove 199 Henry J
  217 John 253 Lemuel 25
  Maria 167 Mark S 25 Mary
  A 253 Silas 167
MORGAN, Huldah 183
  Jonathan 183
MORRISON, Alma 254 Miranda
  234 Orville 100
MOSBY, 129
MOSELEY, Abisha 40 Abishai
  100-101 Dr 100 John 40
MOSES, Widow 200
MOSHER, Clarissa 30 231
  Elder 148 Thomas C 25 30
  231
MOTHERS, Of The Town 103
MURDOCK, Rev Mr 137
MURPHY, James 25
MURRAY, Francis 30 Maria 30
MUSIC, 69
NARMON, Nathaniel 103
NELSON, B H 148 Daniel D
  203 Emeroy 203 Huldah 251
  Jane 197 John W 256
  Nehemiah 185 251 Samuel
  W 25 Sophia 185
NEWTON, Polly 263 Thomas 25
  Thomas T 263
NICHOLS, C C 122 Calvin S 25
  Dr 122 William T 134
NORCROSS, Sarah 266
NORTON, James 183 270

NORTON (cont.)
   Mr 217-218 Phebe 167
   Sylvester 98 Theron 60 98
   217 220
NYE, Edward 25 269 Jonathan
   152 Louisa 218 Mrs
   Timothy 104 Nathaniel 218
   269 Timothy 218
OATMAN, Eli 237 Mary 237
   Sylvia 226
OCCUM, Sampson 216
OLD, School House 73
OLDS, A W 149 Abel W 218
OLIPHANT, Capt 162
ORCUTT, Hugh 218 Philinda
   218
ORR, George S 22 25 39 131 218
   220 Henrietta 218 Horace J
   25 John A 43 98 208 256
   Lena 220 Lucinda 256 Maj
   219 Moses E 22 25 131 220
ORVIS, Elihu 98 220 251
   Joseph U 220 Sina 220 251
OTTARSON, B Fitch 213 John
   213 Margaret 213
PACKER, Joseph 147
PAGE, Martha 204 Sophia 208
PARDEE, Amos 145
PARK, Paul 224 Sarah 224
PARKER, Col 256 Helen 237
   Joseph 237 Mary 256
PARRIS, Caleb 180 Hannah 180
   Harvey 220 Isaac T 208 Levi
   27 220 Merritt C 25 Orla
   220 Rachel 208
PATTERSON, Levi 25
PAUL, Alva 100-101 Phineas 37
PAWLET, And Wells
   Agricultural Society 122
PEARL, Col 221 Stephen 37 40
   98 111 220
PECK, David B 132 Harriet 210
   265 Joseph 265

PELTON, Charles 21
PEMBER, Emily 167 Russell
   167
PENFIELD, Alma 221
   Amoretta 221 Amorette 164
   Betsey S 221 Caroline 221
   Daniel 221 Deacon 252
   Eunice 221 Fanny A 221
   Franklin 176 Harriet D 221
   Horace 36 221 John 142 164
   221 236 245 John Jr 152
   Laura 221 Lemira 176
   Maria 221 Mary Ann 198
   221 Patience 221 Sarah 221
PENTONY, John 25
PEPPER, Amelia 222 Anna 221-
   222 Asahel 221 Ashbel H 27
   221 Caroline 222 Chauncey
   P 183 Chauncy P 221-222
   Clarinda 255 Danforth 221
   Esther 192 221-222 Flotilla
   222 Hamilton 222 Helotia
   221 Hiram 222 James 222
   John 192 221 Julia 222
   Katie 222 Lefa 222 Louisa
   221 Lovina 197 221 Lucy
   221 Margaret 169 Mary 202
   221 Melissa 222 Mr 222 Mrs
   222 Narcissa 183 221
   Orcelia 222 Philena 221
   Philene 221 Seba 183 222
   Seth B 169 221 Simeon 20
   27 183 197 221 255 Simeon
   Jr 197 221 Warren D 222
   Willard 221
PERHAM, Charlotte 254
   Hubert 25 Merritt 25
PERKINS, 55 147 Electa 222
   Jacob 116 197 222 Lucy 197
   Lydia 222 Mary 222 Mr 222
   Mrs Jacob 104 Olive 222
   Rufus 179 222 Salinda 222
   Walter 222 Wesley 60

PERKINS (cont.)
   William F 223
PERRY, David 137 Rev Mr 137
   Roxana 254
PHELPS, Ann 223 J Wolcott
   131 Lophelia 210 Mary 171
   Merritt C 183 223 Rachel S
   244 William U 210
PHILLIPS, Alkanah 217 Ardelia
   264 Axa 217 Betsey 205
   Charles 165 251 Elkanah
   223 264 Mary 223 Mrs
   Elkanah 104-105 Samuel
   223
PHYSICIANS, And Diseases 99
PIAGET, Ellen S 266 Louis 266
PIERCE, Dilla 183 William 183
PITKIN, Hannah 223 Mary Ann
   223 Sylvester 36 86 146 223
PLUMB, Alta 223 Elijah W 67-
   68 141 223 Rev Dr 170
   Sarah 223
POETRY, 550
POMROY, John 224 Lucy 201
   Olive 248
POOR, David 147
POPE, Gen 129 131 219
PORTER, 82 Benjamin 225
   Caroline 225 Dea 224
   Deacon 225 Deidamia 197
   Dorothy 225 Elijah 101 225
   Experience 224 Helen 247
   Hervey 225 John K 103 189
   224-225 Joseph 40 86 142
   225 Moses 20 37 40 139 142
   171 189 224-225 253 Moses
   2nd 101 247 Moses Jr 101
   Moses R 225 Mrs Moses 105
   Robert 101 Sally 189 225
   Samuel 223 Sarah 224-225
   Sophia 225 Thomas 224
POSTMASTERS, 42
POTTER, Amanda 182 226

POTTER (cont.)
   Betsey 182 226 C W 101
   Charles W 43 98 226 Collins
   226 Edwin 103 226 Ellen L
   226 Fanny 212 Fayette 39
   67 102-103 226 George 101
   226 Helen L 232 James 226
   Jane 226 234 Joshua 40 42
   89 182 225-226 Keyes 25 Mr
   226 Phebe 226 Samuel 100-
   101 212 225-226 232 Samuel
   Jr 101 Sylvia 226 William
   20 40 225
PRATT, Alta 227 Alva 36 227
   Byron A 227 Capt 166 181
   193 Caroline 227 Charlotte
   180 Dorcas 190 227 Elisha
   87 105 226-227 Ervin 42 218
   226-227 Esther 227
   Francelia 227 Harvey 180
   Henrietta 218 227 James 20
   35 40 87 190 226-227 James
   Jr 36 Lucy 226-227
   Marrietta 227 Martin V B
   43 98 227 Mary 227 Miner
   67 142 227 Minor 227 Mr 98
   Phebe 227 Philene 227
   Quincy 227 Sally 227
   Samuel 20 227 Sarah 227
PRESCOTT, G A 252 Gustavus
   A 214 228 John C 214
   Nancy 228 252 Prudence
   214
PRESTON, Caroline 222 Jamon
   22
PRIEST, Josiah 20
PRINDLE, Cyrus 147
PURPLE, George H 36 42 97
   228 Sophia 228
PUTNAM, 224 Betsey 250 Gen
   11 Jacob 250 Mary 257 Ruth
   250
QUINLAND, 147 Michael 27

RAID, Road 105
RANDALL, Anna 168 228 Caleb 201 Hannah 223 Jonathan 41 110 153 168 228 Maria 201 Mr 154
RANSOM, Albert A 222 Flotilla 222
RAYNOR, Alonzo 210 Lettie T 210
REDDING, 19 David 18
REED, Abial 228-229 Abigail 228 Allen H 229 Almira 168 229 Alta 229 Annette 254-255 Benjamin 222 Betsey 229 Calvin 25 Charles A 229 Colby 228 Curtis 168 229 Delia L 229 Elbridge J 25 Eliakim 228-229 Elijah 230 Elliott 229 Enoch 228-229 Esther 184-185 228 Ezra 184 199 228-229 Fanny 229 Harriet 229 Ira S 229 Isaac 21 230 James 228 Jedediah 14 20 39-40 137 139 229-230 238 Julia A 222 Julia Ann 229 Laura 229 Louise 229 Lyman 36 230 Mary 229 Mary Ann 229 Mr 228 Mrs Simeon 105 Phebe 229 Philip 39-40 139 230 Ruth 228 Sarah 199 229 Silas 184 199 228-229 Simeon 20 228-229 Solomon 88 230 Sophia 199 229 Stephen 35 228-229
REMINGTON, Annis 175 Frank 261 Henry 175 261 Sophia 261 Zadoc 261
REPRESENTATIVES, To Assembly 41
REVIEW, Of Our Wars 31
REVOLUTIONARY, War 11
REYNOLDS, Elder 148 L P 147 Worden P 148-149 230

RICE, Abial 228 Ann 230 Anna 158 Caroline 230 253 Catharine 230 Daniel 230 James 42-43 98 158 230 253 Lois 230 Marcia 230 Warren 27 230
RICHARDSON, David 152
RILEY, Margaret 244 Robert 244
RIPLEY, Edward H 132
RISDEN, Catharine 255
RISDON, Daniel 20 John 20
RISING, Mary 227
ROACH, Anna 221 Betsey 191 James 191 Minerva 264
ROBBINS, Rev Mr 138
ROBERTS, Isaac 149 Marrietta 227
ROBERTSON, Sarah J 178
ROBINNSON, David 27
ROBINSON, Abbot 226 232 Abel 21 197 232 Anna 232 Benjamin 232 Betsey 231 Capt 231-232 Charles 231 Chauncey H 231 Chauncy H 25 Clarissa 30 231 David 211 231-232 David W 232 Denzill F 27 232 Desdia 232 Edward H 27 Eliza Jane 232 Ephraim 21 172 213 232 Ephraim Jr 204 232 Erastus 232 Ezra 232 Ezra H 231 Fayette S 231 Francis 231 Frank 231 George 231-232 George B 232 Hannah 231 Helen L 226 232 Henry M 232 James B 27 176 James N 210 231 Jemima 172 232 Jonathan 152 Julia C 211 232 Laura 231 Laura B 171 Louisa 231 Lucy 210 232 Luthera 232 Lydia 231 Maria 232 Marietta 231

# FULLNAME INDEX.   291

ROBINSON (cont.)
   Mariette 176 Mary 52 54
   231-232 Mary Ann 232 Mr
   231-232 Mrs Jonathan 105
   Mrs Nathaniel 105 Nath'l 20
   Nathaniel 60 153 230-231
   Nathaniel H 232 Nathaniel
   Hollis 27 Nathaniel Jr 152
   231 Otis 232 Rachel 231
   Rhoda 232 254 Richard 21
   232 Rosanna 213 232 Sally
   231 Samuel 232 Sophia 232
   Sophronia 232 Thomas C
   232 William 231 William B
   231 William C 152 Willis
   232 Wm B 30
ROGERS, Deliverance 183
   Elisha F 42 Salina 250
ROLLIN, Ebenezer 60 233
ROOT, William 39
ROSE, Abigail 260 Roger 40 118
   233 260 Samuel 151
ROSS, Rebecca 197
ROWE, Anna 213 Emily 213
   Harvey 213 Hippocrates 67
   142 Wesley 213
ROWLEY, Delia 234 Laura 169
   Lee T 169 234
ROYALS, Benjamin B 26
RUSH, Aboltus 233 George 20
   233 249 Jacob 233
RUSSELL, Charles 25 Charles
   H 27
SAFFORD, Annis 159 233-234
   Caroline 233 Delia 233-234
   Dr 233 Edwin B 234 Eliza
   233-234 267 Horace 233
   Jane 234 Joanthan 233
   Jonathan 40 100-101 159
   187 267 Jonathan W 233-
   234 Joseph B 233 250
   Joshua 234 Rebecca 233
SAFORD, Edwin B 233

SAGE, Benjamin 35 166 Sarah
   M 203
SAMPSON, Sophia 225
SANDERS, Elder 147
SARGEANT, John 21 35
SARGENT, Betsey 235 Chloe
   235 Daniel 234 Delight 142
   234-235 Dr 210 Epenetus A
   234 Helen 73 John 37 40-41
   58 100-101 234 John Jr 67
   100-101 234 Lemuel 235
   Leonard 102-103 234-235
   Martha 234 Mercy 235
   Miranda 234 Mr 235 Nancy
   234 Ralph 35 234 Royal 35
   58 234 Silas 235 Warren B
   67 100-101 234-235
SAVAGE, David 195 Elmira 195
   Mr 60
SCOTT, Charles H 25 John 25
   174 Mary 174 Richard 25
SCOVILL, Erastus 25
SCOVILLE, Henry 110
SEARL, Amyll 252 Helen 252
SEARLE, Amyill B 25 Oliver L
   25
SEARLES, John 147
SEARS, Rhoda 189
SELECT, Men From 1775 40
SELKIRK, Alexander 81
SEMPLE, Marion 238
SHAW, Francis R 25 Harriet
   252 Helen 174 James M 41
   122 174 213 243-244 Mahala
   215
SHEARS, 147
SHEDD, Sarah 158
SHELDEN, Philene 227
SHELDON, Alta 236 Artemas
   101 Chauncy 236 Cornelia
   180 236 Daniel 236 David
   236 David F 236 Esther 228
   236 Ezra R 236

SHELDON (cont.)
   Franklin 236 Hannah 185
   Harvey 236 Heman 228
   Henrietta 186 Henry 236
   Hiram 101 236 Ira 236 Joel
   180 184 229 Joel H 221 236
   Joel Jr 236 Julia 236
   Lucinda 236 Marcia 236
   Mary 229 235-236 Mr 236
   Nancy 236 247 Newton 236
   Philena 184 Philene 236
   Philo 186 Rachel 242 Sally
   184 236 Sarah 236 Seth 36
   40 184 206 235 Seth Jr 236
   247 Seth P 71 95 Sibel 143
   Silas 29 Thaddeus D 98
   Thomas D 43 Tichenor 236
   William 98
SHEPHERD, 172 Fayette 223
   Moses 236 Silas 192 Susan
   192
SHERIDAN, 130 James 26
SHERMAN, 211 Flora 175-176
   Gen 129 Josiah R 178 237
   Lydia S 237
SHERWOOD, Mary E 258
SHIPHERD, Fayette 68 83-84
   86 141 236 Zebulon R 236
SHORT, Joseph 246
SILL, Rev Mr 137
SIMONDS, Alta 214 237 Annis
   237 257 Benjamin 15 238
   Bethiah 237 Col 14-15 238
   Emily 250 Fanny 238
   George O 26 238 Hannah
   237 Harriet 264 Helen 237
   Ira 237 Joel 40-41 112 139
   146 180 237 Joel Jr 39-40
   214 237 248 257 Joel Sr 217
   238 John 27 237 250 Jonah
   237 Joseph 237 Justin F 27
   39 101 237-238 257 Justin F
   2nd 237 Louise 237

SIMONDS (cont.)
   Lucy 237 Marion 238 Mary
   237 Melissa 238 248 Mr 237-
   238 Mrs 14 Mrs Joel 105
   Ossian H 41 237-238 248
   Patience 180 237 Sarah 237
   Tabitha 246
SISCO, Samuel 143
SKEELS, Elder 143
SKINNER, Ashbel 139 John B
   238
SLOANE, James 35
SMITH, 55 Abigail 239 242
   Alonzo 213 241 263 Alta 242
   Amanda 242 Ann 68 213-
   214 239 Anna 239 Arthur
   239-240 Benjamin 239
   Benoni 40 59 144 172 212
   232 238 Betsey 239 David H
   27 David R 160 163 Deborah
   242 Electa 179 214 Elisha
   21 35 Eliza 239 Elizabeth
   239 Emily 239 Ephraim 27
   239 Esther M 187 Frederic
   241 255 George 145 149 240
   Gov 241 Harriet 241-242
   255 Henry 163 Henry H 103
   Hiram 212 Hoel 239-240 Ira
   239-240 260 Irene 240 Israel
   67 102-103 241 James 58
   101 202 240 James H 26
   Jemima 172 232 239 John
   26 115 214 239 241 Joseph
   181 213 Joseph Sr 150
   Josiah 144 202 239 Judson
   O 242 Julia 202 239 Justin
   101 240 Laura 239 Lena 220
   Lisemore 21 Lydia 213 241-
   242 Marcia 230 Maria 212
   240 260 Martin 26 Mary 163
   Melvina 204 232 Mima 239
   Mr 66 137 239 Nancy 212
   Nathan 14

FULLNAME INDEX. 293

SMITH (cont.)
Nathaniel 36 40-41 206 238
Noah 67 102-103 241 Noal
239 O Judson 26 Penelope
202 239 Pliny 238 Reuben
40 112 150 193 214 239 260
Robert H 35 39-42 239 Ruth
239-240 Salinda 222 Sally
251 Samuel 251 Sarah 239
260 Simon 21 242 Sophia
229 Sylvester 187 Thaddeus
212 Vesta Ann 242
Zephaniah H 240 Zephaniah
Hollister 137
SNELL, Hattie 211 242 James
242 John 27 242 Julia 242
Lois 242 Rhoda 242 Samuel
27 242
SOLDIERS', Obituary 28
Record 23
SOULLARD, E S 147 Edward S
217 242 Fanny 242 Julianna
242
SPAULDING, Nathan 26
SPENCER, 147 Chester 242
Stephen 139 242
SPINK, Edwin I 67
SPOONER, Paul 14
SPRAGUE, Betsey 186 Ezra
147 Phebe 226 Rev Mr 186
226
SQUIER, Truman 102-103 242
STANDISH, Miles 224
STANNARD, Amanda 266 Gen
135 Rev Mr 266
STAPLES, Jonathan 41 173 243
256 Phebe 173 Ruth 256
STARK, Gen 19 John 20 36 40
42 167 208 211 243 Rachel
208 Samuel 243 Sarah 260
Widow 258
STARKWEATHER, Stephen
139

STEARNS, David 215 243 Dr
200 James 243 Janett 243
John 27 35 110 149 215 243
John Jr 27 201 Maria 200
Mary 201 243 Nancy 200
243 Seth 61 243
STEPHENS, Isaac 139
STEVENS, Addie 176 Alvira
245 Annis 244 Asa 21 245
Ashbel 204 244-245 Betsey
207 244 David 244 Elijah
172 244-245 Elisha 244
Esther 245 Hoel 244 James
244 Jared 244 Jerusha 244
Joel 125 244 Jonathan 58-59
244 Joseph 243-244 Laura
204 245 Lora 244 Malona
244 Margaret 244 Mary 244
Mercy 243 Minerva 267 Mr
244-245 Peter 20 40 174 207
243-244 Rachel S 244
Robert 59 182 Robert R 244
Sally 245 Samuel 244 Sarah
169 Sector 244 Theodore 98
Thomas 244 Timothy 244
William 21 112 245 248 267
William H 204
STEWART, John 40 Philo P 142
245
STILES, Sally 250 Seth P 147
250
STOCK, 124 Cattle 125 Dogs
128 Horses 124 Poultry 127
Sheep 127
STODDARD, Abigail 245
Judson B 142 245 Nathan
36 Nathan A 245 Rucard 36
Ruth 245 William 245 265
STONE, Levi H 68 141 245
Simon 38
STRATTON, Bulah 246 Hannah
192 Levi 192 Mrs Samuel
105 Roxana 246 254

STRATTON (cont.)
  Samuel 20 246 254 267
  Tabitha 246 Tryphena 246
  267
STREETER, M H 100 246
STRONG, 82 Ann Eliza 248
  Ann F 246-247 Anna 246
  Betsey 246 Betsy 167 Capt
  247 Eliza Ann 159 247
  Gustavus 246-247 Gustavus
  A 248 Guy C 142 246-247
  Helen 225 246-248 James W
  27 John 27 58 244 246-248
  Justin 246 Laura 247-248
  Laura D 247 Marcellus 248
  Martin D 27 39 41 43 98 246
  Melissa 238 248 Nancy 247-
  248 Phineas 39-40 42 97 152
  159 225 246-247 Phineas Jr
  100-101 Return 21-22 39-40
  42 97 139 246-247 255
  Return Jr 247 Rollin F 67
  103 246 Sabra 248 Thomas
  D 101 247 Thomas J 27 248
  Timothy 111 247 Walter 35
  39 42 246-247 Zopher 246
STRONGG, Phineas Jr 101
STUART, 129 John 66
SUMNER, 83
SWALLOW, Joel 229 Lucy 176
  Sophia 229 Thomas J 35 43
  98
SWEET, Elder 147
SWIFT, Alta 248 Ann 248
  Louisa 248 Louise 237 Mary
  248 Nathan 237 248 Rev Mr
  137
SYKES, Augustus 103 Jacob 21
  248 Laura 231 Minerva 248
  Mr 248
TAFT, Austin 26
TAYLOR, Ahira 249 Charles P
  26 30 249 Cyrus P 26 39 249

TAYLOR (cont.)
  Daniel P 43 248 Elias 249
  Elias P 248 Eliza 249
  George 31 George W 26 249
  Hattie 200 Horace 27 John
  P 248 Matilda 187 Neville
  249 Olive 248 Samuel 139
  248 252 Samuel Jr 30-31
  183 209 249 Sylvester 27
  249 William 27 249 Zadoc
  248
TEALL, Anna 202 Asaph 144
  Joseph 202
TEMPERANCE, 84
THOMPSON, Asa 192 264
  Daniel D 177 Dr 88 Festus
  22 Harriet 160 249 Henry H
  26 James 137 Jemima 192
  John 40 Judith 249 Laura A
  264 Lucy 171 Mary 244
  Oscar F 244 Phebe 193
  Prudence 249 Samuel 160
  170 233 249 Warren 193
THORN, Mary 156
TILDEN, Chloe 249 Ithamar
  100-101 233 249 Philo 101
  Rebecca 233
TINGUE, Emily A 266 George
  266
TOBY, Abigail 169 250 Arthur
  169 250 Azro 249 Betsey
  174 249-250 Chipman I 26
  Chipman J 122 249 Chloe
  249 Deacon 249 Emily 250
  George 162 249 251 Hannah
  249 John 214 249 Josiah 35
  40 143 174 181 249 251
  Josiah Jr 249 Laura 249
  Lorette 249 251 Lydia 249
  Margaret 181 Mercy 249
  Mrs Reuben 105 Rebecca
  249-250 Reuben 40 147 249-
  250 Ruth 250 Salina 250

FULLNAME INDEX.    295

TOBY (cont.)
   Sally 250 Zenas 250 Zeno
     249
TODD, Dr 100 Eliel 21 100-101
   233 250 Jonathan 250
TOOLEY, Lucy 215 Sally 207
TOPOGRAPHY, 5
TOWN, 209 Clerks From 1769
   39 Farm 114 William 26
TOWSLEE, Charles W 26
   Henry 26 Norman 101
TRACY, Amasa S 131
TRAIN, Sally 187
TREAT, Joan 202
TRUMBULL, Alexander 143
TRYON, David 36 250 Dennis
   250-251 Jesse 182 250
   Jonathan 250 Mary 250
   Nancy 250 Penelope 250
   Sally 250-251 Socrates H 67
   101 251
TUTTLE, Huldah 251 Rosabella
   105 251
TYLER, Anna 239 Benjamin
   239
U, S Deposit Fund 119
UPHAM, Ann 251 Clarisa 251
   Clarissa 251 Huldah 251
   John 169 251 Joseph 251
   Joseph P 40 150 220 249 251
   Lorette 249 251 Maria 251
   Mr 251 Paulina 251 Pauline
   169 Sina 220 251
URAN, James 11 21 Sally 165
USAGES, And Customs And
   Observances 90
UTLEY, Fidelia 251 Jane 251
   Leonard 36 60 251
VAIL, 111 Allen 195 Amasa 196
   Chester M 26 Polly 195
VAUGHN, Ann Eliza 248
   Daniel 149 Edna 248
VIETS, Deborah 208

VIETS (cont.)
   Emeline 252 Eunice 252
   Fayette 252 Harriet 208 252
   Harvey 36 252 Helen 252
   Henry 36 208 252 Lura 252
   Martin 252 Mary 252 Mrs
   Seth 105 Seth 21 249 251-
   252 Seth Jr 252 Seth Sr 177
   W, L 196
WADE, Alpheus 228 252 Anne
   252 Hiram 252 John 252
   Mary 252 Mr 252 Nancy 228
   252 Nelson 252 Rachel 252
WAIT, A 147 Archibald 147 256
   Celestia 172 David 22
   Densia 172 Dewitt C 172
   265 Elder 143 148 Hiram
   177 Josephine 265 Lorene
   256 Rachel 255 Washington
   G 172 Washington Z 147
   255-256
WALBRIDGE, Ebenezer 15
WALDEN, 36
WALKER, Chandler 149 J F
   147 Jason F 66 146 149 252
   Lydia S 237 Mr 149
   Sylvester 147
WALL, Edward 242 Vesta Ann
   242
WALLACE, William 40 97-98
   153-154 252
WAR, Of 1812 21 Of 1861 To
   1865 22
WARNER, Angelia 253 Col 12
   19 Elisha 253 Gen 15 James
   M 133 Julia 203 253 Katie
   222 Lucy 253 Marcia 253
   Mark 253 Mark Jr 203 253
   Mary 253 Mary A 253 Mr
   253 Olive J 197 253 Oliver L
   253 Seth 224 Spencer 253
   Walter S 197 253 William
   253

WARREN, Daniel D 26 George
    M 26 Ira C 26 John 26 269
WARRINER, Chester 253 Drue
    253 Gad 253 Nancy 253
    Willis 253
WASHINGTON, 43 Benevolent
    Society 154 Gen 212
WATERS, Edwin L 26
WATTS, Dr 33
WAUGH, Bishop 146
WEED, Caroline 253 James 253
    Sherman 180 209
WEEKS, Abigail 254 Alma 254
    Almira 254 Annette 254
    Catharine 176 254
    Charlotte 254 Chauncy K
    254 Clara 254 Clarinda 254-
    255 Curtis 60 241 254 Cyrus
    254 David 60 253 258
    Edward P 254 Elijah 36 254
    Eliza 254 Fanny 254 Harriet
    241 254-255 Harvey R 161
    254 Henry 254 Hiram 246
    254 John 254 Laura 254
    Matilda 254 258 Mrs David
    105 Nancy 254 Rebecca 249
    Rhoda 232 254 Rich 60 176
    254 Roxana 246 254 Safford
    254 Salmon 37 232 254
    Samuel 192 254 Sarah 208
    254 Seth B 60 254 Wheeler
    254 William C 26 254
    William P 254
WELCH, Catharine 255 Daniel
    21 137 139 160 176 246 255
    Daniel Jr 35 Gov 255 Polly
    255 Polly B 176 Walter 22
WELLS, Cyrus 35 139 Estelle
    203 Pomroy 169 Rebecca
    169 William 133
WENTWORTH, Benning 9 116
    Gov 116
WESTCOTT, Reuben 147

WETHERELL, Elder 147
WHEDON, Agnes 255 Allen 122
    142 148 255-256 Ann 265
    Anne 256 Ansel 88 158 255-
    256 Charles 256 Charlotte
    256 David 35 158 255-256
    David Jr 98 256 Edmund 40
    60 142-143 162 255-256
    James 71 73 208 217 256
    265 Jane 158 255 John 255
    John M 256 John Samuel
    255 Julia 256 265 Lorene
    255-256 Lovice 255 Lucinda
    197 256 Lucy 217 256
    Mahala 208 Maria 256 Mary
    201 256 Mehala 256 Mr 256
    Oscar 256 265 Rachel 255
    Roxana 256 Ruth 256
WHEELER, Benjamin P 26
    John 26 Julia 258 Lyman
    116 Margaret 105 115 258
    Moses E 26 Russel C 97
    Russell C 42 258
WHICKHAM, Hiram 256
WHITCOMB, Alzina 258 Austin
    S 41 175 230 258 Harriet
    160 Lucinda 264 Moses 160
    264
WHITE, Eunice 206 George 185
    James W 26 Mary 248
    Philander 248 Pliny H 139
    Sophia 185 William 206
WHITELAW, James 209
WHITING, Charlotte 258
    Edmund C 110 258 267 Lois
    242
WICKHAM, Eunice 258 Hiram
    35 39 98 109 254 258 Isaac
    173 256-257 Issac 147
    Joseph D 141 Louisa 185
    258 Maria 256 258 Mary E
    258 Matilda 254 258 Merritt
    258 Mrs Isaac 105 R C 154

FULLNAME INDEX. 297

WICKHAM (cont.)
  Robert 36 174 185 257-258
  Rollin C 98 258 270 Ruth
  257 Warren 27 William 27
  258 Willis 258
WIID, Willard 30
WILCOX, Amos 257 Annis 237
  257 Artemus 174 237-238
  257 Betsey 172 256
  Catharine 174 257 Cyrus
  256 Edmund 256 Edward
  257 Electa 256-257 Emma
  257 Eugene 257 Francis H
  257 Harvey 257 Helen 257
  Horace 42 257 James 256
  Jared 172 256 Jerome 257
  Joel S 27 257 John 257 John
  H 103 257 Laura 257 Louise
  257 Lydia 143 172 256
  Marcia 257 Maria 257 Mary
  256-257 Merrien 257 Mr 257
  Olive 222 256 Sophia 257
  Walter 256
WILKINS, John R 26
WILLARD, 205 Aaron 22
  Abigail 260 Andrew 116
  261-262 Archibald 260
  Benjamin 260 Betsey 261
  Capt 258 260 262 Clara 254
  Col 261 Cyrenius M 263
  Cyrenus 103 Ersa 263
  Eunice 263 George 35 142
  175 241 261 263 Henry 258
  260-261 263 James H 100-
  101 190 263 John 261
  Jonathan 8-9 36 40 111 144
  158 179 247 258 260-261
  Joseph 258 261-262 Lemuel
  22 Lucretia 175 263
  Margaret 261 Maria 240 260
  Mary 179 258 261-263 Mrs
  Joseph 105 Nancy 190 263
  Robert 260

WILLARD (cont.)
  Samuel 37 39-40 59 239-240
  258 260 Sarah 239 258 260-
  261 Silas 22 263 Simon 260
WILLEY, Abigail 263 Asa 192
  263 Betsey 192 263 David
  11 21 Israel 263 Lucy 263
  Lydia 263 Patience 263
  Polly 263 Rachel 263 Sally
  263 Zechariah 263
WILLIAMS, Abigail 242 Daniel
  264 David 264 Edward 264
  George 26 James 207 242
  264 John 26 254 264 Laura
  254 Laura A 264 Minerva
  264 Nathan 21 263 Oliver
  161 264 Orcelia 222 Reuben
  H 26 Ruth 207 Sarah 254
WILLIS, Adeline 264 Allen 164
  264 Alvarado 264 Ann 160
  Eliza 181 264 Emily 264
  Fanny 264 Guild 160 181
  264 Mahala 164 Nancy 264
  Sally 164 Sally Ann 264
WILMARTH, Dan 152 Lucy 196
  Nathaniel 196
WILSON, Benjamin 164 Maggie
  E 164
WINCHESTER, Andrew 21 264
  Ardelia 264 Charles 67 103
  264 Ellen 158 264-265
  Harriet 264-265 Horace 264
  Joel 146 158 256 264 Julia
  256 264-265 Lucinda 264
  Lydia 264-265 Mary Ann
  264 Norman 41 264 Sophia
  264
WINTER, Lucy 159 Richard H
  159
WINTHROP, 129 218
WISEMAN, Ann 265 John 21 67
  265 John Jr 265 Josephine
  265 Milton 265 Milton B 265

WOOD, Ahira E 26 Calvin 265
David 21 265 E T 149
Ebenezer 15 Hannah 189
Henry C 26 265 Lucinda 217
Luther B 22 30 245 265
Martin P 26 30 265 Minerva 248 Mr 265 Samuel 248
Samuel M 141 206 266
Stephen 26 Timothy 22 265
Welcome 217 Willard 26
William H 26.
WOODARD, Abraham 173
David 112 John J 39 98 266
Margaret 266 Phebe 227
WOODEN, Olive 205
WOODFIN, Frances 73 185
John 185 Mr 185-186
WOODMAN, Austin E 26 Eliza 205 Fanny M 205 Sarah 223
WOODWARD, Abram 147
Anderson D 266 Ellen S 266
Emily A 266 Jane 169 John J 98 Sally 231 Sarah 266
William 217
WOODWORTH, Betsey 206
Harmony 206
WOOSTER, Aaron 266 Albert 266 Alpheus 266

WOOSTER (cont.)
Amanda 266 Amos 146 149 191 266-267 Andrew 266
Asa 266 Avery 246 266
Deborah 211 266 Dorastus 225 Dorothy 266 Gen 166
Henry 21 40 144 252 266
Henry Jr 144 211 266
Manda 266 Maria 266 Mark 159 Martha 266 Mary 252 266 Mercy 266 Mr 267 Mrs 267 Sarah Ann 159 Sophia 225 Tryphena 246 267
Zeriah 266
WRIGHT, Augustus L 26 30
Aurelia 267 Eliza 234 267
Grove 186 Hoel 267 Jane 172 Lucien B 67 267
Minerva 267 Mr 16 267
Rebecca 267 Resha 267
Samuel 40 169 258 267
Samuel Jr 40 60 267 Sidney 172 Sophia 186 William 30
Zerah 234 267
WYMAN, Charlotte 186
YORK, Duke Of 116
YOUNG, Brigham 150

www.ingramcontent.com/pod-product-compliance
Lightning Source LLC
Chambersburg PA
CBHW062002220426
43662CB00010B/1207